DOUBLE VICTORY

How African American Women Broke Race and Gender Barriers to Help Win World War II

CHERYL MULLENBACH

CHICAGO
REVIEW
PRESS

Copyright © 2017 by Cheryl Mullenbach
First hardcover edition published 2013
First paperback edition published 2017
Published by Chicago Review Press, Incorporated
814 North Franklin Street
Chicago, Illinois 60610
ISBN 978-1-61373-523-7

The Library of Congress has cataloged the hardcover edition as follows:

Mullenbach, Cheryl.
Double victory : how African American women broke race and gender
barriers to help win World War II / Cheryl Mullenbach. — 1st ed.
p. cm.
Includes bibliographical references and index.
ISBN 978-1-56976-808-2 (hardcover)
1. World War, 1939–1945—African Americans. 2. World War, 1939–1945—
Women—United States. 3. African American women--History—20th century.
4. African American women—Employment—History—20th century. 5.
United States—Race relations—History—20th century. 6. African American
women—Civil rights—History—20th century. 7. African Americans—
Employment. 8. African Americans—Civil rights. I. Title.
D810.N4M85 2012
940.53082'0973—dc23
2012021343

Cover and interior design: Sarah Olson
Front cover photos: (top) Bertha Stallworth inspects the end of a 40 mm artillery
cartridge case at Frankford Arsenal, courtesy National Archives AFRO/AM
in WW II List #253; (bottom, left to right) Vera Campbell, courtesy Fort Des
Moines Museum and Education Center; Willa Brown, courtesy Photographs
and Prints Division, Schomburg Center for Research in Black Culture, The New
York Public Library, Astor, Lenox and Tilden Foundations; Pvt. Ruth L. James,
courtesy National Archives, AFRO/AM in WW II List #148

Printed in the United States of America
5 4 3 2 1

For

Zola (Emerson) Mullenbach—
One of the greatest of the "greatest generation"

Richard L. Wohlgamuth

Jake, Bailey, Zack, Brooklyn, Ty, Sophia, and Emerson

In memory of Ralph Mullenbach

CONTENTS

Introduction 1

1 WAR WORKERS
   "Negroes Cannot Be Accepted" 5

2 POLITICAL ACTIVISTS
   "I Am Not a Party Girl, I Want to Build a Movement" 39

3 IN THE MILITARY
   "Will All the Colored Girls Move Over on This Side" 87

4 VOLUNTEERS
   "Back the Attack" 141

5 ENTERTAINERS
   "We Don't Take Your Kind" 195

   Epilogue. 235
   Notes. 239
   Bibliography 245
   Index 255

INTRODUCTION

In 2002, Thomasina Walker Johnson Norford died quietly in her sleep at the age of 94. The *New York Amsterdam News* described her as "the epitome of elegant refinement, culture, and determination." Her parents, who were long dead, would have been pleased and proud to know that their daughter had retained her elegance and refinement in her old age. But they most likely would have been surprised, considering the direction their daughter's career had taken.

When Thomasina was growing up, her parents had tried to convince her that "nice little girls are not interested in politics and labor unions, they teach." Thomasina tried to obey her parents—she became a teacher. But when she ran into problems because she was black, she left the teaching profession. Thomasina turned to politics and labor unions—becoming an influential lobbyist in Washington, DC, where a woman in the halls of Congress was an unusual sight and where a *black* woman in a prominent professional position was almost unheard of in the 1940s.

Professional opportunities for women of Thomasina's generation were limited. But for women who were not white, the options were more restrictive. Yet Thomasina managed to overcome the double barriers of gender discrimination and race discrimination. She was one of a generation of women who did so.

Thomasina was a young adult in the early 1940s, a time that was a turning point in American history. The world was at war—America entered World War II in 1941. As more and more men were needed to fight at the fronts, women were reluctantly accepted in now-vacant positions that had been previously closed to them. They entered the workforce in unprecedented numbers and became official members of the military for the first time in history. Female news reporters followed stories to the battlefields across war-torn lands. Female entertainers sang and danced across continents, performing for the fighting armies in Europe, Asia, and Africa. Women served in hospitals around the world, caring for the wounded and comforting dying soldiers.

Although it was expected that, after the war, women would return to the lives they had led previously, there was no turning back for many—especially for black women. These women were part of what became known as "the greatest generation."

Thomasina was born in 1908—when the first Ford automobiles were selling for about $800. But in 1908 it was illegal for women to drive cars in some cities. It was the year before the National Association for the Advancement of Colored People (NAACP) was formed. Eighty-nine black citizens were lynched in the United States that year.

The women of the greatest generation were teenagers in the 1920s and '30s. In 1920 the 19th Amendment was passed, allowing women to vote for the first time; however, black men and women were kept from voting through intimidation in most southern states. In 1925 the state of Georgia introduced a bill that made it illegal for a black person to marry a white person. In 1935 the NAACP petitioned the University of Maryland to explain its policy of admitting only whites to the university. In 1939 famed singer Marian Anderson was denied permission by the Daughters of the American Revolution (DAR) to sing at their hall—Constitution Hall—in Washington, DC, because she was black.

When America entered the war in 1941 no one could have anticipated the changes that would shape the future for women. But postwar America held hope for many black women. The opportunities that they took advantage of during the war years in the 1940s set the stage for the 1950s, '60s, and '70s—decades that saw the emergence of the civil rights movement and the women's movement.

In the 1950s the women of Thomasina Walker Johnson Norford's generation wondered what it would mean for their children when the US Supreme Court ruled that racial segregation in public schools was unconstitutional. They heard about a black woman named Rosa Parks who challenged life as it was in the South by refusing to give up her seat on a city bus in Montgomery, Alabama.

Many Americans participated in marches that resulted in equal rights for women and minorities in the 1960s. In 1963 a man named Martin Luther King Jr. spoke about having a dream for future generations. The Civil Rights Act of 1964—outlawing discrimination in the workplace on the basis of sex or race—was passed by Congress.

As the 1970s and '80s dawned, Thomasina and the women of her generation began to enter their elder years. The US Supreme Court again took actions that were intended to bring equality to the nation's education system when it ruled that busing of students could be used as a tool to force integration of public schools in America. Black and white women entered political life as never before. Many were encouraged when Sandra Day

O'Connor became the first woman to serve on the US Supreme Court. And some wondered if victory over racism had really been achieved when race riots broke out in Los Angeles after a jury acquitted four white police officers of beating a black man.

By the end of the 20th century, fewer and fewer women of Thomasina Walker Johnson Norford's generation remained. Throughout their lives, many of their stories of triumph over the challenges they faced as women were overlooked. Many of their accounts of victory over racism were ignored. It's up to the children, grandchildren, and great-grandchildren to recover the stories of the women who have gone—and to pay attention to the stories of the women who survive. It is their responsibility to ensure these victorious women are not forgotten. It will be a double victory.

1

WAR WORKERS

"Negroes Cannot Be Accepted"

I stood in line with the others, but a guard came up and said it was no need to wait; that there was no hiring of colored women.
—*Miss Ethel Bell*

In August 1944, factories across the country were in dire need of workers to build guns, bombs, planes, and ships for the US military. The country had been at war for almost three years. The government contracted with factory owners to provide the military with critical supplies, but thousands of men had left their factory jobs to join the fighting overseas. With the urgent need for skilled workers, defense plants looked first to unmarried white women to fill the positions. As the war effort mounted and the need for defense workers increased, the plants began to recruit and hire married white women. Some plants hired black men. Last to be considered for employment were black women. But in some plants the hiring of "colored" women was never a consideration because racial discrimination was an accepted practice in the America of the 1940s.

When Ethel Bell responded to a newspaper advertisement seeking workers for jobs at a plant in St. Louis, Missouri, a guard made it clear to her that she wouldn't be considered for employment because she was black. In 1944 it wasn't against the law for a factory to refuse to hire someone because of race or gender. There was nothing Ethel could do to force the factory owner to look beyond the color of her skin and consider her skills and qualifications. Ethel went home without a job, and the factory owner continued with the profitable government contract.

The Negro Problem

Ethel was one of the many women who were eager to get jobs in the defense plants in the war years. The jobs paid well. Some of the jobs required special expertise and the workers were given opportunities to learn new skills. In addition, the women felt they were doing something to support the war effort at home while other family members were fighting the enemy overseas.

The idea of women of any color working in factories was new to Americans in the 1940s. It was a time when most married women stayed home and worked as housewives while their husbands went to work outside the home. Some women worked in professional positions—as doctors, lawyers, teachers, and writers, for example—but those professions were dominated by men. Women with high school educations or less who worked outside the home often worked in service jobs as store clerks, waitresses, or house cleaners. Many black women worked as maids or "domestics" for white families.

Life as a domestic included long hours and little pay. A typical workday was 12 hours, and most employers expected their domestics to be "on call" six days a week. The job duties included cooking, washing, ironing, cleaning, and serving meals. Sometimes domestics cared for the white families' young children, too. The typical wage for a domestic worker was $7 a week. Domestic workers in southern states made as little as $3 to $4 a week. So when black women who worked as domestics heard about war jobs in defense plants that paid as much as $35 per week, they were interested in applying for those positions.

The federal government created agencies to deal with issues related to war work. The War Manpower Commission was formed to deal with the labor shortage caused by the large number of men entering military service. The Office of War Information relayed news and information about the war to the public. The two agencies worked together to recruit women for the war industries.

A government official from the War Manpower Commission said in an interview with *Time* magazine that as the nation geared up for war it would need to look for workers in untapped sources. He predicted that over 7 million people outside the paid workforce in the United States—92 percent of whom were women—could be convinced to "forsake kitchen or lounge for office and factory." He warned that such a move would "shake U.S. living habits." He explained, "More women in the war effort means fewer women in the home—as wives, daughters, or servants; it means eating more meals out, fewer socks darned, fewer guests entertained at home, and many another change in the American way of living." The same official cautioned that "the Negro problem" was "far from licked." With so many white men entering the military and creating vacancies in the workforce, he warned, "Employers had better get set for a big increase in pressure for jobs for Negroes." And some white people saw this as a problem. Many white business owners would not want to hire black workers, and they would resist pressure from anyone who tried to make them do so.

Wanted: Women Workers

Newspapers and magazines carried advertisements showing women working in defense plants. Radio ads also encouraged women to work in war jobs. The government printed posters and hung them in public places. They showed women happily working for the war effort. The posters carried slogans: THE MORE WOMEN AT WORK—THE SOONER WE WIN, DO THE JOB HE LEFT BEHIND, and WOMEN IN THE WAR—WE CAN'T WIN WITHOUT THEM.

However, the idea of women in nontraditional jobs was a new and very different idea for many Americans. The government published pamphlets that revealed the beliefs of the time—women were not equal to men in the workplace. The pamphlets—titled *When You Hire Women, Safety Caps for Women in War Factories, Women's Effective War Work Requires Good Posture,* and *Washing and Toilet Facilities for Women in Industry*—indicated that women required special handling. The pamphlets encouraged factory owners who were considering hiring women to first "sell" the idea to men. Although many women *did* work before the war, the pamphlets reminded those who were hiring that women were "without work experience of any kind." The pamphlets reinforced the sexist beliefs of the time by encouraging employers to hire women for "certain type of work that women do particularly well"—work that required "care and constant alertness," "good eyesight," and "use of light instruments."

The government also set up special divisions dedicated to black workers within the Labor Division of the War Production Board. The purpose of the division's Negro Employment and Training Branch was "to help qualified Negro workers participate in the employment and training opportunities of the national defense program." It helped place black workers in defense jobs by removing barriers put in place by some white employers or labor organizations. The duties of the Minority Groups Branch of the Labor Division of the War Production Board included making investigations into complaints involving minority groups that had been filed with the government.

Early in 1941, before the United States entered the war, black leaders had pressured President Franklin Roosevelt to do something about job discrimination against black people. The president issued a statement—Executive Order 8802—that said, "It is the policy of the United States to encourage full participation in the national defense program by all citizens of the United States, regardless of race, creed, color, or national origin." To help enforce this order at businesses and manufacturing plants that had government contracts, the president formed the Fair Employment Practices Committee (FEPC). Although the United States hadn't yet entered the war, fighting was in full force in Europe, and factories in the United States were already providing the warring countries with supplies. Many black people saw this gearing up of industries and the establishment of the FEPC as signs of hope for their employment opportunities.

After the Japanese attack on Pearl Harbor in December 1941, the United States entered the war. Leaders in black communities and women's organizations encouraged women to consider working in war-related jobs. They believed black women faced a brighter future with wartime employment. They urged women to enroll in free courses offered by the government to teach workers skills that would prepare them for work in defense plants. They could learn welding, drafting, riveting, drilling, radio construction, code receiving and sending, engine repair, and shipbuilding. Some factories offered on-the-job training, allowing women to learn skills while getting paid.

A government training center in Marcy, New York, offered a course to women in its Women Ordnance Workers (WOW) program. At the same center women trained in a program called Women in Ground Service (WINGS). The women could choose from among six areas in the aviation field: aviation engines; aircraft fabrication; welding; electrical equipment; repair and maintenance; or parachute repair, maintenance, and packing. After three to four months of training, the women were qualified to accept employment in any war industry related to aviation. While they were in training the women earned $49 a month and were provided a place to live. The training center offered a recreation facility, religious worship, hobby and hiking clubs, glee clubs, and theater groups. It was open to all races, and it all sounded very good to women who had been working as domestics.

A Baltimore employment agency reported that in 1941 over 23,000 individuals worked as domestics—cooks, maids, laundresses, gardeners, and chauffeurs—in the city. By October 1942 the number had dropped to 15,000. A spokesman for the agency said he had 500 openings for domestics and was unable to fill them. He blamed it on the war. A high school graduate working as a domestic earned $30 a *month,* while a high school graduate working in a war plant earned $35 a *week* with overtime. A cook/maid worked 70 hours a week for 20 cents an hour; women making gas masks at a war plant earned 42 cents an hour, while women assembling small machine parts earned 63 cents an hour. The situation was similar in New York. A private employment agency reported that it had 23 women on its list of domestic workers. Recently, 10 had left for night jobs washing airplanes for a defense plant. At their new jobs, they earned $18 for a 40-hour week and worked only five days a week. As domestics they earned $10 to $15 per week—and their "week" was six or seven days. A state-run employment agency reported it had 118 workers available to fill 667 unfilled orders. A Florida newspaper reported that housewives there were adjusting: "While agencies struggle toward a nationwide solution of the servant problem, the individual housewife turns mournfully toward her kitchen sink—and washes her own dishes."

Sweaty-Handed Women Need Not Apply

Many women—both black and white—answered the call to enter the workforce and help win the war through their work in the factories. But not all businesses were ready to hire black women, despite President Roosevelt's Executive Order 8802. All across the country black women met with open discrimination as they applied for work.

In Washington, DC, an employment agency ran an ad in a newspaper for women to apply as trainees for work in a war plant. The qualifications were: "Resident of D.C. Age: 21–40. Minimum height: 5 ft. 4 inches. 125 lbs. Must pass physical and rigid character investigation." Applicants were asked to report to the employment agency for an interview. When a black woman applied at the agency she was told that the company had "not yet started taking Negro women."

In June 1942 in Chicago, 40 women completed courses at a technology school that prepared them for work as ordnance inspectors, chemists, and draftsmen. The director of the program reported that the demand for workers was so urgent that all 40 women were placed in positions on the day they completed the course—"except for the five Negro women." They were three ordnance inspectors, one draftsman, and one

chemist. The director boasted that since December 1940 close
to 15,000 men and women had been trained for defense jobs at
the institute—but he could remember only one black trainee,
a female chemist, who had been placed in a job. Despite that,
the director predicted that the five black women waiting for
employment would eventually be placed "when the imperative need of utilizing all trained personnel is realized." In other
words, when the situation got desperate enough—when no
more white workers were available—the black women would
be considered.

In 1943 an East Coast war plant explained its racist position
on hiring black women. The statement represented a common
belief that many white people had about black people at the
time: black people are dirty. Representatives of the plant stated
that black women who had applied for jobs could not be hired
because the work required "handling of small mechanisms"
and that the women were rejected because they "all had sweaty
hands." And a Baltimore company reflected its racist reason-
ing—that blacks were less intelligent than whites—when it
refused to hire black women even though they had completed a
course through a government training center. A spokesperson
at the company explained, "Colored women just do not have the
native intelligence necessary to do highly skilled work."

In New Orleans, Louisiana, Hattie Combre and Burneda
Coleman, two black women who had passed government tests
as machine operators, received letters telling them to report to
work at an army camp in a city 200 miles from New Orleans.
When they arrived, however, they were told "Negroes cannot
be accepted." The commanding officer of the camp told them
that it was not known that they were black when officials sent
the letters and that "Negroes could not be used in such a capacity

to work." The two women had left their jobs in New Orleans for the defense jobs at the camp, and they asked for reimbursement for their travel expenses. Hattie and Burneda were told nothing could be done about their situation.

Two black women in Ohio in 1942 decided they *would* do something about their situations when they were faced with discrimination. Effie Mae Turner and Claretta Johnson brought lawsuits against the companies that refused to hire them. Turner had completed over 240 hours in a defense training center before she applied for a job with a plant that manufactured war munitions. She believed she had been denied a job based solely on her race, because the company had advertised for women war workers every day in the newspaper. Johnson sued one of the biggest aircraft plants in the country when she also was denied work for which she felt she was qualified. The plant owner had received money from the government to build the plant. The women's suits claimed the two companies did not believe in democracy and the principles for which the war was being fought and were therefore giving "comfort to the enemy."

A lower Ohio state court ruled against the two women. Although the lawyers for the two women had argued that the plants were required to hire the women under Executive Order 8802, the judge in the case said he didn't believe the order applied. He said that, during wartime, individual rights were outweighed by maximum production. In other words, the judge believed it was more important for the discriminating companies to keep producing products for the war effort than for Effie Mae and Claretta to enjoy their rights. The women appealed the decision to the Ohio Supreme Court. Their cases were dismissed because, the court said, "no debatable constitutional question" was involved. This confirmed what many believed at the time: Executive Order 8802 carried little legal weight—in the workplace or in the courts.

Toothless Government Programs

Gradually, as the war continued and fewer white workers were available for jobs, employers began to hire black women. Thousands found work in defense plants and other wartime industries. Sometimes it was only after intervention by the FEPC that jobs opened up for black women. A plant in Columbus, Ohio, agreed to hire black women only after months of negotiations with black community groups that had complained to the FEPC about the company's discrimination against black women. In February 1943 the Washington, DC, Navy Yard hired black women for the first time in its history. For the first time in its existence, the Brooklyn Navy Yard hired black women. In March 1945 a St. Louis plant that manufactured electrical equipment hired its first black women after the FEPC negotiated with the management at the plant.

In March 1945 another Missouri company agreed to begin hiring black women. The electrical firm had been employing black men, and a personnel manager stated that the plant "has experienced no difficulty as a result of its Negro men workers." However, the company agreed to hire the women only after several months of negotiations with the FEPC.

Although the FEPC successfully encouraged some employers to hire black workers, it had little authority to force them to open their doors to all qualified workers. It was often criticized for not doing its job. A black social worker commented about the FEPC, "It is as toothless as a month-old baby." Another government agency—the United States Employment Service (USES)—also often came under fire from black leaders.

In September 1942 the *Afro American* newspaper reported that USES—an agency that helped hire workers for defense plants—had published an "operations bulletin." The bulletin stated that USES would refer workers to companies "without regard to race, color or creed" except when the company specified a preference. This meant that any company could tell USES not to send black job applicants—and USES would comply. When officials at USES were questioned about this, they said they couldn't force a company to accept an applicant it didn't want.

In May 1943 the same newspaper reported that USES discriminated against black women who tried to apply for defense plant jobs. The *Afro American* interviewed black women who had applied for war jobs at the USES office in Baltimore and were told that jobs were "not available." This came as a surprise to the women, as they had seen ads in the newspapers and heard reports on the radio that women were needed at the plants. Instead, the women reported that they were referred to menial jobs in canneries, hospitals, hotels, and bus terminals. Some black women reportedly took jobs as street sweepers for the city when they were turned down for war jobs by USES.

In some businesses, the only positions open to black women were cleaning jobs. And in some cases, black women were assigned to the night shifts only. Dirty and dangerous jobs were sometimes the only war jobs open to black women.

When an arsenal in New Jersey needed ammunition workers it embarked on a campaign to recruit black women in nearby Harlem, New York. The plant was praised by government officials for showing "faith and appreciation in the colored workers." Other plants that "show[ed] less enthusiasm for employing Negro workers" were encouraged to follow the example of the New Jersey arsenal. But what the officials didn't mention was the highly dangerous nature of ammunition jobs. Explosions occurred frequently, and injuries were common. Most people looking for war work did not consider ammunition jobs in arsenals highly desirable. However, over 1,700 black women responded to the arsenal's "urgent call" for workers.

Although defense plants were desperate for workers, some were unsure about hiring black women in jobs that required special skills such as riveting and drilling. At a plant that built military airplanes for the army and navy in St. Louis, Missouri, a program was started to train and hire black men as an experiment. After the men proved they were capable students and responsible workers, the experiment was expanded to include black women. The first group of women successfully completed five weeks of training and were "hard at work along with their men folks" a newspaper reported. The experiment was considered a success, and the plant was "hiring Negro women as fast as they can be trained."

On-the-Job Discrimination

After they were hired, many black women faced additional discrimination. In November 1944 white women workers at a plant in St. Louis walked out of their jobs to protest the hiring of a black woman. In the same year black women who made up the night shift at a plant in New York were fired when they protested the lack of sanitary facilities and the poor working conditions at the plant. White women were quickly hired to replace them. In 1942, after only nine days on the job at an East Coast navy yard, 18-year-old black welder Corona Browner was fired, even though she had completed a 320-hour welding course at a government training center. Her firing came after a trade union protested the navy yard hiring a black woman for a job other than janitor. The union leaders knew that many white workers would refuse to work with a black woman, and they encouraged the racist beliefs by protesting the hiring of Corona. They claimed the hiring of black women in skilled trades would "lead to serious trouble between the races." But in reality, the trouble was caused by the white workers who refused to work with anyone of a different race. When black women removed signs designating toilets for "coloreds" in an arsenal plant in Maryland, plant managers replaced the signs with black silhouettes over the toilets.

Toilets became a major issue for Western Electric Company in Baltimore, Maryland, late in 1943. The company had a government contract to provide war materials to the military. About 7,000 people—both black and white—worked at the plant. In October, 1,800 union employees voted to strike after the company refused to provide separate toilets for black and white women. Twenty-two white women walked off their jobs. Since Western Electric had a contract to supply the government with war materials, President Roosevelt became involved in the situation. The president said that, by calling a strike, the striking workers were engaging in actions that "impair the war effort." He ordered the US Army to seize control of the plant in order to keep production going.

Despite the presence of the army at the plant, employee attendance and the level of production fell. Eventually the union leader and some of the plant managers were fired. The War Department and the union finally reached an agreement. A new and enlarged locker and toilet area was constructed. The lockers were assigned in blocks—some sections that "happened" to be assigned only to whites, other sections that happened to be assigned only to blacks. And of course it only made sense that the workers would use the toilets closest to their block of lockers. That meant black workers used the toilets near their locker blocks—separate from the whites. It was still segregation and discrimination, but no one admitted it.

Black Rosie the Riveters

Despite the barriers black women faced during World War II, thousands contributed to the war effort. Their work in shipyards, steel mills, arsenals, ordnance plants, electrical equipment factories, and aircraft plants helped their employers fulfill their government contracts.

The days were long and hard. Women in defense plants worked eight-hour days, six days a week. Some of the jobs

Welders Alivia Scott, Hattie Carpenter, and Flossie Burtos prepare to weld their first piece of steel on the ship SS *George Washington Carver*, Kaiser Shipyards, Richmond, California, 1943. *National Archives AFRO/ AM in WW II List #252*

required them to stand in a production line completing the same task all day with only occasional breaks. The women had to purchase the tools they used on the assembly line—usually at a cost of about $30. After the workday ended, many women faced long commutes by bus or train to their homes. Some black families lived in housing that the government provided. Old buildings were converted into "dormitories" for defense plant workers who had traveled from their homes to work in the plants. But some of the housing the government provided was in the form of trailer camps and tents.

The work could be boring and monotonous. It could be dirty and dangerous. In arsenals women worked as inspectors, carefully examining ammunition storage boxes or binocular lenses. Or they could be found shoveling and mixing sand at steel mills. In other factories they made molds for military equipment. Black women in electrical factories assembled equipment and tested finished products. In aircraft plants they operated machinery, assembled parts for airplanes, and inspected the finished planes. Black women in ordnance plants tested guns, tanks, and other fighting equipment before it was shipped to soldiers at the battlefront.

Women performed various duties in the country's steel mills during the war. They fabricated shells, guns, nails, spikes, and bolts. As raw materials such as iron ore, coal, and limestone arrived at ports by boat, cranes scooped up tons of the material and dumped it inside the mills. But every bit of ore was needed for the war effort; none could be wasted, so workers had to go into the bottoms of the boats to shovel and sweep the ore that the huge cranes missed. Most of the women performing these dirty, backbreaking jobs were black. Inside the steel mills they worked in blast furnaces shoveling mud and mixing clay. They operated machines that cut huge plates of steel for aircraft guns.

Mary Newson left her family farm in Texas and moved to California during the war. At first she worked cleaning train cars, but she soon took a job as a riveter in a naval yard. After a few months Mary's supervisor wanted to move her to the night shift. She had a new baby and didn't like the idea of working nights, so she found a job at another plant. Although Mary was a skilled worker, at the new plant she was given a job as a janitor—a job typically assigned to black employees. But Mary soon moved up to an assembly line job.

Willie Mae Cotright left her home in Louisiana for a job in California. As she boarded the train bound for Richmond she was sent to a special section with a curtain across the door—the Jim Crow section. Behind the curtain the air was hot and stuffy. This is where she and other black riders rode—sitting on long wooden benches and separated from the white travelers who rode on padded individual seats in air-conditioned cars. As soon as the train left the southern states

Bertha Stallworth inspects the end of a 40 mm artillery cartridge case at Frankford Arsenal. *National Archives AFRO/ AM in WW II List #253*

behind, Willie Mae and the other black passengers began to experience liberties that were inconceivable in the Jim Crow South. Their first taste of freedom occurred as they learned they could move to any section of the train as they continued their journey west. And when Willie Mae arrived in California, she began to experience some of the opportunities that she had heard about back in Louisiana. She was offered a job at a shipyard where she received on-the-job training to learn the best techniques for welding. She needed to know how to weld because she was helping to build a ship that would carry American military personnel and materials to war.

Willie Mae lived in an apartment with several other war workers. The roommates worked different shifts—some at night, some during the day. They joked that their beds were always warm because when one roommate left for her shift, another returned, falling into the bed before it got cold.

Aller Hunter was working as a domestic for a white family in Texas in 1943 when she heard that black women could get well-paying jobs at war plants in sunny California. Before she knew it, she was on a train headed west. Aller arrived in the San Francisco Bay area, where the damp ocean breezes were foreign to this Texas girl. But she soon landed a job at a shipyard in Richmond. While Aller was happy to find work, she knew welding wasn't the job for her. She was happy to get a job cleaning up after the welders. Using a broom and pails of water, she scrubbed up the metal shavings that dropped to the factory floor as welders joined the seams of the ships together. Sometimes she had to climb ladders on the outside of the ship and walk on scaffolding as she carried her broom and water pail. She liked her job, but there were times when the winds coming off the bay made her wish she was back in Texas.

A Man's Job for a Man's Wages

While the war provided black women like Mary Newson, Willie Mae Cotright, and Aller Hunter opportunities in plants that held government contracts, it also opened doors for black women in other areas of work. In civilian industries black women worked in food processing plants, restaurants, hotels, garment factories, and in the railroad industry. Lula King, a 64-year-old farm worker, supervised 80 celery pullers and bean pickers on a 2,700-acre farm in Florida. Although she was near retirement age, she said she wanted to do her share to win the war: "They say they need food to win the war, and I'm trying to do my part. I work every day—ain't missed but three Sundays since August. I'll be 65 next year and eligible for a pension, but I am going to keep right on working if the war's going on."

In Chicago Fannie Currie and Hattie Alexander went to work for the Illinois Central Railroad in 1943. They were part of the first group of women hired by the railroad to be section hands—"shoveling cinders, swinging a pick and in general doing a man's job for a man's wages." When the railroad foreman saw the group of "ten husky, cheerful Negro women," he was skeptical. "When I first saw the gang, I nearly dropped in my tracks," he commented to a newspaper reporter. "I didn't know how much work we were going to get done with women, but they sure surprised me. I wouldn't say they are as good as men yet, but they seem to be doing all right and they certainly are good natured. They even sing."

Fannie and Hattie both enjoyed their work.

"My arm gets a little sore slinging a shovel or a pick, but then I forget about it when I think about all those boys over in the Solomons," Fannie said. (American armed forces were fighting the Japanese in the Solomon Islands.) "We women have to pitch in now and do our men's work until they come home. I was a maid in a hotel before I took this job and this isn't any harder than that. Besides, I like to wave at the railroad men as the trains go by," Fannie told a reporter for a black newspaper, the *Chicago Defender*.

Hattie added, "I never get tired and I like being out in the open. I enjoy shoveling. 'A heavy hand with a shovel and a light hand with a biscuit,' I always say. When I go home tonight, I have to bake a batch of biscuits for my man's dinner or he won't be happy. They'll be good too."

The railroad hired women between the ages of 21 and 47 to work as section hands, where they were responsible for an assigned section of the railroad track. The newspaper reported that the women who could afford to would "dress for their role as carefully as actresses, donning overalls, railroad men's caps, and bandannas." Others wore "men's trousers, old sweaters, and scarves around their heads." It was reported that the women "permit themselves one feminine touch—nail polish."

In Chicago a YWCA established a counseling center for women working in war plants and offices. The center was designed to "aid women to make the most of their present opportunity." Roberta Bell, a counselor with the program, said many of the women "feel they are attempting to establish themselves in a working world that is primarily for men." She added, "This feeling together with the fact that they are inexperienced and are Negroes keeps many from making the most of their opportunities." Roberta said she encouraged the women who came to her to ask themselves several questions: "Am I making the best possible use of work experience I am getting right now?" "Am I fitting myself for advancement?" "Am I taking special training in any new skill?" Roberta advised the women about training courses and trends in business and industry.

Workers Unite

Labor unions of the 1940s represented the voices of the workers. But few unions allowed black members. And even fewer allowed black women. In some cases, auxiliaries were formed for black workers. They were segregated groups that operated outside the regular union. Even the Brotherhood of Sleeping Car Porters, the first labor organization led by blacks, did a poor job of representing black women.

The International Ladies' Garment Workers' Union and the Amalgamated Clothing Workers Union, however, encouraged black membership. The *Afro American* newspaper admitted that the garment industry unions had "commendable records on the matter of taking colored workers into the unions." And it encouraged women who were going into the garment industries to join the unions.

Although many black women left jobs as domestics during the war years, working conditions for those who remained in domestic work improved somewhat as a result of the war. With the pool of women willing to work as domestics shrinking, employers were forced to pay more and offer better working conditions in order to convince women to take the jobs. And in 1942 a historical event took place—one that dramatically affected domestic workers.

For five days in November 1942 the Congress of Industrial Organizations (CIO) held its annual meeting in Boston. Rose Burrell of Baltimore was described by a newspaper reporter as "one of the happiest delegates" at the convention. Rose was a member of the CIO's new United Domestic Workers Union. Earlier in the year the first branch of the new union had been organized in Baltimore. All the members were black women. Rose was at the annual CIO meeting representing that local union as their president. She was happy because in Baltimore the union wage scale was $3.20 for an eight-hour day. Full-time union domestics earned $15.50 for a 48-hour week. And Rose and her union "sisters" would get Sundays off. The union's goal was "to protect and dignify the maid." A month after the Boston convention a second local of the United Domestic Workers' Union was organized in Washington, DC. The union wage was $20 a week for a 48-hour week. Inexperienced union workers earned $15 a week. Unlike the Baltimore local, the Washington membership consisted of both black and white women. In Washington the union tried to place workers in homes where the husband and wife both worked outside the home. The union considered this their contribution to the war effort—taking care of housework and children so wives could work in a war industry. The organizer of the Washington local said, "The organization of domestic workers should result in an attitude of mutual respect between a servant and employer, which is of prime importance in a well-run home."

Rebecca Eaton, a field worker for the National Negro Congress in Wilmington, Delaware, helped set up the Domestic Workers Alliance. The alliance acted as combination union/employment agency. Members paid dues of 25 cents per month. In addition to helping women find domestic positions, the alliance worked to improve wage levels and working conditions. It also helped women who wanted to leave domestic service find jobs in industrial plants.

Not a Social Experiment

Always hanging over the heads of the women who worked in the wartime jobs was the belief that the jobs were only temporary. It was expected that when the war ended, women—black and white—would give up their positions to returning servicemen. Black women especially feared the temporary status of their positions. For some white women it simply would mean they would go back to their former lives as housewives as their returning husbands once again became their families' breadwinners. But for those black women who had always worked outside the home—usually in low-paying domestic or service jobs—the postwar job situation looked gloomy. It would be ludicrous for them to go back to their former positions after holding well-paying war jobs. A well-known black leader, Jeanetta Welch Brown, reminded women of the difference between white and black women workers: "The employment of Negro women is not a social experiment but an economic necessity." She predicted that, because many men would not return from the war, there would be a shortage of workers to fill jobs after the war. Historically, black women had worked outside the home in order to survive economically—and they would continue to do so after the war. She wanted to ensure that black women would be considered for any job opportunities after the war.

Life in a Castle

Some black women followed their soldier husbands to army posts across the United States until the men were shipped overseas. Those women worked in the post laundry on the graveyard shifts, in warehouses, and sometimes as clerks and typists. Some worked as maids in the post hospital or in white officers' homes. Salaries varied for these workers. Those who were lucky enough to get work as typists earned $120 a month. Laundry and warehouse workers made $50 to $60 a month. Hospital maids earned $90 a month, but maids in officers' homes made "whatever their employers felt like paying."

It was the custom to segregate black and white soldiers, and that meant black soldiers were sent to military installations that housed only black soldiers. Fort Huachuca in Arizona was one destination for black soldiers. The women who followed their soldier husbands to the camp in January 1943 shared an "unpainted plywood shack" with 11 black soldiers. There were 11 rooms about seven feet square—each furnished with two army cots and bedding. All shared the same shower, toilet, and two sinks. The sinks served as laundry tubs as well. The soldiers and their wives were charged $12 a month for rent for these accommodations, which they jokingly called the Castle on the Hill.

A Woman with Her Head in the Clouds

Willa Brown of Chicago, Illinois, captured the attention of Americans because she broke through barriers that most black men and most women of any race were not able to breach. In the 1930s and '40s *any* woman who held a commercial pilot's license and a master mechanic's certificate was a rarity, but a black woman with those credentials was especially noticeable. Willa earned her pilot's license in 1938 and worked for a Chicago flight service. She took passengers who paid one dollar for a 10-minute ride. In 1939, she helped form the National Negro Airmen's Association of America. Membership was open to any "Negro pursuing work related to aviation." About the same time, she started teaching aviation subjects for the Works Progress Administration (WPA), a government program that provided jobs in public works projects. She became certified as a flight instructor by the Civil Aeronautics Authority (CAA), a federal agency that regulated the aeronautics industry. And she taught aviation mechanics classes in Chicago public schools. In

1940, Willa and her husband, Cornelius Coffey, established the
Coffey School of Aeronautics—open to both blacks and whites.

Willa fought for years to gain racial equality in the aviation industry. Government-supported aviation programs were
closed to black pilots. Black men were not accepted in the US
Army Air Corps. The government-funded aviation training program that was started to prepare a reserve supply of civilian
pilots who could be called in the event of a national emergency,
the Civilian Pilot Training Program (CPTP), was also closed to
black pilots. Willa worked to change that.

Willa Brown was one of the first black women licensed as pilots in the
United States. She directed a government-supported flying school for
the training of black pilots for the war in 1941. *Photographs and Prints Division, Schomburg Center for Research in Black Culture, The New York Public Library,
Astor, Lenox and Tilden Foundations*

"It was a discouraging process the first few years. For several years I wrote to aviation officials in Washington," she told a reporter for the *Chicago Daily Tribune* when discussing her efforts to provide black pilots with training equal to that offered white students. "They were always polite but evasive, and it was significant that during those early years, we never received anything but promises."

Willa Brown's persistence finally paid off in the winter of 1940. The CAA allowed her to set up an experiment with black pilot candidates. The government supplied the equipment, and Brown provided the training. The CAA said if the black pilots "measured up to comparable white pilots," then "something more permanent" would be set up for the training of black pilots. On May 1, 1940, Willa introduced to the public 20 black men who had finished the experimental training course. She said they were "average American youth" between the ages of 18 and 25, recruited from across the country. After an inspection, the CAA officials concluded the men were "good."

Willa's successful experiment resulted in the establishment of programs to train black pilots for civilian work and for the military. Two government-supported flying schools for the training of black pilots for the war program were established in 1941. The Coffey School of Aeronautics, with Willa as its director, was one. The other was a newly created military training field at Tuskegee Institute in Alabama. The Coffey School taught men to be civilian pilots, and it provided preliminary training for men who would go on to military school. Those individuals who had completed their initial training at the Coffey School could take examinations to qualify for training as pilots with the US Army Air Forces at Tuskegee. The instructors there had been trained at the Coffey School. After successfully completing training at Tuskegee, the pilots were ready to go into combat.

The civilian pilot program administered at the Coffey School trained young people to become members of the Civil Air Patrol (CAP). The CAP used civilian pilots to help patrol the shores and borders of the United States during the war. In February 1942, Willa became the first black member of the Civil Air Patrol in Illinois. She was assigned to the 111th flight squadron, an all-black CAP group based at Harlem Field in Chicago. The squadron included 25 pilots who flew planes provided by the government.

In 1944 the all-black National Airman's Association of America, with Willa as its director, began a drive to recruit young people—both boys and girls—10 years or older as junior airmen and as CAP members. The two-month-long drive was aimed at enrolling 5,000 young people. Youths aged 10 to 15 formed the junior airmen's group; those aged 15 to 18 became CAP cadets. Those over 18 were full-fledged CAP members.

Youths over 16 who joined the association took flight training at the Coffey School, but all recruits studied subjects related to aviation in classes scheduled on Monday and Thursday evenings. Students were on call for guard duty at the airport during the day. New enrollees automatically became members of the National Airmen's Association of America and took part in the association's activities, which included entertaining black members of the army air corps when they visited Chicago.

In August 1944, Willa claimed that black youths who were members of the CAP were being discriminated against by the national organization. The all-black Chicago squadron was the only group in the state not invited to the annual summer camp. Willa said she was told that "no provisions were available for Negro cadets."

"Every cadet in all the CAP squadrons looked forward to this event," Willa said. "I feel keenly about this discrimination, prejudice, and disappointment directed toward the youth of my race." She added that black cadets had selected aviation as the branch of service in which they preferred to serve their country and that many of them had older brothers who had distinguished themselves in the air and some of them had "paid the supreme sacrifice."

Spreading the News

Willa Brown wasn't going to stand for the discrimination she saw in the aviation industry. She wanted everyone to know of the injustices she witnessed, and she knew where to go to make people aware of them.

Black Americans learned about the experiences of women like Ethel Bell, Hattie Combre, and Burneda Coleman and heard the charges of discrimination made by Willa Brown through the black press. During the war years, black female journalists did all they could to bring the stories of other black women to the attention of newspaper readers. As with many other areas of society in the 1940s, newspaper ownership and readership was segregated by race. Black-owned newspapers were widely read in black communities. Readers learned about upcoming events sponsored by community organizations and women's clubs. They read about what was happening at their children's schools. And they followed the movements of black troops in the war. It was through the newspapers that black people learned about events in Washington that would have an impact on their lives. Black newspapers were a source for information that they couldn't get from white newspapers—in which the accomplishments of black citizens were ignored.

Lula Jones Garrett, Rebecca Stiles Taylor, Diana Briggs, Venice T. Spragg, and Bettye Murphy Phillips were journalists who devoted their careers to improving the lives of black women. And they were passionate about their work.

Lula Jones Garrett reported for the *Afro American,* a black newspaper that had been in existence since 1892. She wrote news articles and editorial columns. In her column "These Versatile Women" she highlighted the lives of famous black women in entertainment and the arts. Her "Lipstick" column was a lighthearted look at women's lives, sprinkled with a little advice: "The most delicate job any wife has is to feed her husband the proper dose of flattery." But Lula was not confined to "soft" news—articles about hair, makeup, and fashions. She also wrote "hard" news—articles about black women in the workforce and in the military. In the winter of 1944 she wrote a series of articles about how black women lived and worked in the Women's Army Corps (WAC). And in her book review of the popular book *Strange Fruit* she wrote, "For though I have witnessed two lynchings, I had not until today, understood the look of unhuman blood lust on the face of a lyncher."

Lula Jones Garrett was a reporter and columnist for the *Afro American.*
National Park Service; Mary McLeod Bethune Council House National Historic Site; National Archives for Black Women's History/Photo Courtesy of the Afro-American Newspapers Archives and Research Center

Newspaper publisher Charlotta Bass published the *California Eagle* in Los Angeles. *Courtesy of the Southern California Library for Social Studies and Research/Photographer George M. Cutler Jr.*

Charlotta Bass was a businesswoman who made a living from journalism. Not only did she do the day-to-day reporting for the *California Eagle*, but she also owned the paper. Charlotta used her newspaper as a vehicle to demand rights for black citizens in Los Angeles. She used her editorial column "On the Sidewalk" to make her opinions known and to call readers to action. She encouraged readers to write to politicians about racial injustices and to become involved in their communities. In the 1930s she led a move to boycott businesses that would not serve or hire black people in the Los Angeles area. She sent telegrams to President Roosevelt to demand action against racial injustices in Los Angeles. When a white columnist from another paper attacked black newspapers she called him "one of the biggest skunks in the history of American journalism." One of Charlotta's biographers wrote, "Indeed, visibility in the community characterized nearly all of Charlotta's actions through the 1940s."

Female journalists were highly visible on the pages of the *Chicago Defender*, a black newspaper, during the war years. Rebecca Stiles Taylor, Venice T. Spragg, and Diana Briggs wrote about issues that affected women's lives.

Rebecca Stiles Taylor started her career as a junior high school English teacher in Savannah, Georgia. Her work led to her involvement in the women's club movement. Black women's clubs in the 1940s were instruments of social and political change. And Rebecca was a vital part of several clubs at the local, state, and national levels. During the war years she wrote a weekly column, "Activities of Women's National Organizations," in which she kept readers up to date about women's organizations across the country. In her column late in 1942 she issued her opinions about the role of women in the 1940s, "There is a world revolution. . . . Woman shall pitch in to take her proper place in the stern business of running—not the world—but the community in which she lives."

Venice Spragg reported on women's issues at the national level. In her column "Women in the National Picture" she reported on happenings of the National Council of Negro Women, the National Association of Colored Women, and the National Negro Congress. She kept readers up to date about legislation in Washington that affected the lives of black women. She recommended readings from professional publications such as the *Journal of Educational Sociology*. Venice encouraged black women to take every opportunity to get more education. She wrote, "One thing seems certain, the educated woman will continue to come to the fore."

In her feature article "Women Power in War" in September 1942, Diana Briggs reminded readers, "It's a man's war no longer. Today women power is playing an increasing role in every factory and every battlefront." Diana's weekly column, "In a

Man's World" highlighted Chicago women who were making headlines in a "man's world." She profiled Esther Woods, Sarah Harris, Gwendolyn Parkman, Mildred Anderson, and Juanita Jackson in "Gals Take Over Bikes and Keep Wire Buzzin'." The women had been hired by Western Union to deliver telegrams on the South Side of Chicago, where they would replace men who had left for the war. Wearing Western Union uniforms, the women rode through the streets on bicycles delivering messages to homes and businesses. They came from a variety of backgrounds. Juanita Jackson had been a high school student, and Mildred Anderson had worked in a sculptor studio before going to work for Western Union. Sarah Harris had tried to get a job as a telegraph operator but learned that job "was closed to Negro girls." The women enjoyed their jobs but said one difficult part of the job was avoiding dogs who tried to chase them.

Diana Briggs profiled "Peaches, the Cabbie," in her column in March 1942. Lois Mae Davis—"Evanston's only female cabbie"—started driving a cab in 1939 after checking with the chief of police to make sure there was no law on the books that outlawed black women cabbies. The chief said, "I don't see any law against it." By August 1940 she was in business. When she tried to get the men cabbies to allow her to receive calls at one of the cabstands, the men refused. When one agreed to her request, the other men went on strike. So Peaches had to take calls at her house. Soon the "lady cabbie" was in demand.

Bettye Murphy Phillips of the *Afro American* was a journalist with one of the most envious assignments a journalist could get in wartime—war zone correspondent. And she was the *first* black female overseas war correspondent. Late in 1944 she rode a military transport plane for over 26 hours from New York to Scotland and then had a two-hour flight to London. Shortly after her arrival in London, she heard the air-raid sirens and

Bettye Murphy Phillips was the only black woman war correspondent sent overseas in World War II, 1945. *Courtesy of the Afro-American Newspapers Archives and Research Center*

headed for the nearest cellar. That was her introduction to wartime London.

And for a woman who made her living using the English language, the peculiarities of the British version of English were intriguing. In one of her first articles she wrote about unfamiliar terms used by the British—"torch" for flashlight, "underground" for subway, "pub" for tavern, "cinema" for movie, "tram" for streetcar, and "married but not churched" for a love affair without benefit of marriage. But Bettye hadn't come to England to report on the oddities of the English language.

Before leaving for the war zone Bettye had said she hoped to do the job of a regular correspondent. But she also planned to get into "some places where a man can't go." She wanted to see how the soldiers were faring in London and Paris and learn what they were thinking. She wanted to discover what England and France "think of our boys." Bettye was able to do what she had hoped—but it was from a hospital bed in London. Soon after her arrival she was afflicted with paralysis of her left side. She was hospitalized for a couple of months and then sent back to the States. But her hospital stay didn't stop her from reporting. She sent "dispatches" from her hospital bed based on reports brought to her from visitors to her bedside.

Some of those visitors were black soldiers who were eager to talk to a woman from back home. They "tell me their troubles, ask my advice, inquire what I think about people back home," she wrote. Most had been injured in France and were recovering in the London hospital before being sent home or back to the war zone.

One of her visitors was Seaman Alexander (Jake) Williams, a 17-year-old sailor whose ship had been torpedoed by enemy subs in the port of Antwerp, Belgium. He described to Bettye how he had been asleep when the attack occurred. He was forced to abandon ship and jump into the icy waters. After about 30 minutes in the water, he and his shipmates had managed to get to a lifeboat, and they were later picked up by an Allied ship. The sailor was in the hospital undergoing treatment for a spine injury. Bettye reported that Jake said while he was in the water he pictured his mother's face when she got the telegram reporting that he was dead. Happily, that was one telegram that was never sent.

Unwise to Forget

In April 1945 the Women's Bureau of the US Department of Labor issued a bulletin titled "Negro Women War Workers."

The document highlighted the work that black women had contributed across a variety of industries and businesses. Readers were reminded that "their contribution is one which this Nation would be unwise to forget or to evaluate falsely." But throughout the war years the nation ignored and devalued the contributions black women made in every facet of war work. And after the war ended, the nation *did* forget. It was not only unwise; it was wrong.

2
POLITICAL ACTIVISTS

"I Am Not a Party Girl, I Want
to Build a Movement"

Black bodies swinging in the southern breeze . . .
The bulging eyes and the twisted mouth . . .
— *"Strange Fruit" by Abel Meeropol*

Those words are the haunting lyrics of a protest song made
famous by black jazz singer Billie Holiday in 1939. The symbol-
ism of rotting fruit hanging on trees was used to tell the story of
the lynching of a black man in the South in the 1930s. The words
from the song "Strange Fruit" were still meaningful during the
war years of the 1940s.

Some people believed there was good news in the Tuskegee
Institute report released at the beginning of 1944: lynchings in
the United States were down. Only three persons were reported
lynched in 1943—down from five in 1942. Those numbers were
little comfort to the families of two 14-year-old black boys from
Shubuta, Mississippi.

Ernest Green and Charlie Lang were good friends who wanted to do their part for the war effort. They were almost always together. When people in Shubuta saw Charlie, they knew Ernest wasn't far behind. And when they saw Ernest, they knew Charlie was right around the corner. It would be difficult to find anybody in Shubuta who would say the two were good students, but everybody said they were ace scrap collectors. Around the tiny town of Shubuta the two boys were often seen digging through ruins of deserted houses or rummaging through dump piles. They were looking for iron, copper, aluminum, or old tires to turn in to government centers that made the scrap materials into valuable war supplies. Ernest and Charlie were too young to join the military, but at home in Shubuta they could do their part to win the war.

That's what the two were doing on a Tuesday afternoon in October 1942—collecting scrap for the war effort. They were concentrating on an area around a bridge on the edge of town. Ernest was under the bridge and Charlie was on top when a 13-year-old white girl who knew the boys came along on her way home from school.

What happened next is unclear. One report stated that a white passerby driving over the bridge saw the three together. He went to town and told the girl's father that Charlie was "annoying" the girl. Another report stated the girl escaped from the boys after they attacked her and that she ran home and told her parents about the attack. There were other accounts—all with varying details. It's uncertain what actually happened on that October day. But by the following Monday there was no uncertainty about the fate of Ernest and Charlie.

The local sheriff was swift in reacting to the situation. He quickly arrested the two boys. They were taken to the county jail at Quitman, Mississippi. At about 1 AM on Sunday a mob pounded on the door of the jailhouse. According to the county sheriff, a blanket was thrown over his head, he was locked in a cell—and that was the last he saw of the two black boys.

The next day the local citizens were having a gala celebration in honor of Columbus Day. Someone removed two black bodies—Ernest Green and Charlie Lang—hanging from the bridge at the edge of town. They were delivered to the black undertaker in Shubuta. Some reports said there were signs the victims had been tortured. There was a great deal of ambiguity in the reporting of the circumstances surrounding the deaths of the two boys in their little town in Mississippi.

How could people get away with such horrific acts in 1942 in the United States? That was a question many people asked. It seemed especially outrageous at a time when black men and women were fighting for their country in a war for democracy. Was this the America they were fighting and dying for? Roy Wilkins of the National Association for the Advancement of Colored People (NAACP) said that the lynching of black Americans hurt the nation's war effort "as much as a bomb in an airplane factory or shipyard."

When black men were discriminated against by the United States military, when black women were denied employment in war plants that received government contracts, when black citizens could not eat at cafeterias in government buildings, black students could not attend public universities, black nurses could not treat white soldiers, and black Americans could not attend a July 4th celebration, these, too, were situations that hurt the war effort in the eyes of black Americans.

But most black citizens refused to let the injustices keep them from contributing. Many found ways to continue to support their country, while protesting the indignities. Many who led the protests were women. And they laid the groundwork for a bigger struggle that was to come in later years.

The Right to Work and Fight

Some people called A. Philip Randolph "the most dangerous Negro in America" in 1941. He was considered "dangerous" because he wanted to change America. He wanted to change the way black people were treated in employment and in the armed forces. Philip was a well-respected man who had organized black railroad porters into a union in 1925. It was the first labor union for black workers. He had proved things could change when he organized the Brotherhood of Sleeping Car Porters (BSCP).

So when A. Philip Randolph announced plans for a massive march on Washington, DC, in January 1941, black and white people paid attention. They knew he could make it happen. He wanted the president of the United States to do something to help black citizens. And he intended to make it happen—not in a dangerous way—but in a way that would get everyone's attention.

"I suggest that 10,000 Negroes march on Washington, D.C., the capital of the nation with the slogan: 'We loyal Negro American citizens demand the right to work and fight for our country.' Our demand would be simple . . . jobs in national defense and placement as soldiers and officers of all ranks we are qualified for in the armed forces. What an impressive sight 10,000 Negroes would make marching down Pennsylvania Avenue in Washington, D.C., with banners preaching their cause for justice, freedom, and equality," Philip said. The event would be called the March on Washington.

The very same month that Philip called for the March on Washington, President Franklin Roosevelt gave the annual

State of the Union address to the nation. In his speech he outlined "four freedoms" that he said "all Americans" enjoyed.

"We look forward to a world founded upon four essential human freedoms. The first is freedom of speech and expression. . . . The second is freedom of every person to worship God in his own way. . . . The third is freedom from want. . . . The fourth is freedom from fear."

Many black Americans thought the president's words were meant for them. This president seemed to believe in a world free of discrimination. But it didn't take long for them to realize that things were not going to change.

In March 1941 the US Congress passed a law called the Lend-Lease Act. It allowed the United States to provide billions of dollars of war materials to countries "vital to the defense of the United States." President Roosevelt had asked Congress to pass the Lend-Lease Act after British prime minister Winston Churchill asked for help.

Not everyone was happy about the passage of the act because it appeared that the United States was getting involved in the war that was being fought, not on its own soil, but in Europe. A group of about 500 protested the signing of the Lend-Lease Act in a demonstration in front of the White House in April 1941. They carried signs: GET OUT AND STAY OUT OF WORLD WAR NO. 2, FIGHT EVERY STEP TO WAR, and ALL OUT AID FOR BRITAIN MEANS TOTAL WAR FOR AMERICA. In his campaign for the presidency in 1940, Franklin Roosevelt had promised that the United States would *not* get involved in the war. "I have said this before, but I shall say it again and again and again; your boys are not going to be sent into any foreign wars."

The Lend-Lease Act was good news for owners of companies that manufactured products needed by the warring countries. It meant the US government was issuing billions of dollars in contracts with these companies to produce materials to ship to the countries that were "vital to the defense of the United States." That meant the companies with the government contracts needed more workers. These companies were willing to pay workers well for their work. And the government was willing to train workers to learn skills needed to work at the jobs.

All of this was good news to black people who were eager to improve their job opportunities and to learn new skills. Companies that had never considered hiring black people were beginning to hire black men and women because they needed all the workers they could get. But reports of discrimination in the defense industries, the military, and in everyday life made people realize that things were not different. It was difficult to sustain hope when discrimination persisted. Many black Americans did not believe others in their country felt the four freedoms were meant for black people too.

Although the United States was not yet at war, the government wanted to be ready for any possibility. In September President Roosevelt had signed the Selective Training and Service Act of 1940. It required all men between the ages of 21 and 35 to register with the government for military service. The government began to draft men for service. At first black Americans were hopeful. There were many black men and women who were eager to serve in the US military. The act specifically stated, "In the selection and training of men under this act, there shall be no discrimination against any person on account of race or color."

But early in 1941 the military *did* discriminate. Black men in the army lived and worked in segregated units. They were not allowed to join the Army Air Corps. They were allowed to join the navy—but were assigned only to "mess" duties. This meant they were like servants. The Marine Corps did not accept black men. Women of any color were banned from all branches of the military.

So when A. Philip Randolph called for a "nonviolent" march through the streets of Washington, DC, on July 1, 1941, many black Americans thought it was a good idea. Philip said black people wanted the four freedoms that President Roosevelt had mentioned in his State of the Union address—freedom of speech and religion and freedom from want and fear. But they also wanted a fifth freedom—freedom from discrimination.

Philip was a powerful man, a passionate speaker, and a convincing motivator. But he wasn't much of an organizer. He needed other people who could do the day-to-day work of organizing a massive march of thousands of people. Marchers would be coming from all over the country to the nation's capital. Philip needed help, and he had someone in mind for the job.

The Woman Behind a March

Layle Lane was a tiny woman—only five feet, two inches tall. She was the only black teacher at Benjamin Franklin High School in New York City, where she taught history and English. Although she was very strict, students wanted to get into her classes. Layle was the first black female vice president of a teachers' labor union—the American Federation of Teachers. Most important, Layle Lane was as passionate as A. Philip Randolph when it came to fighting discrimination. And Layle was a great organizer. Philip wanted Layle to help with the March on Washington because she had worked for him in the 1920s when he organized the black porters into the BSCP. She had encouraged workers to join the union, and they did. So he knew she could be very persuasive.

When Philip asked Layle to help organize the March on Washington, she said yes. Together with a committee of men and women, Layle put together plans for a silent, dignified march down the streets of the nation's capital. It would end in a mammoth demonstration at the Lincoln Memorial.

Plans were laid out with military precision. Each state would send a brigade of three to five divisions of men, women, boys, and girls. The brigades would be headed by veterans from the Great War (that is, World War I). Ministers from churches across the country pledged their support. Local committees throughout the country registered participants. Organizers sold buttons to raise money for transportation by car, train, bus, or by foot. They spread the word through newspapers and by going door-to-door in cities across the country handing out flyers. And Layle—who was opposed to the drinking of alcohol—even marched into taverns in New York City to pass out information.

By May 1941 the number of marchers who planned to march to Washington in support of equal treatment in the military and employment was estimated at 100,000. The Washington police were preparing for the worst. They didn't know what they would do if 100,000 "additional

Layle Lane was a leader in the planning of the March on Washington.

Courtesy of the Afro-American News-papers Archives and Research Center/ Photographer James L. Allen

Negroes" came to the city since they were already experiencing "difficulty in coping with problems of handling 170,000" who lived in the city.

But A. Philip Randolph said, "The people who will be there from all over America are not hoodlums and ruffians. They represent the finest citizens of the nation, sincere in their desire to have justice."

And Layle Lane said black Americans needed to "hammer away at the walls of segregation 'til they come tumblin' down." She said black citizens needed to "make life uncomfortable for all those who have to be reminded of the meaning of our fundamental principles." As the nation moved closer to war—a war *against* tyranny and injustice and *for* the principles of democracy—the time was right to demand equal treatment in America for all citizens.

As the day of the march neared, government officials got very nervous. Finally, President Roosevelt sent word to the march organizers that he didn't want the March on Washington to take place.

But the organizers wouldn't back down. The March on Washington organizing committee said they had met and decided to continue their "efforts to make the March on Washington the greatest demonstration of Negro mass power for our economic liberation ever conceived."

Suddenly, a few days before the march, the organizing committee and A. Philip Randolph were invited to the White House for a conference. Layle Lane was part of the group that made the trip to Washington, DC, to talk to President Roosevelt.

During the conference the president said a march to Washington by a large group of black Americans would do more harm than good. He said that the discrimination faced by some black people had to be dealt with through methods that were carefully thought out and planned. A. Philip Randolph told the president that the march *had* been carefully planned by a committee of "sane, sober and responsible Negro citizens."

The president kept insisting that the march was a bad idea. After about 30 minutes the president had to leave the meeting, but he asked his advisers to remain and continue the conference without him. The members of the March on Washington committee tried to convince the government officials that the president should issue an executive order that would require companies with government contracts to hire black workers. They tried to convince the officials to do something about discrimination in the armed forces.

When Layle Lane had the opportunity to speak, she said it was time for America to fully integrate black citizens into American democracy. She said if America really wanted to take the lead in fighting for preservation of democratic institutions and traditions—as it appeared to be doing by becoming involved in the war in Europe—it needed to recognize that it couldn't ignore the rights of the black citizens of the United States.

President Roosevelt must have been convinced by Layle Lane and the men who went to the White House. Just a few days after the group had gone to see the president, he signed Executive Order 8802. The order banned companies with government contracts from discriminating against anyone who applied for jobs—regardless of the color of their skin. The order also established the Fair Employment Practices Committee (FEPC), a six-man board charged with implementing and enforcing the order. There were two black men on the commission. The rest were white. Complaints about discrimination could be made to the FEPC. When a complaint was issued, the FEPC would investigate.

The government had posters printed and sent to 12,000 plants around the country. The 24-inch-by-28-inch blue posters bore the words of the president—"I DO HEREBY REAFFIRM THE POLICY OF THE UNITED STATES THAT THERE SHALL BE NO DISCRIMINATION IN THE EMPLOYMENT OF WORKERS IN DEFENSE INDUSTRIES OR GOVERNMENT . . . AND THAT IT IS THE DUTY OF EMPLOYERS . . . TO PROVIDE FOR THE FULL AND EQUITABLE PARTICIPATION OF ALL WORKERS IN DEFENSE INDUSTRIES." A letter was sent with the posters asking that they be displayed where all workers could see them.

Because the president had issued Executive Order 8802, Randolph cancelled the March on Washington. Some black people were excited about the possibilities for nondiscrimination in hiring. But others were disappointed and angry that the march had been called off.

The march may have been cancelled, but the fight for civil rights in the military and equality in defense hiring did not end. As the nation moved toward war, the need for equal treatment of all Americans was intensified in the view of many black people. At a time when the president of the United States talked about freedoms for *all* Americans, it seemed a good time to talk about a fifth freedom—freedom from discrimination. A movement that began in wartime would have lasting impact. And that movement was orchestrated by some determined black women.

The Women Behind a Movement

When A. Philip Randolph cancelled the March on Washington in 1941, he knew that much work still needed to be done. The establishment of Executive Order 8802 as a result of the threatened March on Washington proved that black citizens could make change occur. If Layle Lane and her committee could motivate 100,000 people to march to the capital from all over the country, they knew they could accomplish more. The people who had planned the march continued to work against discrimination. They called their work the March on Washington Movement (MOWM). Some very determined black women were leaders in the movement.

When A. Philip Randolph asked E. Pauline Myers to host a social event for some members of a national labor union she said, "I am not a party girl; I want to build a movement." And she did.

Philip knew that Pauline was much more than an event planner. E. Pauline Myers had worked with Layle Lane to help organize the March on Washington. So when Philip was looking for skilled organizers to manage the national office of the MOWM, he convinced Pauline to oversee the local chapters around the country. She also planned mass meetings, designed flyers, and raised money for the organization.

One way she raised money was by writing pamphlets that the MOWM could sell. She wrote one titled *The War's Greatest Scandal: Jim Crow in American Uniform*. It sold for five cents. She also wrote *Non-Violent, Good Will, Direct Action*, which sold for 10 cents.

Pauline called the discrimination practices of the military "antidemocratic" and "anti-American." She spoke out against them across the country. She printed a flyer advertising her speech. It read, "Coming soon to your city. The daring young woman whose brilliant exposé of the United States Army's racial bias is now helping to shape new military policy. In a ringing lecture discussion."

Some people considered Pauline a troublemaker, but nothing could be further from the truth. In fact, she was behind the movement called Non-Violent, Good Will, Direct Action. This was an idea that encouraged black citizens to resist discrimination by direct action. But the *action* should be taken with *good will* in mind. And the actions should be *nonviolent*.

This was a new idea. It was a turning point in the fight against discrimination. In the past, black leaders had encouraged citizens to fight discrimination by writing letters and telegrams to government leaders. Black leaders had sponsored conferences where citizens heard speakers talk about fighting discrimination. Through talking and writing, they had tried to get white leaders to listen.

But E. Pauline Myers felt that "the old method . . . has been exploded. The patience of Negro America is sorely tried." She explained the plan for the new direction: "The need is for mass organization with an action program—aggressive, bold, and challenging in spirit, but nonviolent in character. It invites attack, meeting it with a stubborn and nonviolent resistance that seeks to recondition the mind and weaken the will of the oppressor."

The new direction included huge rallies in major cities in the summer of 1942. A. Philip Randolph called for mass protests in New York City, Chicago, St. Louis, and Washington. He asked all black citizens in those cities to march together to protest discrimination in the military and in war plants. He wanted blackouts during the rallies. He asked business owners to lock up their shops, ministers to close their churches, homeowners to pull their shades, and partygoers to stop their partying for a few hours on the nights of the rallies. He wanted black communities to be "dark, dry, and silent." Once again it was women who did much of the planning, promoting, and coordinating.

It was surprising that anyone showed up for the June 16 rally in New York City considering all the obstacles planners Layle Lane and E. Pauline Myers had to overcome. They ran into one problem after another. They were denied city permits required for large gatherings. They wanted to rent Madison Square

Garden, but the managers were reluctant to rent to the March on Washington Movement. Most white newspapers failed to publicize the rally. But finally all problems were overcome, and on the night of the event an estimated 25,000 black citizens of New York City converged on the Garden.

It was a spectacular affair with speeches, music, and drama. Bessye Bearden, president of the Harlem Housewives League, and Mary McLeod Bethune, from the National Council of Negro Women, gave speeches.

The crowd cheered when Mary McLeod Bethune said, "I want all America to understand that we will never strike our flag. On the contrary, we will eternally protect it with all that we have in courage, in faith, in endurance. At the same time, we want our flag to protect us—at home in our right to produce and live, abroad in our willingness to sacrifice and die."

The crowd burst into laughter and applause when the Reverend S. T. Eldridge proclaimed, "After this world conflict is over, we want to be a part of this democracy. We don't want to be like a label on a bottle—all around it, but not in it."

The New York event was considered a huge success. The management of the Madison Square Garden facility must have been surprised at the big turnout. Usually when an event took place at the Garden, the marquee on the outside of the building flamboyantly announced the event in bright lights. But the March on Washington Movement rally was never lit up on the marquee.

In Chicago, Ethel Payne was a key organizer for the June 26 rally at the Chicago Coliseum. Thousands of black citizens crowded into the sports arena. They even overflowed into the streets, where amplifiers broadcast the voices of the speakers from inside the building. Working men and women as well as professionals joined the rally. Speakers demanded an end to discrimination in employment, the armed forces, and government.

Southern congressmen who controlled key committees in Congress were blasted for denying black citizens their civil rights. The businesses and homes in the predominately black neighborhoods of the South Side were darkened from 9 to 10 PM to show support.

In St. Louis, Thelma McNeal was a leader in organizing the black citizens to rally on August 14, 1942, at the municipal auditorium. Even some white business owners in parts of the city agreed to participate in the blackout for 15 minutes on the night of the rally. Volunteers distributed flyers and bumper stickers to promote the event. Speakers, musicians, and actors entertained the estimated crowd of 9,000 citizens who turned out for the rally. Protestors carried signs that read HOW CAN WE DIE FREELY FOR DEMOCRACY ABROAD IF WE CAN'T WORK EQUALLY FOR DEMOCRACY AT HOME? and LET'S PRACTICE DEMOCRACY AS WE PREACH IT!

The Washington, DC, event never happened. But rallies in New York City, Chicago, and St. Louis made up for the disappointment in the nation's capital.

For five days in June 1943 delegates from across the country gathered for a convention in Chicago called We Are Americans, Too. A. Philip Randolph had asked E. Pauline Myers and Ethel Payne to organize the event. At the convention delegates voiced their support of the Non-Violent, Good Will, Direct Action campaign. They agreed to use the technique to fight discrimination in employment, transportation, and any situation where discrimination was obvious. They also agreed to set up educational institutes around the country to train people in how to use the technique. Part of the training would include teaching people how to organize and participate in pickets and parades in nonviolent ways. The institutes would teach people how to remain quiet when they were being insulted. And, most important, the nonviolent training showed people how to endure physical assaults without striking back. During the final day of the convention, after two hours of debate, a controversial decision was reached. The delegates voted to bar whites from participation in the March on Washington Movement.

Many speakers gave talks during the five days. Some were women. Senora B. Lawson from Richmond, Virginia, said she supported the work of the March on Washington Movement because "it remembers the forgotten men, the men of the street, and gives them a chance to work and exercise their talents." Cordelia Green Johnson, president of the Beauty Culturists League in New Jersey, said, "We're not asking to sit at the banquet table of white people, but we are asking to sit at a banquet table and eat of the Bill of Rights. It is not necessary to have freedom in heaven, we won't need it there. We want freedom here and now when we can enjoy it." Layle Lane said black people had tools to use in the fight for equality. She said they had tools in "numbers." She meant there were millions of black people living in the United States who, she said, had "purchasing power" of billions of dollars annually. She also reminded the delegates that black people—especially in the northern states where blacks could vote without restrictions—needed to use their voting power to elect candidates who were in support of equality. And E. Pauline Myers reminded the delegates that "colored citizens have the right to disobey unjust laws."

Some black women began to experiment with the idea of taking actions that were nonviolent but bold and challenging. They began to invite attacks and meet them with stubborn resistance.

Stubbornly Resistant

Pauli Murray had applied for graduate school at the University of North Carolina in 1938. She was refused. The letter she received was very clear: "Members of your race are not admitted to the university."

Pauli tried the old method of fighting discrimination. She wrote letters—one to President Roosevelt. A copy of that letter went to First Lady Eleanor Roosevelt. The president didn't answer, but the First Lady responded to Pauli's letter. It led to a lasting friendship between the two women, but it didn't get Pauli into the University of North Carolina.

Being multiracial—black, white, and Cherokee Indian—Pauli Murray knew all about racial discrimination. But "colored" was the only part that a bus driver in Virginia saw on Easter night 1940. And that, along with Pauli's stubborn resistance to segregation practices, was enough to get her arrested.

Pauli and a friend were on their way that night to visit Pauli's family in Durham, North Carolina. They were traveling by bus from New York. The two young women were sitting toward the back of the bus but close to the center. Other black passengers were sitting behind them. The white passengers were seated in front of the women. When more white passengers arrived, the driver told Pauli and her friend to move farther back. But Pauli could see more black passengers coming onto the bus. She knew they would fill up the empty spaces in the back. So she said there was no reason to move from her seat.

The driver left and returned with the police, who arrested Pauli and her friend for creating a disturbance and violating the segregation laws of Virginia. Before the two women left the bus, Pauli gave another passenger her mother's name and telephone number. By that evening Pauli was visited in her jail cell by lawyers from the NAACP.

The lawyers were very impressed that Pauli and her friend had taken great care to write in detail everything that had happened to them on the bus. Pauli and her friend got out of jail.

The NAACP lawyers made plans to file a lawsuit. Before they could do that, the charges of violating the segregation laws were dropped. But the disturbance charge remained.

This was a turning point in Pauli Murray's life. It was one event that led her to law school in 1941 and led her to become a pioneer in the fight for civil rights.

Sit-ins

On a warm July day in 1944, Hattie Duvall, a middle-aged woman from St. Louis, Missouri, walked back and forth in front of a department store carrying a sign that read: I INVESTED FIVE SONS IN THE SERVICE. Hattie wasn't simply boasting about her sons. She was protesting the discrimination she would face if she went into the store and sat at the lunch counter. She knew no one would serve her. In fact, they might ask her to leave the store.

This was especially hurtful for Hattie. She had indeed "invested five sons" in the war effort. Her sons had been part of the D-day invasion in France—the largest amphibious invasion of all time. She thought her contribution to the war effort gave her the right to eat where she wanted.

A year before Hattie protested outside the St. Louis department store, a group of black citizens in Washington, DC, carried signs as they protested in front of a restaurant there. It was the spring of 1943, and the protestors were students at Howard University—a predominantly black university. They were trying the direct-action approach in an attempt to bring civil rights to black citizens in the nation's capital city.

The students carried signs too:

OUR BOYS, OUR BONDS, OUR BROTHERS ARE FIGHTING FOR YOU. WHY CAN'T WE EAT HERE?

WE DIE TOGETHER—WHY CAN'T WE EAT TOGETHER?

They felt that since their friends and family members were fighting and dying in a war for democracy they should have the right to eat where they wanted.

The Howard students were led by a female law student— Pauli Murray. The students were studying civil liberty laws in their classes at the university and knew they were not doing anything illegal. For about a week before the protest the students rallied other students to support the planned protest at a nearby restaurant that had a whites-only policy.

On the day of the "direct action sit-in"—a Saturday—12 students went to the restaurant. The students entered in groups of three and asked for service. When they were refused, they took seats and pulled out magazines, books, pens, and paper. They sat quietly and studied. Police arrived and remained outside. The students weren't doing anything illegal.

Black students continued to enter the restaurant in groups of three. They asked for service, were refused, and sat quietly reading. Soon most of the seats in the restaurant were taken

Pauli Murray led sit-ins at lunch counters in Washington, DC.
The Schlesinger Library, Radcliffe Institute, Harvard University

by black students who were willing to eat and pay for their food—but whom the owner refused to serve. Only a few seats remained for paying white customers.

Finally, the owner closed the business for the day. He said, "I'll lose money, but I'd rather close up than practice democracy this way."

The students remained outside the restaurant and formed a picket line. When customers tried to enter the restaurant, the students explained the situation. Some white customers expressed support for the students' actions.

"I think it's reasonable. Negroes are fighting to win this war for democracy just like the whites. If it had to come to a vote, it would get my vote!" one white customer said.

Another said, "Well now, isn't that something! I eat here regularly, and I don't care who else eats here. All I want is to eat. I want the place to stay open. After all, we're all human."

On the following Monday, the students again set up their picket line in front of the restaurant. Within two days, the restaurant owner had given in and changed his policy. No more "whites only" at this restaurant.

A year later the Howard students decided to try to integrate the heart of Washington, DC. They went to a restaurant near the White House. On a Saturday afternoon in 1944, groups of two or three students dressed in their best clothes entered the restaurant. Every ten minutes more black students strolled into the restaurant.

Outside a picket line of black students formed as well. They were well dressed and well behaved. Even when a group of white soldiers taunted the picketers, they refused to react. They remembered the training they'd had. They were quiet and dignified.

Meanwhile, 55 black students had taken seats inside. The manager called the corporate office of the establishment and reported that the restaurant was filling with black customers. The manager was ordered to serve the students.

In Chicago, Bernice Fisher, Rita Baham, Gladys Hoover, Shirley Walowitz, Sylvia Barger, Eleanor Wrights, and Priscilla Jackson, members of a student group at the University of Chicago, had also sworn themselves to the elimination of discrimination by means of nonviolent action.

The women and some of their male classmates formed a group of about 20 students intent on integrating a South Side restaurant in May 1943. The restaurant had always discriminated against black customers. The group—consisting of black and white students—entered the restaurant and seated themselves. Five of the group were black—three men and two women.

The three men went up to the counter. The two black women sat in a booth with some of the white students. The waitress told the three men at the counter that they could be served in the basement—where blacks had been served in the past. They declined. They preferred to sit upstairs at the counter.

The manager tried to get the black women to move to a booth in the back of the restaurant. When they refused to move, the manager called the police. The police arrived but said no one was breaking the law.

With all the tables occupied and the seats at the counter taken by the protestors, the manager and waiters held out. They wouldn't serve any black people. But the protestors weren't going anywhere. They sat and sat. Finally, after two hours, the manager gave in. Everyone was served.

The students were surprised but happy. They had lined up enough students to take turns coming into the restaurant in groups of 20. But the first group achieved results—so the second and third groups weren't needed.

When Hattie Duvall participated in the movement in St. Louis she joined other black professional women and college students who had learned from the protestors in Washington and Chicago. The St. Louis group also stood up to discrimination with "stubborn and nonviolent resistance" in the form of a series of sit-ins that summer. Sometimes men joined the women. And sometimes white people joined. But it was a core group of black women who planned, organized, and led the effort. Marie Harding Pace, Thelma Grant, Modestine Crute Thornton, and others organized and participated in about a dozen sit-ins in department store restaurants between May and August 1944 in St. Louis. On May 15, 1944, Pearl Maddox and Birdie Beal Anderson—joined by three college students, Vora Thompson, Shermine Smith, and Ruth Mattie Wheeler—went into a popular department store and asked to be served in the store's restaurant. The manager invited Vora Thompson to a private meeting in his office. He explained to Vora that she couldn't be served because it would "create a disturbance" and "the American pattern would not permit the serving of Negro customers." Vora told the manager that black men were suffering and dying in a war for democracy. Certainly, blacks should be allowed to eat where they chose in a democratic America. Vora said it was "time to begin training Americans to respect Americans. Our brothers and our sweethearts are suffering and dying all over the world to destroy Fascism, and you and I must get rid of it at home."

While Vora was in the meeting with the store manager, the other women were enjoying a soda and a sandwich in the restaurant. Their lunch had been purchased by a white man who had been in the protest group. The black women quietly ate their lunch at the counter and left. Vora's visit with the store manager failed to change the store's policy of discrimination. The manager and waiters continued to make it clear that black diners were not welcome at the lunch counter.

In July, 55 women enjoyed ice cream at a department store restaurant in St. Louis. Forty of the women were black. Fifteen were white women. The white women had purchased the ice cream and given it to the black women. Sometimes the sit-ins by the black women of St. Louis caused a stir. At another sit-in at a drugstore counter, for instance, Shermine Smith had eaten only part of her sandwich when the manager took the sandwich from her hands, grabbed Shermine by the arm, and lifted her from her seat. Shermine remembered what she had been taught. She met the attack with nonviolent resistance. She didn't kick, or scream, or resist the manager. She didn't say anything as he escorted her from the store.

Usually when these black women entered a restaurant the waiters refused to serve them. Sometimes the white customers complained and left because they didn't want to eat with black people. When that happened, the managers sometimes closed the stores for the day—which meant the stores were losing money.

As the summer of 1944 wore on in St. Louis, the protestors learned new tactics. They started moving their sit-ins from Mondays to Saturdays. The weekends were busier, and closing the restaurants caused more loss of money for the store owners and white workers.

Sometimes the police were called to remove the protestors. The women began to plan sit-ins at more than one restaurant at the same time to cause delays in the police arrivals. That gave the protestors more time to sit at the counters—and more time for people to notice them.

And like Hattie Duvall, the women used signs to call attention to their cause. As they silently walked back and forth in front of the stores where they were refused service, they carried big signs:

WHY CAN'T I EAT HERE?

WHAT DOES DEMOCRACY MEAN TO YOU?

A NAZI'S BULLET KNOWS NO PREJUDICE

MY MOTHER SERVES, MY BROTHER SERVES, MAY I BE SERVED?

Maybe white people who saw them would think about the four freedoms that President Roosevelt had spoken about in his State of the Union address in 1941. Maybe they would think about the injustice of discrimination when they witnessed black people quietly and politely asking for basic civil rights. Maybe they would think that the contributions black Americans were making to the war effort should give them the right to eat where they wanted. However, it was long after the war ended that black customers were finally welcomed at St. Louis lunch counters. The women who led the sit-ins during the war years laid the foundation for what was to come years later.

The VV Campaign

At a time when everyone in the world was paying attention to the ideas of democracy and freedom, it seemed like a logical time to talk about democracy and freedom for blacks in the United States. That's why a black newspaper called the *Pittsburgh Courier* started the Double V campaign in 1942. "Double V" stood for victory at the war front and victory at home—victory for democracy in Europe, Africa, and Asia, and victory for democracy in America.

The campaign spread quickly across the country. Black citizens of all ages talked about the Double V. It was a symbol of pride. Double Victory Clubs were started. People wore Double V pins and flashed the Double V sign with their fingers to show their support for the campaign. They stuck bumper stickers that read DEMOCRACY: AT HOME + ABROAD on their cars. Women were crowned Double V Girls. When Irene Hunter of Chicago was featured in the newspaper as the Double V Girl of the Week, she was swamped with letters from soldiers stationed all over the world. A teacher in Texas named Ruth Chumley won $25 when her song lyrics were chosen as the theme song for the Double V campaign.

Some black leaders opposed the Double V campaign. They thought movements like the Double V might appear unpatriotic. They thought black activism should be "on hold" for the duration of the war. But others believed it was a perfect time to be active. Movements like the Double V campaign gave some black people the courage to act.

The Double Victory Girls Club of Cincinnati, Ohio, conducted a demonstration in front of a federal government employment building to protest discrimination by the office staff in December 1943. They claimed the government workers at the office generally ignored black applicants for jobs. And they said that when black applicants were considered, they were only offered jobs as maids or maintenance workers regardless of their training and qualifications.

Ethel Payne decided to act when she faced discrimination by a government employee. Ethel knew about discrimination; she had witnessed it more than once in her life. That's why she became involved in the March on Washington in 1941. And she was encouraged when the president signed Executive Order 8802. The order had been directed at the government as well as businesses. Government agencies were reminded that discrimination in hiring for government jobs had to stop.

In December 1942, Ethel had taken a civil service test. She passed the test, which meant she was qualified to be a librarian with the government. She applied for an opening in a government agency in Washington, DC. Ethel was ready to go to work—but over a year later she still hadn't been offered a job. She happened to be in Washington in 1944 and decided to inquire about the status of her application. She set up an appointment to talk to an official at the agency. When Ethel arrived, she was directed to the fifth floor and was greeted by a man who introduced himself as Mr. Mc Pherson. He said, "You've come about the job. Well, I'm sorry to say that I can't give it to you." When Ethel asked why, he admitted she had scored at the top of the grade but that he couldn't hire her because she was black. "I'm sorry," Mr. Mc Pherson said, "but that's just the policy." Ethel thought it was ironic that Mr. Mc Pherson had rejected her application based on the color of her skin. The department where Mr. Mc Pherson worked and where Ethel had been discriminated against was the US Department of Justice!

Anna Arnold Hedgeman was a black woman who was executive director of a national committee that was lobbying for a permanent FEPC—the committee that oversaw Executive Order 8802. In the fall of 1944 she had been invited by the US Senate to answer questions about the need for a permanent FEPC. Some members of Congress wanted the commission to end when the war ended. Anna and others knew that it was an important committee that must continue after the war.

While Anna was at the Senate answering questions from the senators, she experienced discrimination, which only underscored FEPC's importance for her. During a break for lunch, Anna joined a group of white people who were testifying at the hearing too, and they all went to a government cafeteria in the Senate Building. It was there that an employee told one of the white women in the group, "We have orders from the management not to serve Negroes." The group went to another restaurant—in the Senate Office Building. They were again told they could not be served. Finally, the group went to the US Supreme Court building and had lunch in its cafeteria.

One of the white women in the group wrote a letter to President Roosevelt telling him about the injustice. She reported that two restaurants in a government building had refused service to the women because Anna was black. But she added, "I am proud to report here in the building of the highest court of our land we found food and freedom."

The March on Annapolis

When news about the Double V campaign reached Maryland many black residents were inspired. Black soldiers were already fighting for victory on the war front. And now black citizens were prepared to fight for victory at home—in Annapolis, Maryland. They also listened when E. Pauline Myers talked about "mass organization" that was "nonviolent in character."

Black citizens in Maryland were fed up. They claimed too many blacks had been killed by the Baltimore police department. The police said the killings were justified; the black citizens said they were signs of police brutality. Black leaders orchestrated a letter writing campaign to Governor Herbert R. O'Conor. But no one ever got a response from the governor. Was he ignoring the black community's concerns?

A black woman named Juanita Jackson Mitchell managed to *finally* get the attention of Governor O'Conor. She did it by bringing 2,000 black people to the state capitol in May 1942 to make their demands heard. That was impossible for the governor to ignore.

The well-organized event was supported by the Citizens Committee for Justice, which was made up of representatives from 125 black organizations. They contributed $800 to cover transportation costs for anyone who wanted to join the march. People traveled by train, bus, and car. They gathered in front of the state capitol and made their way into the stately old building with its marble halls and crystal chandeliers. A newspaper reporter commented on the "many occupied seats that had never held a colored body before."

The protestors were serious, quiet, and resolute. The governor listened for two hours as individuals explained what actions they wanted. They demanded an end to police brutality. They wanted a new police commissioner and a black judge. They wanted more black police officers—in uniform—so they were visible to all in the community. Lillie M. Jackson asked for an additional black *female* police officer. The group also demanded at least one black person on boards that oversaw institutions in the state. Virgie Waters, the president of the Master Beauticians Association, spoke about the need for a black representative on the state board of beauty culturists and hairdressers. And she wanted an additional black state inspector of beauty shops.

After listening to everything that was said, Governor O'Conor said he would establish a biracial committee to study conditions in the areas of concern. He said the committee would act promptly on some matters but that others would have to be dealt with "gradually."

Juanita Jackson Mitchell gave the final speech. She said, "This demonstration was born out of the desperation of the people and we demand immediate redress." And Juanita explained what they meant by "immediate." She said they expected action from the governor "not within the next year, nor the next month, but next week." Juanita didn't wait for the governor to take actions when it came to helping his black constituents. Later that year she directed the citywide Register and Vote campaign—getting 11,000 black citizens to register, making them eligible to vote in local and national elections. With 11,000 more black voters at the polls, the governor's political career was more tenuous than it had been.

A Maker of History

As Pauli Murray, Layle Lane, and Juanita Mitchell applied their revolutionary approaches in organizing black Americans, other black women utilized their distinctive styles to bring about change through more traditional channels. Crystal Bird Fauset was one who chose a more conventional path.

Crystal Bird Fauset started her career as a teacher, but her efforts in getting black women out to vote for Democratic presidential candidate Franklin Roosevelt in 1932 led to another career. When Roosevelt became president, he appointed Crystal to a position in the Works Progress Administration (WPA)—a federal program designed to carry out public works projects, including the construction of public buildings and roads. In 1938, Crystal ran for a seat in the Pennsylvania state legislature and won. This made her the first black woman elected to the Pennsylvania House of Representatives—and the first black woman in America to be elected to a state legislature. While serving as a state representative, she worked on issues related to working women.

When the war broke out, Crystal was appointed to a position with the Office of Civil Defense (OCD). The OCD was a federal agency that worked to protect the United States from attacks by its enemies. It also worked to keep morale high during wartime. Crystal was assigned to direct race relations within the OCD. Her duties involved working to encourage community leaders to include blacks in civil defense work in their communities.

Crystal Fauset was known for her engaging speaking skills. She drew big crowds. When she spoke to a group of 300 at a meeting of the National Association of Negro Business and Professional Women's Clubs in October 1942, she recommended that a study of all high schools and colleges should be undertaken to learn what white students were learning about "dark-skinned peoples of America." Crystal said students should learn about other races but that "color prejudices" should be targeted "in order to make democracy a greater reality in America." She told the audience that it would be up to women to assume this work because the men were overseas fighting the war. She reminded the women that "this is our war and anyone who tries to shirk is a traitor to the future of the colored American."

Crystal believed black women should become involved in politics, and she encouraged them to vote. She said that by becoming involved in politics blacks could become "makers of history." Crystal was so highly regarded in politics that when President Roosevelt ran for reelection in 1944, he consulted with her on how to appeal to black voters. Despite Crystal's position in the Roosevelt administration and her friendship with Eleanor Roosevelt, her political loyalties shifted to Roosevelt's challenger. Crystal announced in October that she was supporting Republican candidate Thomas E. Dewey for president in the November election. One southern newspaper gloated that "friends of Mrs. Roosevelt who haven't been enthusiastic over her association with Negro leaders are now saying 'I told you so.'" According to the newspaper, it was long believed that "despite all the advantages received under the Roosevelt administration, [blacks] would turn against the President."

Crystal left the Democratic Party because she was disappointed in the party's lack of support for civil rights causes. She continued her political activism in the Republican Party, where she became the adviser on Negro affairs for the Republican National Committee. Although Crystal changed her mind about which political *party* she wanted to support, she had always been an advocate for participation in the political *process*. She believed that black citizens could make economic, educational, and social gains by working within the political system. She continued to promote that message—regardless of which party she represented.

Daughter of Slave, Adviser to President

Another high-profile activist in the 1940s was Mary McLeod Bethune. A personal friend of First Lady Eleanor Roosevelt, Mary became a prominent official in the Roosevelt administration. That friendship had its start in the 1920s when, at a women's luncheon where Mary was the only black woman, she was introduced to Eleanor Roosevelt, years before she became First Lady. By the time Eleanor's husband became president of the United States, Mary and Mrs. Roosevelt were close friends. President Roosevelt appointed Mary to the post of director of the Division of Negro Affairs within the National Youth Administration (NYA). The NYA had been established by President Roosevelt in 1935 to help young people during the Great Depression get training and jobs. It continued into the war years. The NYA served all youth between the ages of 16 and 24 who needed work—and Mary Bethune worked to make sure black youth weren't overlooked by administrators of the program. It was through the NYA that many black women completed specialized training that made them eligible for defense plant jobs.

Mary made it her job to make sure white America did not overlook black America. Her parents and some of her siblings had been slaves. Mary grew up in South Carolina and attended schools there. When she graduated from college she enrolled in a Bible college planning to become a missionary in Africa. She was surprised and disappointed when her application was denied—the mission did not accept black applicants. She turned to teaching and eventually started her own school in Florida. The school, which started as an elementary school for black girls, expanded into a high school and college. It became Bethune-Cookman College. Mary Bethune believed that education was a key to racial equality.

Mary became president of a black women's group, the National Association of Colored Women (NACW). When Mary became dissatisfied with the organization, she started her own group, the National Council of Negro Women (NCNW). Through this organization black women had a voice in Washington.

During the war years, the NCNW sponsored Hold Your Job clinics. These weeklong events were held across the country in areas where large numbers of black women worked in war jobs. It was assumed that black women would probably be fired when white soldiers returned from the war. The Hold Your Job clinics were designed to help black women make themselves valuable to their employers so that when the men returned—it was hoped—the black women might keep their jobs. At the clinics women learned to be "particular about their dress" at work. They were offered courses on "behavior and attitude on the job and in public places." The women were encouraged to take any training available and to join labor unions.

Mary McLeod Bethune was the force behind the admission of black women into the newly formed Women's Army Auxiliary Corps (WAAC) in 1941. When Congress voted to establish the

Mary McLeod Bethune (left) inspected the Women's Army Corps (WAC) training center in Fort Des Moines, Iowa, where she shared a meal with WAC captain Dovey Johnson (right). *National Park Service; Mary McLeod Bethune Council House National Historic Site; National Archives for Black Women's History. Official US Army photo from Office of War Information*

WAAC, the plan called for an all-white organization. Mary Bethune convinced officials to admit black women, and she helped recruit black women for the first class of officer candidates.

Mary became the leader of a group of black leaders who were known as the Black Cabinet in the Roosevelt administration. The official name of the group was the Federal Council on Negro Affairs. It was made up of influential black men and women who studied black issues and problems and made recommendations to government officials. Because of Mary's reputation, she was able to get officials to take action on some of the causes the

Black Cabinet championed. Mary became known as one of the most influential women in the Roosevelt administration.

"Nice Little Girls Teach"

"I was brought up in a family where politics was a daily evening mealtime discussion. But my parents were always keen to admonish, 'nice little girls are not interested in politics and labor unions, they teach.'"

Fortunately, Thomasina "Tommie" Walker Johnson disobeyed her parents. She grew up to become the "first full-time Negro lobbyist in America"—a job that required her to be interested in politics *and* labor unions.

At first, however, Thomasina *did* take her parents' advice— she became a teacher. But when she encountered racism while she was looking for work in Boston, Massachusetts, she got angry and decided she would do something about discrimination in America. This led her to a job as a lobbyist in the US Congress.

The National Non-Partisan Council on Public Affairs was a division of a national black women's sorority called Alpha Kappa Alpha (AKA). The AKA was started in 1908 and had taken on numerous causes to improve the lives of black people—providing healthcare clinics, education assistance, and community betterment projects. One of the women who had started the sorority, Norma E. Boyd, decided to form a division of the sorority that would lobby for black causes in Congress. That's when Thomasina became the first full-time lobbyist representing black interests in Washington, DC.

Walking the halls of Congress dressed in a pastel business suit with a sprig of pink roses pinned to her jacket, Thomasina could "drive a hard bargain where it counts most for Negro people." She led the fight for antidiscrimination in many bills that were brought to votes in both the House of Representatives and the Senate. One was the National Nurse Training Act, which provided for the training of black nurses, and the admittance of black nurse trainees at over 30 hospitals that had not allowed black nurses. Another was an antidiscrimination clause in the bill to draft nurses in wartime.

One of the toughest fights came in the struggle to have black women accepted by the US Navy. When the navy finally agreed to admit black women in May 1945, the plan was riddled with discriminatory provisions. Thomasina helped lead the opposition against the navy's original plan to ban black women from being officers. She also opposed the segregated training schools. Thomasina's fight to eliminate these injustices led the navy to form a committee of black women leaders to iron out a solution. In the end, when black women were admitted to the navy, they were allowed as officers as well as enlistees, and they served in integrated units.

Fighting for Nurses in the Military

Does a wounded or dying soldier care about the skin color of the nurse caring for him? In the 1940s some people felt he would. Most nurses were female in those days. And white nurses cared for white soldiers. Black nurses cared for black soldiers.

When the major general of the US Army told Mabel Staupers he would allow black nurses to serve only black soldiers it was discouraging. But things had been worse before the United States went to war. Although a very small number of black nurses had been allowed to serve during World War I, they were not allowed to remain in the corps after the war. Because Mabel and many others protested that policy, the Army Nurse Corps changed its policy—allowing black nurses in segregated units under a quota system beginning in 1941. The US Navy, however, refused to allow black women in their nurse corps.

Mabel was determined to bring about change for black nurses. And she believed this was a good time to do it. With the nation's leaders talking about the need for thousands of nurses to care for wounded and dying soldiers, it made sense that a quota system for black nurses should be abandoned. But Mabel had a tough fight ahead of her.

The policy of the US Army in regard to black nurses was very clear in 1941: "Negro nurses and other Negro professional personnel would only be called to service in hospitals and wards devoted exclusively to the treatment of Negro soldiers."

Mabel Staupers met with army officials to persuade them to lift the limits on the number of black nurses accepted in the army. The army wouldn't budge. Officials said the army would not "place white soldiers in the position where they would have to accept service from Negro professionals."

Mabel was a resolute and determined activist to prove that black nurses could provide care equal to that of their white counterparts. She was the leader of the National Association of Colored Graduate Nurses (NACGN), a group that fought for the rights of black nurses. It was similar to the American Association of Nurses (ANA), another group that fought for the rights of nurses—but that organization was only open to white women.

Mabel led the NACGN for years, and she didn't give in when it came to fighting for equality for black nurses. She wanted a few simple things. She wanted black nurses and white nurses to be able to attend nursing schools together. She wanted black and white nurses to work together in hospitals. She wanted the armed forces to be integrated. And, although nurses in the armed forces might not be safe from the enemy in a war zone,

Mabel wanted to know her nurses would be safe with their fellow Americans. Because of the racism and discrimination that existed in the nursing profession and the armed forces, Mabel knew none of those things would be simple to attain. But what better time to fight for these basic civil rights? The nation was at war and needed every medical professional available.

Many hospitals around the country operated nursing schools where women could learn how to become skilled nurses. Few accepted black women, and some accepted only a few black applicants each year, so black hospitals established nursing schools where black nurses could get an education.

Norma Green was a black army nurse stationed at the Tuskegee Veterans Administration Hospital at the Tuskegee Institute in Alabama in October 1942. She had volunteered for service overseas and was preparing to ship out. In preparation for her departure, Norma took a bus to Montgomery, Alabama, to do some shopping. But, when she tried to board a bus for her return trip, she said, the driver tried to stop her. There were only whites on the bus. When Norma refused to leave the bus, a policeman was summoned. Norma said he threw her into a patrol wagon and four other officers beat her, blackening her eyes and breaking her nose. The officers stole her money and planted a bottle of whiskey in her bag after dousing her with most of the contents. She was taken to the police station, where she was booked for disorderly conduct. When the police learned that Norma was an army nurse, they released her.

When Mabel Staupers learned of Norma's experience, she sent a letter to the secretary of war. She demanded that all nurses be provided protection. She wrote, "It becomes increasingly difficult for the association [the NACGN] to urge young women to enroll in the Army Nurses Corps unless guarantees are assured."

Early in 1943, Mabel spoke at a conference in Chicago called Negro Nurses in the War. The event was attended by nurses from around the country. A statement was issued by the black nurses: "We believe Negro nurses should be integrated into army hospitals in those sections of the country where these nurses are now accepted by white physicians and staff. We further believe that the morale of the Negro nurse and her whole attitude toward the war program would be strengthened by this action."

As the war wore on, the need for nurses to care for the wounded soldiers in the United States and on the battlefront increased. The military said there was a shortage of qualified nurses and that it needed 10,000 more. So Congress decided to draft nurses for duty—similar to the way it drafted men for the armed forces.

This idea made black nurses furious. Why *draft* nurses when there were hundreds of black nurses who were willing and qualified to *enlist* for work in military hospitals? They were ready to go, but the military insisted on keeping the number of black nurses low. In fact, there were fewer than 200 black nurses in the military in 1943 compared to about 20,000 white nurses. And the military still insisted that black nurses care only for black soldiers.

Jane Edna Hunter, the head of the Ohio State Federation of Colored Women's Clubs, joined with Mabel Staupers to oppose the draft. "Allow all black nurses to enlist, and the draft won't be necessary," they said. "If nurses are needed so desperately, why isn't the Army using colored nurses?"

Another question asked by activists was "Why are black nurses treated with less respect than prisoners of war?" This question came after it was learned that black nurses who worked in a US military camp for German prisoners of war in

Florence, Arizona, were forced to eat in a segregated dining room. The order for this had come from the army major who oversaw the camp. The first day the order was to take effect the nurses decided to ignore it and sat where they had always sat—with the white personnel. The major called the chief nurse and told her that the segregated arrangement had been implemented because he had ordered it. He reminded the nurses that they were in the army and had sworn to obey orders from their superior officers.

The NAACP sent a letter to the US War Department explaining how the nurses felt: "They feel especially humiliated and degraded because, even though in the uniform of the United States Army, they were set apart under the very noses of German war prisoners who serve as cooks and waiters in the hospital officers' mess."

It seemed especially unfair that while the country was engaged in a world war to preserve democracy, black citizens faced discrimination at a US government military installation. Enemy prisoners of war were granted freedoms that some Americans—including black nurses—could not enjoy—just because they were black.

Success!

After fighting for the rights of black nurses in the military for years, Mabel Staupers finally saw results. In January 1945 the Army Nurse Corps lifted its quota on black women. A few months later the US Navy accepted black nurses into its nurse corps. These were encouraging moves for black women. But by the time these changes were made, the war was almost over.

In March 1945, Phyllis Mae Dailey from New York City became the first black woman admitted to the navy. She was 25 years old and had applied several times to the Navy Nurse Corps. She had always received the reply that the navy did not accept Negroes. But Phyllis was determined, and she kept trying. "I knew the barriers were going to be broken down eventually," Phyllis said. She was a member of the NACGN and believed the activism of Mabel Staupers led to her acceptance. "I think the NACGN has been largely instrumental in opening the doors of the navy to us," she said. By the middle of May, Helen Turner and Eula Loucille Stimley were also sworn in as navy nurses. The doors had been opened, and there were more women ready to pass through them.

Phyllis Mae Dailey (second from right) was the first black nurse commissioned in the US Navy in March 1945. *National Archives AFRO/AM in WW II List #158*

Civilian Nurses Face Discrimination

The US military openly discriminated against black nurses; even when they were finally accepted, they were forced to live and work in segregated situations—black nurses cared only for black soldiers. Black and white nurses were housed separately. Discrimination existed in civilian hospitals too. Tuberculosis is a highly contagious disease that was quite common in the 1940s. Nurses who worked in tuberculosis wards risked contracting the disease. Though many public hospitals refused to hire black nurses at all, some public hospitals hired them only for their tuberculosis wards.

The practice of discrimination in the hiring of nurses came to a head in Philadelphia in 1942 when a group of black citizens decided to speak out against the continued racism they experienced. One of the city's tax-supported hospitals had a shortage of nurses. But the hospital continually refused to hire qualified black applicants according to the citizens who were bringing a lawsuit against the city. The group claimed that the hospital administrator and the director of nursing were intentionally overlooking black nurses for positions at the hospital. They said that in the five years the administrator had been at the hospital not one black woman had been admitted to the nurse training school. And the group accused the director of nursing of discrimination. The group said that after black nurse applicants passed the state test for nursing, the director required them to take additional tests. One black nurse applicant said she took three or four tests in addition to her state exam. When she passed all the tests, the director of nurses told her to come back after she lost 16 pounds. Then she was told she needed to lose an additional 30 pounds. It seemed that the administrator was looking for excuses to avoid hiring black nurses. The *Afro*

American, a black newspaper, reported the following year that the city's hospitals still had not hired any black nurses.

The city hospital in Baltimore, Maryland, was desperate for nurses in 1943. They were so desperate they were looking for creative ways to train and hire nurses. The hospital board came up with an innovative plan to solve their problem. There were thousands of Japanese American women detained in government internment camps in other parts of the country. Why not bring them to Baltimore and put them to work in the hospital? The hospital would train them as nurses and give them a place to live. It seemed like an ideal plan.

It seemed like a very *unfair* plan to black citizens in Baltimore. Why import women from other parts of the country when there were black women living in Baltimore who could be trained as nurses? After all, there were only a handful of black nurses currently working for the hospital—all in the tuberculosis ward. There were many more black women who *wanted* to enter nurse training programs but were prevented from doing so because of the hospital's policy of discrimination against black applicants.

Black leaders explained that they were not opposed to the plan because it called for bringing in Japanese American women—they were opposed to the idea of bringing *any* women to Baltimore to be nurses when there were plenty of local women who could fill the positions. They organized a letter-writing campaign to the city's mayor protesting the plan. The letter writers urged the mayor to use his influence with hospital officials to open the programs to black women. The hospital did abandon its plan to train Japanese American women from the internment camps, but continued to refuse to accept black women into the nurse training program. They explained that there were no housing facilities available for black women. "But there are housing facilities available for the Japanese American women?" the black leaders asked. Then the hospital administrators explained that patients in the hospital would be more accepting of Japanese American women from the internment camps than of black nurses.

Once again, it appeared that a public hospital—supported by black taxpayers—was discriminating against black nurses. It seemed hospital administrators were inventing flimsy excuses to justify discrimination.

Too Many Questions

Crystal Bird Fauset, Mary McLeod Bethune, Thomasina Walker Johnson, and Mabel Staupers were well-known activists to most black Americans in the war years. Inda DeVerne Lee, on the other hand, was not a name most would recognize. But this black woman made an impression with American servicemen serving in India in 1945 when she protested discrimination on a day that was revered by all Americans as a day to celebrate freedom.

DeVerne Lee was a woman who liked to try on a pair of shoes before buying them. She liked to slip a pretty dress over her head and check out her image in the dressing room mirror before deciding it was the perfect outfit for a special occasion. But DeVerne was a black woman. In some states she couldn't try on a pair of shoes or a dress in a department store. She could purchase the items—but trying them on first wasn't allowed.

DeVerne was always questioning the rules that people of her race were expected to obey in the 1940s. All that questioning didn't go over well in the community where she was a teacher. After a while, her superintendent suggested she find somewhere else to teach. DeVerne did move from that community and that teaching position, but she never stopped questioning.

After leaving her teaching job, DeVerne joined the Red Cross and volunteered to go overseas in 1945. She ended up in Calcutta, India, working as a staff assistant at the Cosmos, the Red Cross club for black soldiers. Both black and white soldiers came to Calcutta for rest and relaxation. There were three Red Cross clubs—two for white soldiers and one for black soldiers.

The heat in Calcutta (today known as Kolkata) could be unbearable, so the US Army built a beautiful new pool for soldiers and Red Cross workers. Black soldiers and Red Cross workers, however, could enjoy the pool just two days a week and every third Sunday. All other days were reserved for white soldiers and white Red Cross workers.

Shortly after the pool was built, the army decided to hold a big grand opening celebration on July 4. It would be a joint celebration for the pool opening and American Independence Day. That is, a celebration on July *4th* for white soldiers and white Red Cross workers but on July *3rd* for the black soldiers and black Red Cross workers!

The black troops and workers, led by DeVerne, decided to boycott the July 3rd celebration. In other words, the army threw a big party, but no one came. It was an embarrassment to the army and the Red Cross party planners.

Some of the black soldiers were punished for their participation in the boycott. To show their displeasure with the discrimination, DeVerne and some of her coworkers at the Red Cross— Geraldine Smith, Eloise Ligon, Mary Robinson, Bertha Shaw, Willie Lee Johnson, and Alice Johnson—sent a letter to the Red Cross headquarters. They wrote, "July 4th is a day long honored and respected by Negroes as well as other Americans for its significance to democracy and the principles upon which our government was founded. Such a day's celebration involving Americans anywhere on the face of the globe becomes an insult to whatever minority group is excluded from participation."

Because of the incident, DeVerne and the other black Red Cross volunteers requested their return to the United States. But it was wartime, and transportation was dependent on the military. Since the women couldn't be sent home immediately, the Red Cross assigned them to other positions until their travel could be arranged. DeVerne was given a position that separated her from the other black women and the black soldiers. The women were on the first ship back to the United States as soon as the war ended a few months later.

The Activists That Never Were

Many black women were actively working to bring about change for black Americans. Activism took many forms—women's clubs, letter-writing campaigns, and political activities. Many black people saw social activism as one way to draw attention to—and eliminate—racism and discrimination. But in the 1940s many white Americans saw this kind of activity as dangerous because it threatened a way of life that they viewed as normal— a way of life that allowed and encouraged discrimination. Those Americans looked for opportunities to portray black activism as a frightening element in American society.

In 1943 a rumor began to circulate among white women who employed black domestics. According to the rumor mill, there was a secret network of black women activists trying to undermine the long tradition of black women working as maids for white women. The current system depended upon the false idea that black women were inferior to their white mistresses, but the (completely fictitious) network was supposedly populated by black maids who preached social equality and formed clubs to further their cause. And, according to the story, they were instigated by America's First Lady, Eleanor Roosevelt. That's why they were known as Eleanor Clubs.

No one knows exactly how the legend started, but by early 1944 many white women who employed black maids believed the rumors—causing alarm among those individuals who saw this as a threat to their way of life. Here's how the network supposedly worked: Black maids formed Eleanor Clubs and pledged loyalty to the First Lady. The maids who joined promised to resign from any job where members of the household spoke unfavorably about Mrs. Roosevelt, whom club members referred to as the Great White Angel or the Great White Mother. The clubs' goal was for all black maids to leave their jobs with white families by Christmas 1943 or January 1944. White women would have to do their own work in the kitchen. The maids' mottos were "Out of the kitchen by Christmas!" and "A white woman in every kitchen by Christmas!"

The rumors were so outrageous that it was surprising anyone believed them. But many did. One story that ran the circuit was that a black maid left during the middle of a meal she was serving because one of the guests had said something she didn't like about Mrs. Roosevelt. And she had been instructed by the Eleanor Club to leave if ever the First Lady was insulted.

Another rumor was that a white woman in South Carolina walked into her dining room one day and saw three places set at the table. She asked her maid if her husband was bringing a guest for lunch. The maid said no. When the woman asked why the extra place was set, the maid replied, "In the Eleanor Club we always sit with the people we work for."

Another widely circulated rumor described a white Florida woman who drove to the house of her maid when the maid didn't show up for work. She arrived at the house and blasted her car horn. The maid didn't come out. When she went to the door, she saw the maid lying down. The white woman asked if she was sick, and the maid said she wasn't. When asked why she hadn't come to work, the maid reportedly said because she had been to an Eleanor Club meeting where they had been told to demand higher wages, and the club leader had told the women not to respond to car horns from white women.

Eleanor Roosevelt was a strong supporter of civil rights for black citizens. Many Americans criticized her because of her support of some civil rights causes and her friendships with black women. Her actions at a time when racial discrimination was acceptable made her a target for people who believed in the separation of the races.

Also, many black maids were leaving domestic service to work in war industries, where the salaries were better and they would receive Social Security benefits. This was an unsettling idea to white women who benefited from the current system, which required black women to work as servants for low wages. It meant white households might have to pay more for maid service, and they might have to provide better working conditions. But the most troubling aspect to them was that it meant black women were making demands—believing they were equal to whites. The Eleanor Clubs seemed like a possible reason for the exodus of black maids from the kitchens of America. And the First Lady's habit of speaking out against discrimination and associating with black people appeared to explain black women's bold demands.

The rumors became so widespread that the Federal Bureau of Investigation (FBI) took them seriously and conducted an investigation to determine if the clubs existed. It released a statement in January 1943 reporting that their agents had failed to verify the existence of the Eleanor Clubs. They were activist groups that never existed—except in the minds of people who were eager to encourage racist beliefs that black women were to be feared and that activism of any sort by black Americans should be squelched.

The women who fought for black Americans to join the military, work in war plants, and participate in July 4th celebrations had no interest in secret clubs like the fabled Eleanor Clubs. Activists like E. Pauline Myers, Pauli Murray, Layle Lane, Mabel Staupers, Mary McLeod Bethune, and Thomasina Walker Johnson wanted to call *attention* to discrimination. Like many American women during World War II, they wanted to do their part for their country. But for these black women, who believed racism hurt the war effort as much as any enemy bomb, supporting the war effort meant fighting discrimination both at home and abroad.

3
IN THE MILITARY

"Will All the Colored Girls Move Over on This Side"

I went to the coffee shop for breakfast, but I was told I could not be served unless I desired to eat in the back of the shop. I left the place unserved because I know that I could be lynched in the U.S. uniform as well as a man in overalls.

—Louise Miller

"Will all the colored girls move over on this side."

Everyone knew it wasn't a question. It was a command.

At the sound of those words, a small group of black women who were about to make history stepped aside as a much larger group of white women were called by name, one by one, and led off to their new living quarters.

New quarters also awaited the black women. But the living quarters that housed the black women were separate from the whites.

The women were the first to serve in a newly formed organization called the Women's Army Auxiliary Corp—the WAAC. The women—or "WAACs" as they were called—were settling into their new homes at Fort Des Moines, Iowa.

The WAAC had been established a few months earlier by the US Congress. With so many men needed to fight on the battlefields, the government decided to use women to help in noncombat jobs. A bill was introduced by Rep. Edith Nourse Rogers, and on May 15, 1942, the WAAC was created.

Women's Army Auxiliary Corps Is Formed

The women who arrived in Fort Des Moines in July 1942 were members of the first WAAC officer candidate class. As officers, these women would train and lead the enlisted WAACs, called the auxiliaries. Most of the officer candidates were women who had attended college; many were college graduates and had been working as teachers, secretaries, or social workers in civilian life.

The plan called for a total of 440 women to make up the first group of officer candidates. Forty were to be black women. In 1942, an estimated 10 percent of the population in the United States was black, so Congress decided to limit the percentage of blacks in the WAAC to 10 percent as well. The group of black candidates became known as the Ten Percenters.

When the idea of forming the WAAC was brought up, owners of black newspapers and leaders in black communities wrote letters asking the president and Congress to include black women in the corps. Mary McLeod Bethune was working in the War Department in Washington, DC, when discussions began about forming the WAAC. Mary did all she could to make sure black women were given a chance to train as officer candidates.

When the decision was made to allow black women to serve in the WAAC, many black people across the country were pleased. But when it became known that the WAAC would "follow the policies of the regular Army," which included segregating the races, they were very disappointed. Military officials explained that the policy of separating black and white soldiers had been in place for a long time and that they believed the practice worked well for "everyone." They ignored the fact that it *didn't* work well for black soldiers who were restricted to certain jobs within the military and denied basic civil rights.

When a woman from a southern state was appointed director of the WAAC, many black women were disheartened and skeptical of her capacity to be fair when racial issues arose. The director, Oveta Culp Hobby, promised that there would be no "deliberate displays of discrimination," but she said the separation of the races would be necessary. She explained, "The Women's Army Auxiliary Corps will follow in general the policies of the regular army of the United States. These policies have been long-formulated and have been found to be workable and time-tested." The army refused to admit that racial segregation was discrimination.

Organizations that had been fighting for equality for black women in the WAAC said they would continue the fight. A spokesperson from the National Council of Negro Women said, "Now is the time to change the 'present procedure' of the army. If we can't have democracy now, when in heaven's name are we going to have it?"

Recruitment

"This is a woman's war as well as a man's war. Every woman must do her part. One way to do your part is to join the Women's

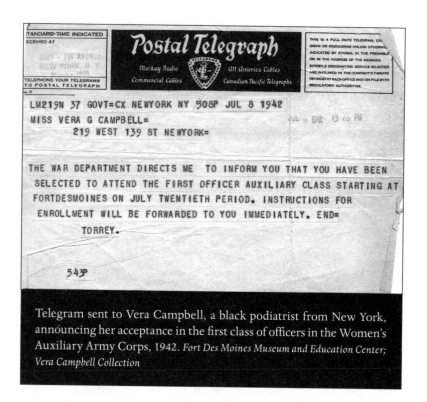

Telegram sent to Vera Campbell, a black podiatrist from New York, announcing her acceptance in the first class of officers in the Women's Auxiliary Army Corps, 1942. *Fort Des Moines Museum and Education Center; Vera Campbell Collection*

Army Auxiliary Corps." These words appeared on the back cover of a government brochure that outlined the requirements for the Women's Army Auxiliary Corps in 1942.

Across the country, posters, brochures, and newspaper ads encouraged women to support the war effort by joining the WAAC. The hope was that women would take the words seriously and apply for the WAAC officer positions or the lower-ranking auxiliary openings.

By May 27, army recruiting stations around the country had been supplied with 90,000 application forms. The response was astonishing. WAAC headquarters in Washington, DC, was swamped with women eager to join. Local recruiting stations were flooded with applicants.

The requirements were straightforward. Candidates had to be between the ages of 21 and 45, stand at least five feet tall, and weigh 100 pounds or more. Single and married woman could apply. If mothers could prove that their children would be cared for during their absence, they could join. Black women were encouraged by leaders in the black communities to apply, but some reported that officials at recruiting stations refused to give them application forms.

All across the country black women responded to the call for women to "do their part." In Chicago two friends, Violet Ward Askins and Mildred Osby, applied together. Charity Adams had just completed her fourth year as a math teacher in Columbia, South Carolina, when she received a written invitation and application form from the WAAC asking her to apply to the first officer training. She had been recommended by the dean of her college. Mildred Carter, a graduate of the New England Conservatory of Music, had danced in Broadway productions and was the first black woman to perform with the Boston Symphony Orchestra. She was operating her dance studio—the Silver Box Studios—in Boston, where she taught ballet, tap, and interpretative dance, when she left to enter the first class of WAAC officers. Vera Campbell, a podiatrist from New York, and Cleopatra Daniels, a school superintendent from Alabama, also volunteered.

Dovey Johnson's grandmother was a personal friend of Mary McLeod Bethune, so when Mary encouraged Dovey to apply to the first WAAC officer class, she entered the recruiting station in Charlotte, North Carolina, with a sense of confidence and asked for an application form. But the white army recruiter tried to squash Dovey's enthusiasm by shouting at her—and ordering her out of the building. He threatened to have her arrested. So Dovey traveled to a city north of Charlotte where she hoped to escape Jim Crow practices. In Richmond, Virginia, Dovey finally was able to complete an application—resulting in her acceptance into the first class of officer candidates.

By June 4—the deadline for submitting completed application forms—over 30,000 women had gotten forms and returned them to local recruiting stations across the country. Four hundred and forty would be chosen to attend officer candidate training. The others would be auxiliaries.

The black women who applied to officer candidate school gave many reasons for their interest in the WAAC. "At this time of history when the entire world is at war, it is the duty of every citizen, regardless of race or creed, to do his share to bring back peace and security to our country," explained Mary Frances Kearney of Bridgeport, Connecticut. "If we are to win the war, it must be won with the help and cooperation of all of us," said Cleopatra Daniels.

Some of the candidates said they were looking for an adventure. Some were bored with their civilian jobs. Some of the black women believed Oveta Culp Hobby when she said that the WAAC would offer "equal opportunity for all."

And Director Hobby reminded everyone that "American women have not failed to realize that they owe a debt to democracy. A debt in return for all the privileges which they have enjoyed as free citizens of a free nation."

With many women applying for the officer candidate slots, the government came up with a way to choose the best candidates. The applicants had to write an essay titled "Why I Desire Service." They were also given an aptitude test. This helped officials learn about the different skills each woman had. Those who passed the aptitude test were interviewed. The next step was a physical exam. Those who passed the physical exam were given another interview. During the second interview many personal questions were asked about the women's school records, families, and hobbies.

Basic Training

Throughout the day and night of July 20, young women—black and white—arrived at Fort Des Moines. They had traveled to Iowa on buses or trains from across the United States. They were met at the station and transported to the fort in army trucks fitted with long wooden benches. The WAAC candidates endured a bumpy ride as the trucks lumbered through the city streets.

As the WAACs passed through the gates of Fort Des Moines they entered a world of neat, red brick buildings and carefully trimmed lawns. The fort had been created as a cavalry post where soldiers who rode horses into battle were trained. Over the years thousands of male soldiers—both black and white—had been trained there. In 1917, when the United States entered World War I, black officers were trained at Fort Des Moines. Now another chapter in American history would begin at the fort. The first black women to enter the WAAC would spend the next few weeks making history there.

Before the WAACs arrived at the fort the old horse stables had been converted into buildings for their use. The street where the barracks stood became known as Stable Row. Some women claimed they could still smell horses in their living quarters!

The very first candidate to arrive at the fort was a black officer candidate named Bessie Mae Jarrett. Just a month before, she had graduated with honors from Prairie View State College in Texas. Soon after her arrival, more candidates began to come from across the country. These new arrivals were white. Several days passed before more black candidates arrived to join Bessie, who was living alone in her segregated barrack.

The black WAACs settled into Building 54, where each woman was assigned a cot and two lockers—a tall green one for uniforms and a smaller one for underclothes, gloves, and equipment. The bathrooms were in the basement.

At the mess hall the black WAACs were again confronted with the ugliness of segregation. A sign had been placed over a table in one area of the room. The sign had the word "Colored" written on it. The black women sat down and ate their meal. But the next day they had a plan. They marched into the mess hall and sat at the table marked "Colored" as they had the day before. Instead of getting into the line to get their food, the black women turned their plates over and refused to eat. The next day when they entered the mess hall the sign had been removed. But a card had been placed on the table. "For C" was printed on the card. Once again the black women turned their plates over and refused to eat. Within a week all the signs had been removed.

Soon after the WAACs were inducted, they were issued uniforms. Much thought and discussion had gone into the design of the clothes. Some officials wanted the uniform to be two shades of blue. Others wanted green. Famous dress designers of the time were asked to help with the designs. It was decided that the uniforms would be dresses—no slacks allowed. Coveralls were provided for WAACs who worked in the motor pool. Hats, coats, and purses were part of the uniform. Galoshes, bedroom slippers, and stockings were issued. And a specially designed "exercise dress" was worn during physical training.

From the first mention of the formation of the WAAC, the general public—tantalized by newspaper reports—was fascinated with the idea of women in a military organization. Newspaper reporters asked about the clothes the WAACs would wear. They wanted to know if the women would be allowed to use makeup. What about nail polish? And one reporter brought up the question of underwear. What would WAAC underwear look like?

Reporters became such a problem that officials limited their contact with the WAACs. After the first day at Fort Des Moines, the reporters were asked to leave. They were not happy about this, but they had gotten many interviews and had taken an assortment of photos of the new WAACs. They had learned that the WAACs could wear makeup and nail polish. And they discovered—and reported in the newspapers around the country—that WAAC underwear was khaki and pink.

During the six weeks of training, the officer candidates had much to learn. Some of the WAACs believed they had to work twice as hard to prove that women could do as well as men in the military. For the black candidates, an additional burden was placed on their shoulders. They had to prove that black women could do as well as men *and* as well as white women.

When Mary McLeod Bethune visited Fort Des Moines during the first week of training she reminded the black WAACs, "We are making history here today."

Women's Auxiliary Army Corps officer candidate in gas mask, 1942.
Fort Des Moines Museum and Education Center; Vera Campbell Collection

"The Negro women whose faces are turned this way are depending upon you to represent us on the ground floor of this new dramatic program that has been set up in America," she added. "Out of the millions of us, you have been selected," Mary pointed out. She stressed the "grave responsibility—a challenging responsibility" that the black WAACs faced.

The WAACs were divided into groups called companies. Each company had three platoons. Each platoon had about 40 members. The first class of black officer candidates was in the First Company, Third Platoon. Only whites were in the First and Second Platoons. All the officer candidates spent their days preparing to relieve male soldiers of their noncombat duties. At the end of the training they would fill jobs as cooks, bakers, truck and ambulance drivers, record keepers, stenographers, telephone operators, and messengers. The army planned to have enough WAACs ready by November 9 to release 450 men for combat. And the plan called for that to occur each week until the war ended.

With only six weeks to learn their new jobs, the WAACs were busy every minute. Reveille was at 6:30 every morning. A loud whistle sounded to wake them. After quickly dressing and making their beds, the black officer candidates rushed from Building 54 across the street to the front of Building 55, where the rest of the company was housed. From there the entire company marched to the mess hall for breakfast.

Classes began at 8 AM and ended at 4:30 PM. The candidates studied military courtesy and customs, organization of the army, first aid, hygiene, and map reading. They learned about current events. And they learned what to do if the enemy attacked by air or with chemicals. They also learned about "property accountability"—how the army kept track of everything it had. Candidates participated in physical training that included handsprings and pushups. They learned how to salute and how to march in formation.

Every Saturday morning the WAACs' quarters were inspected. Inspectors entered the barracks wearing white gloves. They looked for dust under cots, unpolished spots in the latrine, smudges on walls, and dirt on the floors. They inspected footlockers, looking for items that were out of place. Gloves, handkerchiefs, towels, combs, and toothbrushes were to be arranged in a special order in the lockers. And no "unauthorized" items—civilian clothes or food from the mess—were allowed.

Beds were to be made according to army regulations. The fold in the top sheet had to be two inches from the bottom of the pillow and exactly six inches deep. Each bed had two sheets and two blankets. The sheets and blanket were folded in a special way at each corner of the bed. They had to be perfectly smoothed out and tight on top.

The WAACs did have some time for fun. They could take the trolley into the city of Des Moines—a four-mile ride that cost 10 cents. (While they were in training, the WAACs earned $21 per month.) There were movie theaters, shops, and restaurants for entertainment in the city. Some families in Des Moines invited the WAACs to their homes and churches. The Negro Community Center in Des Moines invited the WAACs to tea. Black citizens in the community were eager to meet the black WAACs.

The WAACs didn't have to leave the fort for entertainment. There were service clubs on the base—separate clubs for blacks and whites. There was a golf course, tennis courts, and a movie theater at the fort. There was also a swimming pool—a welcome relief from the humid Iowa heat. But the use of the swimming pool presented another opportunity for the army to inflict racism on the black WAACs. They were allowed to use the pool only one hour a week, on Friday nights. And because many white Americans in the 1940s believed black people were dirty, the pool was "cleansed and purified" after the black WAACs used it.

When the WAACs weren't in classes or enjoying precious free time, they could be found marching in parades. Visitors came to the fort often to see the WAACs "pass in review," or perform in parades. Military and government officials were curious about the WAACs and came to see them. They had never seen women in the military. The Third Platoon, made up of all black women, was an especially unusual sight.

On Saturday, August 8, only three weeks after the first candidates arrived at Fort Des Moines, the WAACs made their first formal public appearance. The gates of the fort were opened for newspaper and magazine reporters and the public. One newspaper reported that the black WAACs marched "with heads high" and "firm of step," "breathing defiance to Hitler, Hirohito, and Mussolini." After the parade the WAACs marched to their barracks, where they changed into their gym suits, marched back to the parade grounds, and demonstrated their physical training for the audience.

Each day ended for the WAACs with "lights out" at 9 PM. There was a "bed check" at 11 PM. Most were so tired by the end of the day that as soon as the lights went out they fell asleep.

The final week of training for the first class of WAAC officer candidates finally arrived. Most of the week was taken up with exams. The WAACs were tested on all the things they had learned in their classes—leadership, military rules and customs, care of equipment, first aid, and sanitation. They were tested on their drills and physical training. The next step was graduation.

One More Opportunity for Racism

Graduation day was Saturday, August 29. It was a hot, sunny day and the ceremonies were held outside. Military and government officials were special guests. Candidates had invited their families. The fort was filled with reporters and photographers eager to record the historic event.

The ceremony was short. There were some speeches, and the national anthem was sung. Finally, the diplomas were awarded. The WAAC officer candidates were no longer "candidates"; they were officers. The new officers wore gold bars on their uniforms as a symbol of their status. Other WAACs were now required to salute them as a sign of respect.

The first class of Women's Army Auxiliary Corps officers had proven themselves to the world. They were ready to move into positions held by men who were needed in battle. It was a momentous day for the black women of the First Company, Third Platoon. They had faced racism and segregation and had responded with grace and dignity.

Vera Campbell, member of the first class of officer candidates in the Women's Army Auxiliary Corps, 1942.
Fort Des Moines Museum and Education Center; Vera Campbell Collection

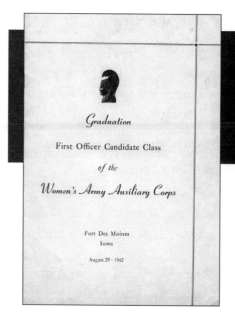

But the discrimination didn't end with the graduation day ceremonies. It would have been natural for the names of the candidates from the entire company to be listed in alphabetical order when awarding the diplomas. For the First Company that meant the first WAAC officer candidate to receive a diploma would have been Charity Adams—a black woman from the Third Platoon. But the army decided to divide the class lists by platoon, so the names of the candidates in the First Platoon and the Second Platoon—all whites—were read first. Last came the Third Platoon.

Despite such treatment, the first black officers of the WAAC were ready for their first assignments—they were eager to learn where they would go and what they would do.

Auxiliaries

As the first class of WAAC officers was undergoing basic training to become commanding officers in the summer of 1942, hundreds of auxiliaries were joining and beginning their basic training. At first the number of black auxiliaries was low, but eventually more and more black women began arriving at Fort Des Moines. All auxiliaries spent one week in a reception center where they received their clothing and equipment and underwent an orientation. Then they had four weeks of basic training. From there some went on to eight weeks of specialist school. Last, the auxiliaries were held in staging companies, waiting for their assignments—where they would begin their new lives replacing men who would move to combat positions.

Those auxiliaries who went to specialist schools after basic training became skilled in administrative duties, cooking and baking, or motor transportation. Administrative specialists learned all about the army's way of keeping records and handling paperwork. Cooks and bakers became responsible for planning and delivering the meals at the camp mess halls. The women in the motor transportation school learned how to drive army vehicles—including the quarter-ton jeep and the one-and-a-half-ton trucks used to transport troops and supplies. Since they were responsible for inspecting vehicles before they were taken out of the motor pool, these women also learned the principles of motor mechanics. In addition, the auxiliaries learned convoy driving so they could move troops and supplies in noncombat operations. Blackout driving—driving in the dark without lights—was also part of the training.

More and more black women joined the WAAC as the war heated up. They signed up for a variety of reasons. Sometimes family members influenced the women's decisions to enter the military. Patricia Gunter's husband was fighting with the American forces in North Africa, and she wanted to do her part to help win the war too. She joined the WAAC and attended administrative specialist school at Fort Des Moines, Iowa. Lessie Ferguson, a correspondent with the *Bluefield Daily Telegraph* in West

Virginia, joined the WAAC the same day her brother joined the army. Hazel and Mazel Greer were the first twins to join the WAAC together. They were from Center, Texas.

The Greer family had nothing on the O'Bryant family of Augusta, Georgia. Tessie O'Bryant sent three daughters off to join the WAACs. Tessie Theresa, Ida Susie, and Essie Dell O'Bryant had decided to join the WAAC together, but when they went to sign up, Essie was sent home because she was underweight. She returned home, and—with the help of family and friends, including the neighborhood grocer—Essie Dell gained enough weight in a month's time to join her sisters. By the time Essie Dell got to Fort Des Moines to begin her basic training, Tessie Theresa had just completed her basic training, and Ida Susie was already an auxiliary stationed at Camp Atterbury, Indiana. But it wasn't only the O'Bryant *women* who were doing their part for the war—five male cousins were serving in the armed forces as well.

In February 1943, Marie Sublett of Springfield, Illinois, joined the WAAC. Marie said she was "rarin' to go" to the training center as soon as possible. It wasn't unusual for a new recruit to feel this way. The idea of serving in the military during wartime sounded exciting to plenty of young girls in the 1940s. But Marie wasn't a young girl. Marie held the distinction of being the first black *grandmother* WAAC!

Marie said she joined the WAAC for a number of reasons. She wanted to work as a recruiter—enlisting other black women. Marie's family and friends thought she'd be good at recruitment work. She seemed to have a knack for judging character in people. One of her favorite pastimes was "watching people." "They fascinate me," she said.

Marie wasn't the first person in her family to serve in the military. Her grandfather had served in the Civil War, and her husband, Robert, had served in the First World War. Robert inspired her to join the WAAC. Marie joked, "I thought I'd serve in the second world war to catch up with my husband."

But Marie wasn't joking when she explained, "I feel that I have served my community by raising a family, and now that a larger opportunity has presented itself to serve my country, I gladly offered my services."

Field Assignments

The idea of women serving in the military wasn't popular with some men in 1942. There were male military leaders who thought women would be more trouble than they were worth. Some thought women could not handle the work required of military personnel. They were reluctant to allow the WAACs on their military bases. And some were especially reluctant to let *black* WAACs on their bases.

WAACs were assigned to bases around the country based on requests from the commanding officers at the installations. Some were willing to use black WAACs—but not for the types of jobs the WAACs were trained to do. Officials said they couldn't imagine how black WAACs could be used other than in "laundries, mess units, or salvage and reclamation shops." These were jobs that required little training or special skills, and they were considered unpleasant assignments. But it was insulting to expect WAACs who had received weeks of specialized training to take these positions just because they were black.

The reluctance of army leaders to request WAACs meant that many of the women who had completed basic training and specialist training and were in the staging centers waited for long periods of time before they were requested at field assignments. The women became very discouraged as the time went on.

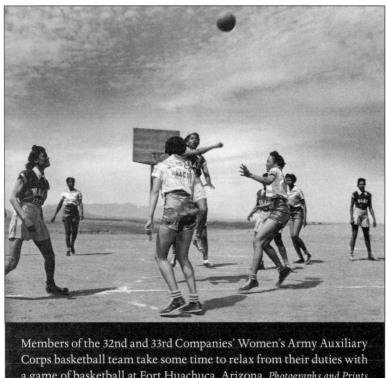

Members of the 32nd and 33rd Companies' Women's Army Auxiliary Corps basketball team take some time to relax from their duties with a game of basketball at Fort Huachuca, Arizona. *Photographs and Prints Division, Schomburg Center for Research in Black Culture; The New York Public Library; Astor, Lenox and Tilden Foundations; United States Office of War Information Army Signal Corps*

One military camp that welcomed WAACs—and specifically black WAACs—was Fort Huachuca, Arizona. Fort Huachuca was eager to welcome black WAACs because it was a base that housed the 92nd Division of the army—an all-black division of men. With the arrival of WAACs, the men would be available for combat duty.

Early in December 1942 two companies of WAACs—the 32nd and 33rd—became the first WAAC companies assigned to an army training post. As they stepped off the train at Fort

Huachuca they were cheered by a "welcoming committee" of thousands of soldiers. They stood in perfect military salute as the national anthem played. They enjoyed a hearty lunch and then were escorted to their spacious, well-equipped barracks—called WAACville—to unpack and begin to settle into their new lives. On Saturday night a dance was held to make the WAACs feel at home—and to give the men a chance to perform some "mad jitterbugging" before shipping out for combat assignments.

The WAACs at Fort Huachuca, two companies that consisted of close to 150 auxiliaries, were commanded by women who had graduated with the first class of officers at Fort Des Moines in August: Frances Alexander, Natalie Donaldson, Violet Askins, Irma Cayton, Vera Harrison, Mary Lewis, and Corrie Sherard.

The auxiliaries were well prepared to take over the jobs of the departing soldiers. They knew they had a tough time ahead. As Clara Monroe, Vernice Weir, Helen Amos, and Eula Daniels hoisted luggage and moved equipment around their barracks, they said they weren't concerned with nail polish or evening dresses "for the duration." They were out to prove that women could "soldier with the best men." They would be working as typists, stenographers, clerks, messengers, receptionists, switchboard operators, librarians, medical technicians, and photographers. Women who worked as postal clerks were lovingly known as "postal packin' mamas."

One of the postal packin' mamas was Consuela Bland from Keokuk, Iowa. Consuela was an accomplished soprano before joining the first class of WAAC auxiliaries in August 1942. At Fort Huachuca she was receptionist and chief mail clerk. This was considered one of the most important jobs on the base because the soldiers were far from family and friends and treasured letters from home. But the soldiers showed they also appreciated

Consuela's musical talents when they gave her a standing ovation at a performance in the base chapel. Auxiliary Mercedes
Welcker-Jordan, another former entertainer, had written the
official WAAC song, "We're the WAACs," and quickly settled in
as a motor transport specialist. Margaret Barnes, a former jav-
elin champ, also began her duties in the motor pool at Fort Huachuca. Myrtle Gowdy from New York City and Glennye Oliver
from Chicago worked in the personnel office. Marjorie Bland
(Consuela's sister), Georgia Harris, and Thelma Johnson worked
in the fort's 950-bed hospital, which was staffed with all black
personnel. Ernestine Hughes, a newspaper reporter before the
war, wrote articles for the post newspaper, the *Apache Sentinel.*

Auxiliaries Ruth Wade and Lucille Mayo demonstrate their ability to
service trucks at Fort Huachuca, Arizona, December 1942. *National
Archives, AFRO/AM in WW II List #145*

Mayvee Ashmore was a librarian at Service Club No. 1. Wilnet Grayson, a former cosmetologist from Richmond, Virginia, had completed motor transport training where she learned how to operate and maintain army vehicles including instruction in engine repair and lubrication, vehicle recovery, blackout driving, and maneuvering trucks and tanks. However, at Fort Huachuca, Wilnet served as a chauffeur for the fort's officers. She said, "I feel it is the duty of every American woman to lend her strength and talent to help win this war."

Hulda Defreese of Hillburn, New York, was a cartographer and blueprint technician at Fort Huachuca. She had majored in fine arts at New York University and put the skills she learned

WAACs trained in the handling of all types of trucks await the command to start their vehicles at the post motor pool, Fort Huachuca, Arizona, December 1942. *National Park Service; Mary McLeod Bethune Council House National Historic Site; National Archives for Black Women's History/Photo by US Army Signal Corps*

there to work in the WAAC. Her duties included drawing contour maps of the mountains surrounding Fort Huachuca. The maps were important for the soldiers when they went on military maneuvers in the mountains. Anna Russell from Philadelphia was an artist at Fort Huachuca too. She designed posters, signs, and the scenery for the post's little theater. Her cartoons, which were featured in the post newspaper, provided light moments for the soldiers. Eleanor Bracey from Toledo, Ohio, was a chemist and had one of the most important jobs on the post. She worked in the water purification and sewage disposal plant. Her job was to prevent odors escaping from the plant.

As the war heated up in Europe, Africa, and the Pacific, more WAACs were needed to fill the jobs on bases left by soldiers going into combat. Third Officer Frances Alexander encouraged black women to join the WAACs. She said the WAAC needed more black women who had the "country's best interest at heart." She warned potential WAACs that "glamour girls are *out* for the duration" but women "interested in the glamour of democracy and world freedom" were welcome in the Women's Army Auxiliary Corps.

WAAC Becomes WAC

On September 1, 1943, a historic event occurred that changed life for the women of the WAAC. It was on this date that the Women's Army Auxiliary Corps became the Women's Army Corps (WAC). When the WAAC had been created in 1942 it was considered a supplement to the army, but was not an official branch of the service. Because of that separation, the WAACs did not get any of the benefits that male soldiers received—such as government life insurance, veterans' medical coverage, or death benefits. If a WAAC was captured by the enemy, she had no protection under the international agreements that covered prisoners of war. All that changed when the WAAC became the WAC. The women who were in the WAAC had a choice—go home or join the WAC.

Most of the black women who had joined the WAAC stayed with the newly formed WAC. And just like black men in the army, black women in the WAC were forced to live under segregated conditions. Segregation was army policy.

Although male army commanders were initially reluctant to request WACs for duty, eventually women began to populate posts around the country. Black WACs were part of those groups. Black WACs were stationed at Fort Knox, Kentucky; Fort Lewis, Washington; Fort Sheridan, Illinois; Fort Sam Houston, Texas; Fort Riley, Kansas; Fort Dix, New Jersey; and many other military posts across the United States. But as the war wore on, black WACs wanted to go overseas—to Europe, North Africa, and the Pacific, where they knew they could do more to help the war effort. They were eager to get closer to the fighting.

WACs Go Overseas

Beginning in January 1943, white WAACs were being sent overseas to highly desired assignments. But no black units were given the opportunity to go until January 1945. The first black Army Nurse Corps members had gone overseas in 1943, but they did not have full military status.

Charity Adams had been part of the first class of officers at Fort Des Moines in 1942. In 1944 she held the rank of major, and she was ordered to report to Washington, DC, late in December. Within a short time she learned that she was going overseas and would command a unit of black WACs. But she had no idea where she was assigned, and she didn't know what her unit would be doing.

When the day of departure arrived, Charity learned she would travel to her destination by cargo plane—not the most comfortable form of transportation. She was handed a sealed envelope and ordered to open it after she had been in the air for an hour. When she tore open the packet, she learned she was headed to London. But the orders also contained information about Paris. She was confused. Was her destination London or Paris?

Charity arrived in London on January 28, 1945, and learned that she was to command a unit called the Postal Directory Service for the European theater of operations—the 6888th Central Postal Directory. It would consist of 31 officers and almost 900 enlisted women—all black. The enlisted WACs would arrive in stages beginning in February.

The 6888th would be in charge of all mail going to US citizens and soldiers in Europe. That was mail for an estimated 7 million people! And to make matters more daunting, mail had been piling up for months because of massive troop movements during recent critical battles across the European continent. Most of the Christmas letters and packages had not yet been delivered when the 6888th arrived in February. They had a big job ahead of them.

A white army band greeted the first contingent of WACs as they departed their train at the station in Birmingham, England. As the townspeople cheered, the band played the "Beer Barrel Polka." The WACs marched through the blacked-out streets to their new home in the former King Edward School for boys. It had steam heat and two spacious dining halls. The WACs' first meal was a tasty roast lamb. They were pleased to see the regulation-size basketball court in the gym. But when the newly arrived WACs sank onto their beds after their long journey that first night, they were in for a surprise. The "mattresses" were sacks of straw. Life was full of little inconveniences in wartime England.

Soon after the arrival of the WACs, Major Charity Adams held a press conference. She said after a brief training period, the women of the 6888th would begin "directing, locating and changing mail addresses of battle casualties, transferees, and hospitalized troops."

That sounded depressing to some of the WACs—some of the mail would be returned to the United States to the families of soldiers who had been killed. But the WACs also knew that mail from home was the biggest morale booster a soldier could have. So they knew their job was helping to keep morale high among the soldiers.

It didn't take long for the WACs to start sorting through the mountains of mail. In some cases the addresses were illegible, and they had to try to decipher the writing. Packages were falling apart, and they had to repack many of the contents. Six airplane hangars overflowed with packages that had been undelivered to soldiers. They worked around the clock, splitting three eight-hour shifts, seven days a week. Sergeant Betty Jane Smith of Kansas City, Kansas, was in charge of 56 of the 6888th WACs in Birmingham. It was her duty to keep the "girls supplied with mail" and ensure that it went out to the soldiers "in the shortest possible time."

Two of those "girls" were sisters Winona and Jacquelyn Fuller from Chicago. The Fuller sisters had volunteered for duty in Europe because they wanted to keep up a family tradition. Their father had recently been discharged with a Purple Heart for his service with the US Navy. And two brothers were serving with the navy and the army in the Southwest Pacific. But the Fuller sisters weren't the only sister team serving with the 6888th in Europe. Two of the three O'Bryant sisters from

Georgia who had joined the WAAC together—Essie and Tessie—went overseas with the 6888th.

Shortly after Victory in Europe Day (VE Day), the 6888th was ordered to leave Birmingham and move to Rouen, France. On June 9, 1945, the WACs crossed the choppy waters of the English Channel and landed in Le Havre, France. It was in Le Havre that the devastation of the war hit the women of the 6888th. They were shocked and heartbroken by what they saw. The entire city seemed to have been leveled by the Germans.

From Le Havre the 6888th boarded a crowded train for the long ride to Rouen. When they arrived, they were taken to six aging red brick buildings. The WACs' home in France was an

Pvt. Ruth L. James on duty at the battalion area gate of the 6888th Central Postal Directory in Rouen, France, May 1945. *National Archives, AFRO/AM in WW II List #148*

old barrack that had housed French troops over the years. It was called the Caserne Tallandier. The WACs learned that the buildings had been used by the Nazis during the German occupation. And they heard that a German sniper was buried in the center of the huge courtyard. It was a chilling reminder that the Germans had occupied the area only a short time before their arrival.

The Caserne Tallandier was surrounded by an eight-foot-high fence. When the WACs arrived, crowds of black soldiers and French men and women gathered outside the gate—trying to catch glimpses of the newly arrived black women. Both black and white military police (MPs) guarded the gate. Helping the male MPs were WAC MPs, including six-foot-tall Thelma Albin from Sterling, Kansas. The male MPs carried guns, but the WAC MPs weren't allowed weapons. However, the WACs had a secret weapon. A British soldier had offered to teach the WAC MPs jujitsu, and they had taken advantage of his lessons.

Some of the WACs were annoyed by the soldiers and the local citizens. They felt the constant attention interfered with their jobs. They appreciated the high fence that protected them from the gawkers. But other WACs felt restricted by the fence. Doris Maxwell of Terre Haute, Indiana, looked at the fence and broke into a song that had been made popular in 1944 by singing cowboy Roy Rogers—"Don't Fence Me In."

In October 1945 the 6888th received orders to move to Paris. The WACs packed up and traveled from Rouen to Paris. When they arrived they were thrilled to find their new "barracks" were three hotels complete with rich furnishings, chefs, and maids. Paris was the last stop for the 6888th. Gradually, groups of WACs were deployed to the United States. By March 1946 all the WACs of the 6888th had left Europe and returned home.

Adele Ricketts, Eloise McNeely, Lucia Pitts, and Bernice Huggar were four black WACs who returned to the United

States on the troop ship the USAT *Thomas Barry* in August 1945. There were 41 WACs onboard with 4,300 white soldiers. When they landed in New York they were taken to Camp Shanks, where they were served a steak dinner with coffee, cake, and ice cream. The four black WACs talked about their experiences.

Adele praised the British people, many of whom had lost their homes to enemy bombs. She was impressed with how they managed to maintain their morale during the war. The French also made a lasting impression on her. "The French underwent terrific bombings and suffered the worst hardships of the war," said Adele. "However, they still have high spirits and a bright outlook on life."

Eloise reminisced about her travels in France and England: "We made tours to Versailles, the Pierre Fonds Castle in Compiegne, and also to Stratford-on-Avon in England. Socializing with the French was no problem, and the English were wonderful to us." Eloise had been in the army for almost three years, and she was eager to see her daughter in California and her son who was in the army.

"I loved the English people, their atmosphere and the beauty of their country," Lucia said.

"Although I am happy to be back again, I'm also glad I had the chance to go overseas," Bernice commented. She was looking forward to seeing her husband, William, who was in the army serving with the 92nd Infantry Division.

Racism Back Home

"We wanted the Negro WACs out because, well, they'd ruin property values," said a member of a neighborhood association in Chicago in June 1945. The group's racist beliefs were made very clear in a letter to the War Department protesting the housing of black WACs near their homes. Among other things, the group said it feared the black WACs might have "colored boyfriends coming to call on them." The group was also worried that the housing of the black WACs near their white neighborhood might "lead to general social intermingling" between white and black residents.

In May a group of 55 WACs (and more were scheduled to come) had been assigned to work at Gardiner General Hospital, where they would help care for wounded soldiers—both black and white. They were living in barracks in Burnham Park next to an exclusive, all-white neighborhood. For years racist members of the white neighborhood had worked to establish restrictive covenants that kept black people from moving into their neighborhood.

In their letter to the War Department, members of the neighborhood association tried to justify their racism by insisting their purpose was noble—"to promote harmonious race relations." They explained, "We believe that a poll of the patients and staff of the Gardiner General Hospital will show that Negro WACs are not wanted or needed for the care, comfort, or welfare of the wounded and convalescent American soldiers." They said that the idea of housing black WACs near their neighborhood was "a plan on the part of a few agitators to impose Negroes upon whites in a white community." One wealthy business owner in the neighborhood didn't try to disguise his racist views. He told a newspaper reporter he wondered where "Negroes got the idea that they had the right to live anywhere they want to."

Not all residents of the white neighborhood agreed with the cruel, racist actions of the neighborhood association. Some wrote letters to the War Department offering their support for the WACs. They wrote that they "welcome these Negro WACs into the community."

The War Department must have listened to the "welcoming" whites and refused to cave to the racist demands of the neighborhood association because it did not move the WACs from the barracks. And the WACs continued to work at Gardiner General Hospital.

Too Hot to Handle

August can be sweltering in Washington, DC. Not all buildings were air-conditioned in 1943. It wasn't completely out of the ordinary for offices to close for a few hours—or maybe even for a day—just until things cooled off a bit. That *could* explain what happened at a recruiting office one day when six black women tried to complete applications to join the US Navy. Or it might have been a case of race discrimination.

When Althea Jefferson, Hazel Lee, Velma Hammond, Bernice Jacobs, Cleomine Lewis, and Cora Wright entered a Navy Women Accepted for Volunteer Emergency Service (WAVES) recruiting office in the nation's capital, the male recruiter handed them the paper application forms. As the women began to write, the recruiter was called from the room. When he returned he told the potential WAVES that he had been ordered to close the office because of the intense heat. He asked them to leave through the rear door of the air-conditioned office. The women went around the corner to a store to do a little shopping and returned to the recruiting office about 25 minutes later. They found the office open. When they entered, the same recruiter explained that he had closed the office for a short time but decided to reopen when a breeze passed through, cooling things off. The women were given some pamphlets about the WAVES and told there was "no place for them at the present time." The recruiter said they would be notified as soon as actions had been taken that would permit enrollment of black women.

Over a year later the navy started to permit black women to join the WAVES. But it took an order from the president of the United States to get it done. In October 1944, President Franklin Roosevelt gave the order requiring the navy to admit black women to the WAVES.

The first two black WAVES were Harriet Pickens and Frances Wills. They were the only black candidates in the officer training school at Northampton, Massachusetts. Harriet finished the training in third place in a class of 186 students. Harriet and Frances's white classmates described their black fellow officers as "swell," "brilliant," and "marvelous." By July 1945—after the war had ended in Europe and a month before the Japanese would surrender—the navy had trained 72 black WAVES.

Lt.(jg.) Harriet Ida Pickens and Ens. Frances Wills, the first black Navy Women Accepted for Volunteer Emergency Service (WAVES) to be commissioned, were members of the final graduating class at Naval Reserve Midshipmen's School in Northampton, Massachusetts, December 1944.
National Archives, AFRO/AM in WW II List #159

Other branches of the military were even slower in allowing black women to join. The women's branch of the Coast Guard—Semper Paratus, Always Ready (SPAR)—admitted black women in March 1945, and only five blacks served in the SPAR during World War II. The Marine Corps had allowed white women to join and serve since 1913—but only during wartime. The women who served during World War II were discharged when the war ended. Black women were not admitted to the Marine Corps during the World War II years.

That's History

When Sammie M. Rice learned she would be going overseas with the US Army, she knew it would be a milestone in her life. But she also understood what it meant for *all* black women. Sammie wrote a friend, "We will be the first group of Negro nurses

Black US Army nurses. Sammie M. Rice is the first on the right. *Sammie Rice Collection WVO257, Betty H. Carter Women Veterans Historical Project; Martha Hodges Special Collections and University Archives; University Libraries, University of North Carolina at Greensboro, North Carolina*

to go overseas during war. That's history, you know. Everybody is excited."

Before shipping out Sammie spent two weeks at Camp Kilmer in New Jersey. Even this was top secret. She could write letters to family and friends, but she was not allowed to disclose her location. And she and the other nurses were forbidden to leave the camp as they prepared for their overseas assignment.

Sammie didn't know *where* she was going; but she knew she would be traveling by ship, and she knew that could be dangerous. Traveling by ship in the waters of the Atlantic meant the possibility of torpedo attack by German submarines. But Sammie was comforted by the fact that the ship would be accompanied by an American convoy all the way to their destination.

Sammie was part of a unit of black army nurses who left America on the USS *James Parker* at 6 AM on February 7, 1943. One of the nurses—Thelma Calloway from Montclair, New

The US Navy transport USS *James Parker. Courtesy of US Naval Institute*

Black US Army nurses serving in Liberia. *American Foreign Service Journal photo from US Office of War Information, AFRO/AM in WW II List #153*

Jersey—wrote a song about the ship titled "James Parker Blues." She sang the song in the ship's dining salon many times during the month-long voyage. The trek across the Atlantic was accomplished without interference from the Germans. The only misfortune occurred when Ellen Robinson, Sarah Thomas, and Esther Stewart contracted the mumps. And Sammie Rice suffered from seasickness throughout the trip.

The USS *James Parker* delivered the army nurses safely to Casablanca, French Morocco, on March 10. The nurses spent several days on "shore leave" enjoying the sites of the beautiful city. They spent time at the Red Cross club and attended a dance held in their honor by American military officers. From Casablanca the nurses set out for Dakar, French West Africa (now Senegal). After a brief stay, they journeyed on to Freetown, British West Africa (now Sierra Leone). Finally, they reached their destination—the 25th Station Hospital in Liberia on the west coast of Africa.

One of the nurses, Alma Favors from Chicago, expected to miss her family while she was overseas. But her homesickness was lessened a little when she ran into one of her cousins thousands of miles from home. Staff Sergeant Paul Favors from Detroit, Michigan, greeted Alma as she settled into her new home. Back in the States, Paul had been a sparring partner with the famous boxer Joe Louis. But in Liberia, Paul was just one of many American soldiers who had been sent to Africa to guard a precious resource.

American soldiers were stationed in Liberia to protect the large rubber plantations owned by an American company that supplied the Allied military with most of its rubber. American and Allied armies used immense amounts of rubber for tires on vehicles. And with the other major world supplier of rubber under enemy control in Malaysia, the security of the Liberian rubber plantations was crucial. But the risk of contracting various diseases was quite high in Liberia in the 1940s. Clean drinking water was hard to come by, and malaria was widespread. There was a critical need for the army nurses who arrived in Liberia in 1943.

It didn't take long for Sammie Rice and the other army nurses to settle into a routine at their new assignment. The 25th Station Hospital staff treated soldiers with diseases and also American pilots who had been injured in battles on the Italian front. Many of the pilots suffered from burns they had sustained when their planes crashed. Lieutenant Susan E. Freeman was in charge of all the nurses. She quickly assigned nurses to key positions. Sammie Rice began her duties as charge nurse in a ward where she cared for 11 patients who were suffering from psychological problems.

Lts. Roby Gill, Beaumont, Texas; Leola M. Green, Houston, Texas; Mattie L. Aikens, Macon, Georgia; Zola Mae Lang, Chicago, Illinois; and Ellen L. Robinson, Hackensack, New Jersey, were US Army nurses sent to Liberia. *Photographs and Prints Division, Schomburg Center for Research in Black Culture; The New York Public Library; Astor, Lenox and Tilden Foundations; US Office of War Information Army Signal Corps*

While the nurses were highly regarded for their medical expertise, the Liberian people quickly learned that the nurses had other skills to offer. Jewell Paterson and Idell Webb had brought a supply of vegetable seeds from America. They began to raise corn, tomatoes, and beans and contributed the produce to the army mess. Native Liberian boys helped cultivate the vegetables and began to enjoy the delicious results too. The boys took seeds back to their villages and started their own gardens.

Both the army mess and the local Liberians began to eat better when Idell, fellow nurse Roby Gill, and the local Liberians teamed up to raise a flock of robust chickens that produced a steady supply of fresh eggs—and the occasional chicken dinner. The Liberians supplied the chickens, but when they arrived, the chickens were scrawny and produced small eggs. The American nurses tried to locate some corn to feed the chickens, but none could be found. Instead, the Liberians gave the nurses some native rice. Idell and Roby mixed the rice with bread soaked in water and fed it to the chickens. The chickens gobbled up the unusual concoction. Everyone—Americans and Liberians—were delighted when their rice-and-bread-fed chickens became chubbier and produced much larger eggs.

When army nurse Eva Boggess from Waco, Texas, wasn't tending patients in the hospital, she could be found looking for African bugs to add to her collection. Chrystalee Maxwell from Los Angeles, California, had bought a secondhand camera and became known as the official photographer. She was also selected by the soldiers as the best dressed nurse in the unit. When Chrystalee wasn't in her nurse uniform, it wasn't unusual to see her in plum-colored slacks and jacket, or fluffy blouses with lace trim, pleated skirts, mesh stockings, and satin shoes. Thelma Calloway, the nurse who had composed and sung "James Parker Blues" on the voyage from the United States, continued to compose and perform. She was working on another piece she called "The Liberia Blues." It was a song about ocean steamers, sea crossings, and "a yen to be back in America." All the nurses took pleasure in the unit's two pet monkeys—until one of the mischievous little creatures found its way into a nurse's room and ate her lipstick.

The nurses joked about the frequency with which malaria struck in the camp. They even invented a mock African Campaign

Ribbon—modeled after the authentic medals bestowed on soldiers who had shown courage in battle. The nurses conferred the African Campaign Ribbon to their colleagues who had endured at least one bout with malaria. But many of the nurses were victims of the disease, and it was not really a laughing matter.

The nurses were able to joke about their malaria attacks, but they couldn't find any humor in events that occurred late in 1943. After only nine months in Liberia, the first contingent of black nurses to serve overseas was ordered back to the United States. By December they had all returned home and were reassigned to new posts.

Officials said the return of the black nurses was "only routine" and that there were many letters "on file" commending the nurses for the "splendid" work they had performed in Liberia. Most of the nurses themselves said they didn't know why they had been reassigned. Gertrude Ivory said she and the other nurses were brought back to the United States because they all had malaria.

The Liberian government was enthusiastic about the services the black American nurses had performed. In April 1944 officials from Liberia asked the US government for permission to grant a medal of honor to Lieutenant Susan E. Freeman, the woman who had led the work of the nurses. The Liberians wanted to honor her for "distinguished contributions" to their country. The US War Department approved the request, and Susan was awarded the Liberian Humane Order of African Redemption—an award that recognized individuals who had performed humanitarian work in Liberia. In addition, Susan Freeman was honored as the 1944 Mary Mahoney Award recipient by the National Association of Colored Graduate Nurses. This award honored nurses who had "significantly advanced opportunities in nursing for members of minority groups."

The black army nurses who had been the first black unit of nurses to serve overseas continued to serve in the Army Nurse Corps at various hospitals around the world. Some were assigned to hospitals in the United States. Several of the nurses who had served in Liberia went to England with a unit of army nurses. Others went to the Southwest Pacific war zone. Rosemary Vinson, Daryle Foister, Fannie Hart, Anna Landrum, and Caroline Schenck were assigned to the China-Burma-India theater of operations.

Sammie Rice was one of the nurses who contracted malaria while in Liberia. She recovered and was with the group that went to England in 1944. Sammie continued to send part of her army paycheck back home to her family as she had while in Liberia. They knew they could count on her. And the wounded servicemen whom the nurses cared for in the hospitals around the globe felt only gratitude for the black "angels of mercy."

There's a War Very Near

Birdie Brown was six feet tall, and people looked up to her. But it wasn't because of her height that her fellow nurses looked up to Birdie. It was because they were the first group of black army nurses in the Pacific theater of operations, and Birdie was their leader. She was the chief nurse of the 268th Station Hospital unit. Part of her duties included helping the nurses adjust to life in a war zone.

Their adjustment started with their voyage from the United States. All but two of the nurses had suffered from seasickness. Louise Miller, Elcena Townscent, Marjorie Mayers, Prudence Burns, Claudia Mathews, Thelma Fisher, Beulah Baldwin, Dorothy Branker, Joan Hamilton, Bessie Evans, Alberta Smith, Inez Holmes, Elnora Jones, and Geneva Culpepper arrived in

Australia in December 1943. The *Pittsburgh Courier* reported that
"bedlam broke loose" among the troops at the sight of the black
nurses and "the nurses received an ovation that befitted a pro-
cession of queens."

Lts. Prudence L. Burns, Inez Holmes, and Birdie E. Brown arrive at
the 268th Station Hospital in Australia and receive their first batch of
mail from home, November 1943. *National Archives, AFRO/AM in WW II
List #187*

The nurses would stay at a staging area for nurses until they received orders sending them to other military hospitals in the Pacific. At the military camp in Australia they learned how to live under GI combat conditions. That included exercising in helmets and combat uniforms.

By spring 1944 the nurses felt impatient to move to their next assignment "somewhere in the southwest Pacific." Birdie summed it up: "We are extremely anxious to get to work. We have enjoyed Australia's hospitality and made lots of friends but we can never get out of our minds the fact that there's a war very near us and we're here to do a job. We shall be happy when we are working."

The nurses did move on to other areas of the war zone. They went to a 250-bed hospital in New Guinea, where Prudence

Army nurses waiting for assignments to hospitals in the Southwest Pacific stretch their muscles in an early-morning workout at a training camp in Australia, February 1944. *National Archives, AFRO/AM in WW II List #183*

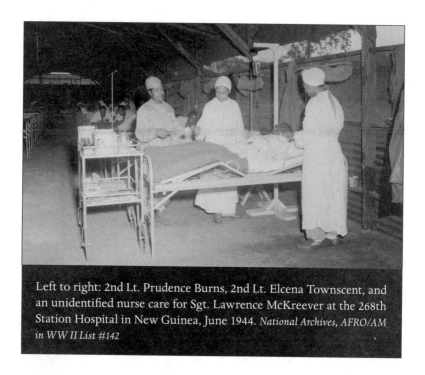

Left to right: 2nd Lt. Prudence Burns, 2nd Lt. Elcena Townscent, and an unidentified nurse care for Sgt. Lawrence McKreever at the 268th Station Hospital in New Guinea, June 1944. *National Archives, AFRO/AM in WW II List #142*

Burns became head surgical nurse. Geneva Culpepper was assigned under her as a surgical nurse. Joan Hamilton was a dietitian. Marjorie Mayers was in charge of recreation at the hospital, which included the enlisted men's basketball team.

At one point during the 268th's time in the Pacific, a US newspaper reported that Birdie and some of her nurses had been captured by the enemy. The report was inaccurate. But when a journalist found Birdie at work in New Guinea and told her about the published article, Birdie had a good laugh. She wanted to assure readers back home that she was very much "uncaptured" and was looking forward to returning to America at the end of the war.

But it wasn't quite time for the nurses of the 268th to leave the Pacific theater of operations for home. The American armed forces had liberated the Philippines from the Japanese in the summer of 1945. The nurses of 268th were needed there. So off they went for one last assignment. While they were in the Philippines the war ended with the bombing of Japan by the United States in August 1945. By October 1945 the nurses' bags were packed, and they were waiting for orders to return home to the United States. But before leaving the Philippines, one of the nurses had one more duty to perform.

Prudence Burns wanted to marry her fiancé, Sgt. Lowell Burrell, who was stationed in the Philippines too. So just before leaving for the United States, Prudence and Lowell were married. Prudence wore a wedding dress designed by one of her friends. It was fashioned from the most luxurious fabric they could find in the war-torn islands—silk from a military parachute.

The America We Live In

Louise Miller had trained with the 268th Station Hospital nurses at Fort Huachuca, Arizona, and she had been with them in Australia and New Guinea. She didn't go to the Philippines with the rest of her unit. In the spring of 1945, Louise received word that her father was sick back home in Atlanta, Georgia. The army sent her back to the United States so she could spend some time with him.

Louise wore her Army Nurse Corps uniform on her long flights home. She passed through Tucson, Arizona, and then went on to her next stop—Dallas, Texas. Louise was tired and worried about her father. She was also hungry. As soon as she arrived in Dallas, she headed to the nearest coffee shop for a bite to eat. She had plenty of time—there was a three-hour layover. She approached the counter, where she was told she could eat— but only in the back of the shop.

Louise's Army Nurse Corps uniform had not impressed the coffee shop worker, and it didn't mean anything to a passenger on the plane she boarded for her flight to Atlanta. She had just settled into her seat on the plane when the flight attendant asked her to move to another seat—the white passenger Louise had sat next to didn't want to sit next to her. Louise was saddened by this harsh welcome back to the United States after her years of service to the country. She predicted, "Our boys will not be willing to come back to the America we live in when victory is won." She felt other returning black veterans would be disappointed that their service to the country in time of need was not appreciated.

Black Nurses in Europe

The first contingent of black army nurses assigned to Europe arrived in August 1944. Captain Mary L. Petty led her unit of 63 nurses as they walked down the gangplank of the ship that had brought them to England. The women knew they had a critical role to play in Europe. Because they were nurses they were committed to caring for the wounded soldiers. But they had another important task ahead. In a ceremony as they disembarked the ship, Captain Petty spoke about the nurses' roles. She said the contingent of black nurses had "come to foreign soil to render the greatest possible service in this theater and to do everything within its power to improve race relations."

Some of the nurses who had served in Liberia—including Thelma Calloway, Idell Webb, Sammie Rice, and Roby Gill— were with the unit that arrived in England. The nurses expected to serve in hospitals in Great Britain and France. And they knew they would treat both black and white soldiers. Black nurses

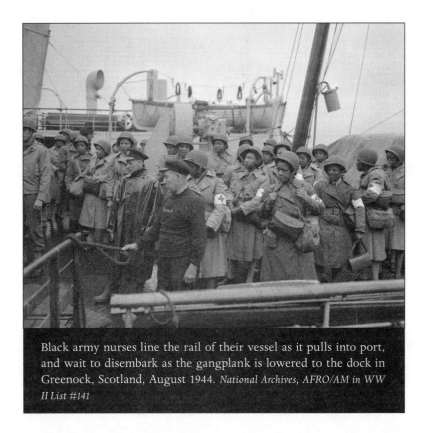

Black army nurses line the rail of their vessel as it pulls into port, and wait to disembark as the gangplank is lowered to the dock in Greenock, Scotland, August 1944. *National Archives, AFRO/AM in WW II List #141*

touching wounded white soldiers had been a problem in some American hospitals.

"When we first entered service in Camp Livingston, Louisiana, we were forbidden to touch white soldiers," Dorcas Taylor remarked. "But before we embarked for Britain, they needed us so badly, we touched everybody."

The army nurses who comprised the first unit of black nurses in Europe did not receive the most prized assignment. They had been sent to England to relieve a unit of white nurses who had been caring for Nazi prisoners of war. It was not a duty most

First black nurses in England, 1944. *National Park Service; Mary McLeod Bethune Council House National Historic Site; National Archives for Black Women's History/Photo by US Army Signal Corps*

American nurses cherished. While it was the responsibility of all nurses to tend to the wounded and help them recover, it was difficult to show compassion for the very men who had wounded and even killed American soldiers. And some black citizens in America believed that the black nurses had been assigned to prisoner of war hospitals intentionally—to keep them from serving in hospitals where they would treat white American soldiers.

After a few months, the army decided to change the assignment of the black nurses. Rather than holding the prisoners in hospitals staffed only with black nurses, the prisoners were transferred to other installations. The nurses continued to serve in England and France—but they cared for American soldiers.

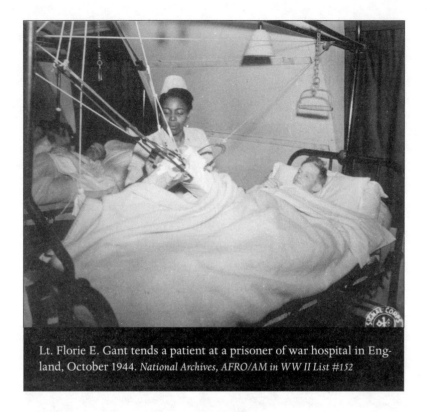

Lt. Florie E. Gant tends a patient at a prisoner of war hospital in England, October 1944. *National Archives, AFRO/AM in WW II List #152*

The Hospital in the Clouds

A picture of a black soldier lying in a hospital bed with a leg and both arms in slings caught the attention of Hazel Neal as she picked up a copy of the black newspaper the *Pittsburgh Courier*. It was the summer of 1945, and Hazel lived in Flagstaff, Arizona, while her husband, Grady, served with the US Army somewhere in the China-Burma-India (CBI) theater of operations. Hazel couldn't believe her eyes when she read the print under the picture—the soldier was Grady!

From the newspaper account Hazel learned that the truck Grady had been driving had plummeted 350 feet over a cliff and landed at the bottom of an embankment. He was carrying supplies over the newly constructed Ledo Road when his truck slipped off the muddy trail and over the cliff. His fellow soldiers pulled him from the truck, called an ambulance, and within a short time he was on his way to the 335th Station Hospital at Tagap, Burma—a hospital staffed entirely with black medical personnel.

The construction of the Ledo Road had been "one of the greatest road building jobs in history." Starting from Ledo, India, the Ledo Road joined with the existing Burma Road—ending up in China. The combined Ledo and Burma Roads were known as the Stilwell Road. The building of the Ledo Road and the rebuilding of the Burma Road were the result of an exhaustive undertaking by thousands of men—a combined

US Army trucks wind along the side of a mountain over the Ledo Road between India and Burma. *National Archives, AFRO/AM in WW II List #009*

force of Indians, Chinese, Burmese, Britons, Australians, and Americans. More than half the Americans were black soldiers.

What made the task so incredible were the conditions under which the soldiers worked. The Ledo Road was being built through some of the most difficult terrain in the world—swamps, jungles, and mountains—treacherous terrain for the men trying to construct a road for use by heavy military vehicles. As the soldiers inched their way through the jungle and over the mountain passes, they encountered torrential rains, extreme heat, and biting cold. If they managed to keep their vehicles on the winding trails they were lucky. But there were no guarantees that they wouldn't become deathly sick from malaria, cholera, or dysentery. And they had to contend with all the wildlife—elephants, monkeys, tigers, panthers, lizards, and snakes.

When Grady Neal was delivered to the 335th Station Hospital—also called the hospital in the clouds—the all-black medical team was waiting for him. Included in the group were a handful of black army nurses. The hospital had been operating on the slope of the Patkai Mountain range—4,500 feet up in the clouds—for only a few months. Before the 335th was established, men who were injured on the Ledo Road were transported by truck, jeep, raft, mule, or oxcart to hospitals that, depending on where the accident occurred, could be several hundred miles away.

In October 1944 a group of black army nurses had arrived in Tagap to help set up the hospital. Rose Robinson, Rosemae Glover, Polly Lathion, Rosemary Vinson, Fannie Hart, Anna Landrum, Caroline Schenck, Agnes B. Glass, Madine H. Davis, Margaret Kendrick, Elestia Cox, Lillie L. Lesesne, Olive Lucas, Eva Wheeler, Doshia Watkins, Rose Elliott, and Daryle Foister knew their work was important. The Ledo Road would be used by Allied armies to get supplies to China—a strategic ally that was struggling to defeat the Japanese armies in the CBI theater. Supplies were transported by planes to China, but it was a dangerous and costly undertaking by air. Planes heavily loaded with fuel and other supplies had to maneuver mountain peaks as high as 16,000 feet. The air trip consumed so much fuel that by the time a plane reached its destination, most of the precious cargo had been eaten up by the aircraft making the delivery. It was crucial that a land connection between India and China be made. The Stilwell Road was that connection.

Before patients could be treated at the 335th Station Hospital, the nurses helped the other members of the medical team convert the abandoned buildings that were to become their medical facilities into a modern laboratory, pharmacy, operating rooms, patient rooms, mess hall, and living quarters. They even had to install a water system—using pipes left behind by the Ledo Road engineers—to carry the water from high in the mountains for use in the hospital. A drainage system had to be built to handle the excess water that rushed down the mountainside during the rainy season. And because there would be *some* time for rest and relaxation, a baseball diamond, basketball court, and movie amphitheater were built into the mountain slope near the hospital.

Back home in Flagstaff, Arizona, Grady Neal's wife, Hazel, learned about the 335th Station Hospital from newspaper articles. Grady had tried to protect his wife from worry—he had told her he was suffering from a bout with malaria. Although Grady's injuries from his tumble over the Ledo Road mountainside were very serious, the all-black medical team at the hospital was well prepared to treat his injuries.

Rose Robinson from Pennsylvania was the chief operating room nurse. Elestia Cox from California and Rosamae Glover from Ohio were nurse supervisors. Rosemary Vinson from

Michigan was the hospital dietitian. Rosemary Vinson, Fannie Hart, Anna Landrum, Caroline Schenck, and Daryl Foister had served in the 25th Station Hospital in Liberia before coming to work at the hospital in Burma. Daryl had worked in hospitals in Pennsylvania and New York before joining the Army Nurse Corps. She was positive about her overseas experiences. "I haven't minded my overseas duty," she remarked. "I've learned a lot about the customs and habits of foreign peoples."

Hazel Neal couldn't help but worry about her husband after seeing his picture in the newspaper and learning about the seriousness of his injuries. But she could be comforted knowing he was being cared for by a top-notch medical team high in the clouds over Burma.

They Just Accept Us

"They just accept us, like us, and no questions are asked," black army nurse Ora Pierce said about the German soldiers she saw every day when she went to work.

Black army nurses had traveled to all corners of the world to care for American soldiers who had been wounded by the enemy. Some black nurses had cared for enemy prisoners in England. Ora Pierce stayed in the United States, and the enemy came to her.

In September 1945, Ora and 29 black army nurses were stationed at a hospital in Florence, Arizona. Over 30,000 German prisoners passed through the distribution center on their way to work in labor camps in other states across the country.

Some of the prisoners had been away from home for as long as seven years, Ora said. Some of them talked about how they had been captured by the Americans. But all of them wanted to tell the nurses about their homes. Ora thought most of the

A group of army nurses. Ora Pierce is third from right. *Courtesy of the Fort Huachuca Museum*

prisoners were like American soldiers—they were homesick and liked to talk about their wives and sweethearts. "I have yet to meet one [soldier] who didn't want to talk, right off the bat, about home—whether it be in Kansas, New York, or Berlin."

Besides caring for sick and injured prisoners, Ora supervised the work of 36 prisoners who worked in the hospital with her nurses. One of the Germans was Ora's assistant in the physical therapy department. He had been a physical therapist in Germany before the war.

"On the whole," Ora remarked, "they are extremely co-operative and polite. As gestures of friendliness, they have made name plaques and jewel boxes carved from wood for every one of the Negro nurses."

While the enemy prisoners were accepting and friendly to the black army nurses, that wasn't the case with some Americans.

When the nurses arrived in Florence, five white civilian nurses worked at the hospital. When they learned that the black army nurses were coming, the white nurses were so displeased that they quit their jobs rather than work with the black nurses.

And although Ora and her nurses were welcome in the white officers' mess hall, this came about only after some of the nurses complained to the National Association for the Advancement of Colored People earlier in the year—when they had been segregated from their white counterparts during meal times.

The situation at Florence had definitely changed between January and September 1945. "Maybe it's being isolated on a desert," Ora commented, "but there is a real feeling of co-operation and friendliness at Florence."

Ora Pierce said the German POWs "just accepted" the black nurses at the Florence prison camp. Injured Germans were cared for by the nurses in the camp hospital. Others worked alongside Ora and the other nurses. If the German prisoners could accept the nurses, maybe white Americans would accept black Americans if they had opportunities to work with them. But in the 1940s, discrimination and segregation prevented those opportunities.

The America They Hoped to Live In

Many black women were eager to serve their country in the military during the war. But for black women it wasn't as simple as signing up. The army allowed black women to join early in the war—although their numbers were restricted—but the other branches of the military were much slower in allowing black women into their ranks. Despite a critical need for nurses during the war, the army and navy nurse corps were reluctant to open their doors to black women. And those nurses who did get into the military and the nurse corps were forced to live in segregated environments. And sometimes they were forced to endure blatant racism.

When the Dallas coffee shop worker had refused to allow Louise Miller to sit in the front of the restaurant in 1945 as she traveled home to visit her sick father, he couldn't see past the color of Louise's skin. He didn't see a woman who had served her country in a war zone. But Louise knew this individual's actions were indicative of a much deeper problem in America. She spoke of "the America we live in."

Louise was talking about the racism that was tolerated and accepted in America—including in the military. The America Louise lived in was one that required black women serving their country to live in separate barracks from white women. It was an America that "purified" the swimming pool at a military post after black officer candidates swam in it. It was an America where a recruiting office closed down rather than give applications to black women. It was an America where the color of a person's skin overshadowed the uniform.

Despite these humiliating experiences, Louise Miller, Charity Adams, Sammie Rice, Ora Pierce, Birdie Brown, and thousands of other black women wore the uniform of the American military and hoped that someday in the future the America they lived in would be able to see beyond the color of their skin.

4

VOLUNTEERS

"Back the Attack"

"When I turned my back, the policeman named Dean kicked me. When I turned, he slapped my face and struck me on the shoulder with his fist."

—Mildred McAdory

Twenty-seven-year-old Mildred McAdory was director of the Fairfield Youth Center in Fairfield, Alabama, and she was preparing for an upcoming tin can collection drive—a project undertaken by a group of black students as part of the Victory Scrap Drive.

In December 1942, scrap drives were common all over the country—often organized by students who wanted to do their part for the war effort. The country had been at war for the past year, and materials such as rubber, paper, and metal were in short supply; scrap drives were a way for citizens to collect everyday items—paper, silk fabric, rubber bands, steel, and iron—needed for the manufacture of wartime products such as parachutes, gas masks, life rafts, bombers, trucks, and tanks. Mildred and the young people at the youth center were ready for their upcoming drive. At the end of one day, Mildred boarded a bus for her ride home. The city buses were segregated, with a black line painted across the ceiling to divide riders. White passengers sat in the seats ahead of the line, and blacks had to sit behind it. The driver of Mildred's bus had even placed a board on a seat to ensure that everyone knew his or her place on the bus.

A black couple paid their fares and took empty seats in front of the board—in the white section. All the seats in the black section were filled. The driver turned to the couple and said, "You'll have to get behind that board." When the couple asked for a refund of their fares, the driver told them he couldn't return their money. They left the bus.

Two black men entered the bus; one of them moved the board, placing it on the floor. The driver told the man he had to sit behind the board. The man pointed to the line on the ceiling and said he was sitting behind the line. The driver called the police. When a policeman arrived, the driver pointed to three men and Mildred, indicating they were the troublemakers. The policeman ordered the men and Mildred to the police car. Mildred asked what crime she was being charged with, and the officer asked her if she knew who had moved the board. She replied that she knew nothing about it.

The policeman pointed to a seat on the bus and said, "Well, come back here and sit down before I slap you down."

"You have no reason to do that," Mildred replied.

"I'll knock hell out of you with the board," the policeman said, and he took the men to the police car.

Incensed, Mildred told the bus driver, "I'm going to report you to the company for being rude to passengers—calling the police on innocent people and having them threatened."

"Call 'em. That won't do you no good," taunted the driver.

Mildred decided to leave the bus. As she stepped down, the driver called to the police, "Hey, take her on too." The officer looked at Mildred and said, "Come on, girl, get in that car," and kicked her.

When Mildred and the two men arrived at the police station, they were questioned. The police asked Mildred which man had moved the board. She repeated that she didn't know. The policeman who had been at the bus said, "She's a g–d— liar." Put her n— a— in jail." He kicked Mildred again, slapped her face, and punched her shoulder. She was led to a cell that held five other women. Mildred spent the night on a dirty mattress trying to ignore the roaches that scurried across the floor—it seemed there were thousands of them.

The next morning Mildred was taken to a hearing, where she was charged with interfering with an officer. The bus driver testified under oath against Mildred, who was fined 10 dollars and set free.

Mildred McAdory and the young people at the Fairfield Youth Center who had spent the day organizing the scrap drive were volunteers. Like thousands of American citizens during the war years, including many black women, they felt they could do their part to help win the war on the home front while their loved ones were fighting on the battlefronts. Why did these women volunteer to help win the war for a country that tolerated the ugliness of segregation and the cruelty of discrimination? For every black woman who did her part for the war, there would be a different answer to that question.

Office of Civilian Defense

Even before the United States joined the war, the federal government had established an agency called the Office of Civilian Defense (OCD). The OCD directed programs that existed to protect and serve citizens on the home front and to promote volunteer involvement in defense. When the Japanese attacked Pearl Harbor in December 1941, the work of the OCD became critical. And the need for volunteers intensified.

The OCD organized Defense Councils that formed Civilian Defense volunteer offices in communities throughout the country. The Defense Councils trained men and women as air raid wardens. It was their job to teach citizens procedures to follow in case of an enemy attack from the air. They supervised blackouts, organized people to fill sandbags, and planned for protection against fires in the event of an enemy attack. Volunteers were trained as fire watchers, auxiliary police and firefighters, nurse aides, first aid workers, road repair crews, messengers, and ambulance drivers. Plans were made to deal with emergency food and housing situations. Volunteers were trained for decontamination, bomb, and rescue corps.

Under the OCD, a block plan system was established that provided information about wartime services and programs in cities, towns, and rural areas. A chief oversaw the block plan system, which divided the city into several zones, each with its own leader. And each zone consisted of 4 to 15 sectors. Under the sector leaders were the block leaders. Each block leader had responsibility for about 15 families. People who volunteered in the block organizations dealt with the *service* rather than the *protective* phase of civilian defense—distributing information about everything from salvage collection and war savings bond drives to services for military personnel and the labor supply.

They provided information to neighbors about services they could access such as childcare programs, and they collected information that would be helpful to the war effort such as reporting the number of spare rooms available for war workers. The OCD depended on volunteer labor from ordinary citizens. Many responded to the call. Many were women. And many were black women.

All across the country black women in cities, towns, and rural areas volunteered through OCD programs. Some were housewives and farm women who participated in classes where they learned how to manage their homes under wartime conditions. Others were women who did their volunteer work after they returned home from their jobs in factories, offices, and businesses. Some women enrolled in childcare courses that consisted of 75 hours of instruction over a period of five weeks. After completion of the course, the women volunteered in daycares, nursery schools, and after-school programs to help care for the children of women who were working in war industries. All these women contributed extra hours of free labor because they wanted to do something to help win the war.

Jessie L. Terry served as "race relations adviser" for the California Council of Defense. It was her job to contact churches and organizations in the black communities and encourage members to participate in civilian defense activities. "Everywhere I go, the women are eager to volunteer for duty," said Jessie. "Already, there are hundreds in every defense activity, and they are tremendously enthused about their jobs. Many of them have sons or husbands in the armed forces, and if you don't think these women take their services seriously, you should watch them work!"

People registered to become Civilian Defense volunteers at libraries, schools, and police stations. They were required to be "able-bodied, self-reliant, of good character," and between 30 and 50 years old. The Committee on Civilian Defense had set a goal of registering 150,000 volunteers in Baltimore, where black public school teachers volunteered their time to register volunteers. After registrants were organized, classes were offered to train them in their specific job duties.

After the registrants completed classes, they were given exams. If they passed the exams, they were evaluated for their "character, reputation and ability to lead other people during a crisis." Typically the classes were segregated, and black volunteers were placed only in black communities. Sometimes black volunteers were delayed in getting into classes because officials practiced discriminatory practices—refusing to place black and white volunteers in classes together. It meant black people who wanted to volunteer sometimes had to wait until there was a group of other black potential volunteers large enough to make up a class.

By March 1942 the city of Baltimore had registered close to 600 volunteers as air raid wardens. But many more were needed. There was a need for auxiliary firefighters and police too. The city was divided into sectors and precincts. Civilian Defense regulations called for four wardens for every 500 persons in a sector. Ten sectors made up a precinct. There were 120 precincts in northwest Baltimore alone. This area of the city was predominantly black. Citizens were urged to volunteer. But because of segregation, blacks who were interested in volunteering couldn't begin classes. The Committee on Civilian Defense promised that if 20 "qualified colored applicants" registered, a class would be offered for black firefighters. In the meantime, eager black volunteers had to wait. The city's discriminatory practices interfered with the country's need for volunteers in critical wartime areas. But racism won out over wartime preparedness.

While segregation could be a barrier to blacks who tried to volunteer, it didn't stop those determined black women who wanted to aid the war effort. In Washington, DC, Blanche Bennett organized housewives in her apartment building into salvage crews. In Brooklyn, New York, two labor leaders—Dolly Lowther and Charlotte Adelmond of the Laundry Workers Union—used their organizational skills to coordinate block volunteers in the Brownsville section of the city. The Metropolitan Council of Negro Women in Manhattan, New York, trained and sent speakers to churches and other organizations to explain the confusing point-rationing system to housewives. The 80-member Women's Motor Corps raised money and bought an ambulance for the 15th Regiment of the New York National Guard.

The Atlanta University School of Social Work in Georgia was the site of a two-week institute in 1942 to train black volunteers to work in social welfare agencies. It was the first program of its kind in the nation for black citizens. The institute was conducted at the request of the OCD for the purpose of preparing volunteers to help staff social welfare offices that were seeing increased demands as a result of the war. Fifty-five black men and women completed the courses. Most were college graduates and were employed as teachers, nurses, librarians, beauticians, or clerks. During the course of the institute, participants completed 12 hours of "practical work" in the agency where they would be assigned. Upon completion of the course, they were awarded special certificates from the university.

In Chicago, Alva Bates organized the Women's Division for the Sale of War Bonds. The women set up booths in hotels and other locations around the city. Also in Chicago a Civilian Defense Corps made up of 53 women operated the Consumer Information Service in a public library. They distributed information about nutrition and tips for housewives on how to make healthy meals as they dealt with food shortages. Ruth Pettiford headed up the only black unit of the Red Cross Motor Corps in Chicago. Members worked with the Wool Conservation Program to collect fabric from shops and homes.

The black New York Beauticians Volunteer Corps was organized in August 1942 by Maude Gadsden. By October 1943 the 250 members of the group had sold $300,000 worth of war bonds. Their goal was to reach the $1 million mark. The Harlem chapter of the Corps led the race. Katherine Burton was the top saleswoman, having sold $7,000 worth of bonds. The women set up booths in beauty shops, churches, and theaters. Citizens were encouraged to "Back the attack" with their purchase of bonds. By early 1944 the Beauticians Volunteer Corps had reached the $500,000 mark in bond sales.

Other black women's organizations and individual women contributed many hours to help finance the war. They promoted war bond drives and rallies, distributed literature, canvassed from door to door—keeping the program before the public and "combing the community for the extra small change which otherwise might be unwisely spent."

Mattie W. Stewart, a waitress in the officers' dining room of the Bowery Savings Bank in New York City, sold a quarter million dollars' worth of bonds. As she sold lunches to the bank officers she told them she was working to promote bond sales for the sake of her son, who was a sergeant in the US Army. Her story inspired the bank officers to contribute generously to her efforts.

Dora Lewis was less successful in her early efforts. Dora was a black woman who tried to do her part for the war. When she set out to get pledges for war bonds in New York City, white residents of one neighborhood refused to sign pledges just because Dora was black. Dora reported the problems she encountered to the National Association for the Advancement of Colored People (NAACP). The problem was reported to the chairman of the New York War Bond Pledge Drive. It was pointed out that the situation was insulting to blacks who volunteered their services to their country. When Dora's experiences were reported in a New York newspaper, pledges poured in to her. One came from the mayor of New York City—Mayor F. H. LaGuardia asked Dora to his office, where he wrote her a check.

Racism in Civilian Defense

Shortly after the attack on Pearl Harbor in December 1941, the Negro Committee for United Action to Defeat Hitler and Hitlerism issued a warning: "Every one of us, no matter where he lives, must find out who the air raid warden is in his area and be prepared." The warning continued, "Failure to understand what to do may mean not only the loss of your own life, but the lives of members of your family. . . . We must remember that in blitz attacks there are only two kinds of people: the quick and the dead."

One night in September 1942 a black couple was driving home to Rutherford, New Jersey, after a visit to New York. Alfonso and Dorothy Jackson heard the sirens signaling a practice blackout. They had taken seriously the warnings about what to do when the air raid sirens sounded. They knew they had to stop and seek shelter. When they pulled their car over on the roadway, an air raid warden told the Jacksons to leave their car and take shelter in a café across the street. There was a crowd of about 25 people moving toward the restaurant. When the group reached the door, an unidentified man emerged from the restaurant and scanned a flashlight over the crowd. There were about 10 black people in the group—including the Jacksons. The man told the blacks to stand aside. He admitted the whites into the restaurant, followed them in, and closed the door!

Although the incident was only a practice, it raised the question—"What if it had been an authentic air raid? Would the Jacksons and the other black people have been left outside to die?" The incident was reported to state officials. An investigation took place. Within a month a state law was passed barring discrimination in air raid shelters in the state of New Jersey. Many black citizens of New Jersey were encouraged by the law, but black residents in other cities were still concerned. In Washington, DC, for example, black people were excluded from theaters and restaurants in the downtown district. What would happen to black people in the nation's capital when the air raid sirens were heard?

When the US Army Air Forces requested volunteers to work on air raid maneuvers at the post on Governor's Island in New York, 58 women were referred to the post by the New York City Council of Defense. Military officials asked 52 of the women to report for duty. The six women denied were black. The NAACP contacted the mayor of New York City. Mayor LaGuardia called officials at the post, and the six black volunteers were immediately assigned to positions.

As in many cities, the OCD in New Orleans, Louisiana, operated segregated programs. Black citizens there voiced complaints about the program. They accused the local OCD office of discriminating against blacks and criticized officials for failing to appoint "a Negro with the authority and respect of the public" to head the black division. They said the black volunteers didn't get equipment that the white volunteers got. In addition, black citizens complained that officials failed to provide civil defense classes for black citizens. During blackout tests, blacks were confused about what they were supposed to do because they were barred from the classes. Black air raid wardens hadn't been well trained and didn't know what to do. Black residents said, when an air raid siren sounded, they had to look for a shelter designated for black citizens. If the closest shelter was one assigned to white residents, black people could try to enter it—but they might not be welcomed with open arms. Black leaders said in sections of the city where there were black air raid wardens and auxiliary police patrolling the districts, whites in the neighborhoods refused to listen to instructions issued by the blacks. And black residents objected to the discourteous attitudes of the white air raid wardens and auxiliary police.

The situation in New Orleans came to a head in March 1942 when a blackout test was staged by the OCD office. These 15-minute practice tests were intended to prepare people to act if an actual air raid by the enemy occurred. All unnecessary lights were supposed to be put out and window shades drawn. All cars, trucks, buses, and street trolleys were to stop and their lights had to be turned off. Streetlights, traffic lights, and advertising signs were to be out during a blackout test.

Because they felt their safety had been neglected by the OCD office, many black citizens decided to protest and show their anger for the way the program was run by ignoring the test. Their lights were out in their houses—as the blackout test required. But that was because the homeowners were at parties, theaters, and taverns. Some black residents and motorists spent the 15-minute blackout period flickering the lights in their homes and cars. They treated the test as a joke, saying the most successful "blackout" was the "blackout of Negroes from full participation in the civilian defense program" in New Orleans.

These troubling events in New Orleans continued apace. In 1943 black war workers were disrespected yet again when Red Cross volunteer nurse aides were refused seats at a war bond rally. The rally started with a parade that began at the Customs

House on Canal Street. The nurse aide corps—made up of white and black volunteers—joined in the parade route. When the group reached the municipal auditorium, where the rally was to take place, the black women corps members were told they could not enter the auditorium with the white section of the corps. The usher told the women that the Red Cross had issued an order forbidding blacks on the first floor. Three of the black women ignored the usher and took seats. After white people complained about having to sit near the black women, the usher approached the women and told them the seats were reserved and they would have to move. When the women asked, "How far back?" the usher said they could not sit on the same floor with whites. He indicated the "buzzard's roost" section of the auditorium—the balcony—was reserved for "coloreds."

Instead, the three women joined the rest of the black nurse aides outside. None wanted to go to the segregated section of the auditorium for the rest of the rally. The nurse aides and other members of the New Orleans black community resented the racist treatment the women received at the bond rally. The women had graduated from a local school of nursing and were volunteering at the hospital to alleviate a critical shortage of nurses in New Orleans. They deserved better treatment.

Although some OCD officials encouraged and supported segregation among wartime volunteers, black women offered their time and labor in all areas of civilian defense that were open to them. If they couldn't work beside white volunteers in serving their country, they offered their services in separate facilities. Nurse aides played a vital role in the war efforts, and many black women were eager to attend the required 80 hours of training to learn the necessary skills and lend their support to hospitals that were in desperate need of help. Some hospitals were willing to let black and white women work together.

In Brooklyn, New York, in 1942 the Civilian Defense volunteer office issued a call for 2,000 nurse aides. Male and female hospital workers were in short supply, as many had left for defense plant jobs or the military. Officials hoped that black women would answer the call. They reported that all the black nurses who were already serving excelled in their work.

The OCD in Brooklyn was looking for more women like Eva White, who was the mother of six children. Eva worked at a paying job three mornings a week but volunteered every Friday at a hospital as a nurse aide.

"My children are all at school, and I enjoy the work," Eva explained. "It isn't hard, and it is a great satisfaction to know that I'm not only helping to make sick people more comfortable but that I am really doing something for my country." Eva was invited by the OCD to make an appeal on the radio to encourage other black women to volunteer.

"Being a nurse aide is a fine thing," Eva said during the radio broadcast. "And I'd like to tell my people how much pleasure I get from serving. I'd like to persuade them to join."

Alphabet Soup

WDCA, WEVS, WAND, USO: there was no shortage of acronyms to symbolize the numerous volunteer organizations during the war. There was no shortage of women to support the work of the various organizations. And there was no shortage of racism across the groups.

WDCA
The motto of the Women's Defense Corps of America (WDCA) was simple and direct: "Service to servicemen." There was little doubt about the purpose of the group. And the women of the

WDCA in their blue military-like uniforms were straightforward in their approach to making a difference in the lives of servicemen and their families. Ordinary citizens, as well as movie
stars and celebrities, were active in the WDCA in major cities
across the country.

In St. Louis, black women in the WDCA raised $1,000 and
bought furniture for a recreation club at the Jefferson Barracks of the Army Air Forces' Technical Training Command.
They provided the servicemen with cigarettes, ashtrays, and 50
pounds of cookies.

Marva Louis, well-known singer and wife of the famous
boxer Joe Louis, was the captain of the Joe Louis chapter of the

Surrounded by recruits, singer Marva Louis, wife of boxing cham-
pion Joe Louis, takes time out from a tour of nightclubs to entertain
men in black regiments at the US Naval Training Station at Great
Lakes, Illinois. *National Archives, AFRO/AM in WW II List #231*

WDCA in Chicago. Marva and 117 other black women who comprised the chapter sent gifts each month to military camps in the Chicago area. Because of Marva's participation in the group, the work of the women was noticed by more people.

But Marva had a falling-out with the WDCA in August 1943 when the group refused to place a black woman on its board of directors. Marva formed an independent organization she called the Joe Louis Service Guild. It was a volunteer organization that was open to all women, including factory workers and teachers. The women took on a variety of activities, such as sending cookies and newspapers to servicemen each month. And with a supporter as well known as Marva as their president, they were able to hold a bond rally that netted $100,000. Thanks to Marva, they auctioned off a pair of Joe's boxing gloves. The gloves went to the highest bidder—for $20,000! Marva was somewhat reluctant to part with the gloves, which she had been saving for her grandchildren. But she felt she could make the sacrifice because "there is a war to win and the country needs money."

WADCA

The Los Angeles unit of the Women's Ambulance Defense Corps of America (WADCA) was one of 54 chapters in June 1942. The organization offered a "widely diversified defense program" including motorcycle and cavalry units. Women between 18 and 45 years of age, who were US citizens and could pass a physical examination "equal to that in any man's army," could join. They were military trained and learned jujitsu. Known as the Glory Gals, their unofficial slogan was "The hell we can't."

WEVS

Fifty black women in Dayton, Ohio, formed the War Emergency Volunteer Services (WEVS) organization in 1942. At the first meeting the group identified immediate needs in the city. They knew 800 women were coming to Dayton to work in war industries, and the women needed places to live. WEVS members were also concerned about 300 black servicemen of the 98th Aviation Squadron who were stationed at Patterson Field. They wanted to do something to make them feel welcome. The women didn't waste time talking. Within three months of its establishment, WEVS had sponsored three dances for the servicemen.

AWVS

The American Women's Volunteer Service (AWVS) was open to black and white women. Their motto was "Unite and serve." While the group members were united in their goals, they did not serve equally. White women held the top leadership roles, while black women were welcome only as workers who had to operate in groups separate from white groups.

Much was accomplished by the AWVS volunteers. Every unit had a junior auxiliary of girls 14 to 18 years old who took training courses and provided a messenger service. The organization offered segregated classes in air raid precautions, communications, map reading, convoy driving, motor mechanics, defense photography, public speaking, navigation, home repairs, and nutrition. Black women completed the classes in their segregated units and were qualified to volunteer in positions in businesses and government agencies that were vacant because workers had left for the armed forces or for defense jobs. Their departures left openings in vital jobs—with few workers available to fill them. The women of the AWVS were ready to step in to do the work. Classes for nurse aides and receptionists prepared women for volunteer work in hospitals, daycare nurseries, social welfare organizations, and government agencies. Any woman who completed 100 hours of volunteer work earned the privilege of wearing the AWVS uniform. Many black women took advantage of the opportunities to learn new skills while serving their country in wartime.

One black AWVS member from Harlem who completed a course in communications and map reading took a volunteer position with the War Department's "interceptor command." She worked with other women who plotted the movement of enemy planes spotted by air raid "spotters" at listening posts.

Another black AWVS member became highly visible when she composed the lyrics and music for the organization's official theme song, "American Women for Defense." Mercedes

Mercedes Welcker-Jordan, member of the AWVS, plays and sings the official AWVS marching song she composed, April 1942. *National Park Service; Mary McLeod Bethune Council House National Historic Site; National Archives for Black Women's History*

Welcker-Jordan, head of an AWVS motor corps in Harlem, wrote the "catchy" tune that one newspaper described as "destined to be a great hit with orchestras and radio programs." Mercedes donated the song to the AWVS on the condition that any proceeds from the performance of the song be divided three ways—among the national AWVS committee and the two Harlem units.

The Harlem AWVS units raised money to purchase an ambulance, and members of the organization were trained to drive it. In Beaumont, Texas, the AWVS unit fingerprinted over 1,600 children in anticipation of an emergency in which children could be separated from their parents, and raised funds to

The Harlem American Women's Volunteer Service (AWVS) raised money for and dedicated an ambulance at city hall in Harlem in July 1942. *National Park Service; Mary McLeod Bethune Council House National Historic Site; National Archives for Black Women's History*

equip four nursery schools. The black AWVS unit in Galveston, Texas, built two air raid shelters in church basements for children and stocked them with fruit juices, water, medicines, and everything that would be needed in an emergency. In Omaha, Nebraska, the AWVS established a daycare for children of defense workers. The nursery was open to both black and white children. In Durham, North Carolina, the black AWVS home nursing classes built an incubator for premature babies and presented it to the city's department of health.

AWVS chapters that were located near military camps offered relaxation and recreation for soldiers. In Baltimore the AWVS held dances every Saturday night for soldiers. In Washington, DC, the AWVS held air raid precaution classes in the spring of 1942. In Chicago AWVS members served as clerical workers at draft boards, trained women as fingerprinting experts, and made hotel and railroad reservations for soldiers and their families. In Los Angeles, when a group of soldiers gathered around the black organist after a church service and called out the titles of religious songs, she eagerly played all their requests. This gave the local AWVS chapter an idea. Each week they offered a weekly event at which entertainers performed hymns and spirituals. The events were packed with soldiers, sailors, and marines.

Because Los Angeles was home to many Hollywood entertainers and sports personalities, the AWVS chapters were sometimes assisted by celebrities. Some entertainers joined the AWVS; others helped raise funds for AWVS projects. In October 1942 the Los Angeles AWVS benefitted from a boxing match between triple titleholder Henry "Hurricane Hank" Armstrong and Juan Zurita when the two boxers donated part of the proceeds from the match to the AWVS. The group's Servicemen's Benefit Fund received $4,000 from the event.

AWVS members were visible to all when they wore their sky blue military-style uniforms. They were proud to be recognized as volunteers for the war effort. Even celebrity volunteers wore the uniforms when they were on AWVS business. The uniform let people know that the women were involved in war work. Sometimes it meant they were given special consideration by people who were grateful for their service. But in October 1942 the AWVS uniform meant little to Southern Pacific Railways employees.

Twelve black AWVS members—including actresses Maggie Fleming, Patsy Hunter, Millie Monroe, Chinkie Grimes, and Alice Keye—had traveled to Arizona from Los Angeles to volunteer at the opening of an officers' club at Fort Huachuca. The actresses performed for the thousands of military personnel stationed at the camp, and after the event the women purchased first-class tickets on Southern Pacific's *Argonaut* for their return to California. When they boarded the train they were directed to the dirty, overcrowded Jim Crow car and told to find seats. The AWVS members told the usher they had already purchased first-class tickets and wanted to purchase sleeping berths for the overnight trip. They were ignored.

The women decided they would not stay in the Jim Crow section of the *Argonaut*. They moved from car to car looking for open seats and ended up standing in the aisles throughout the 100-mile trip from Hereford to Tucson. Finally, after a "stormy session" with a conductor, they were given temporary seats. When passengers holding reservations for those seats got on the train at the various stops, the black AWVS volunteers had to move. When the women threatened to get off the train, rail personnel found seats for them. But they never got their sleeping berths. They sat up all night on the 500-mile ride.

A rift occurred within the AWVS between white and black members in the spring of 1942 when three prominent black women resigned as a result of discrimination. The AWVS called it a "wrong impression."

Grace Nail Johnson, Lugenia Burns Hope, and Osceola Macarthy Adams, all volunteers in the AWVS, were well-known socialites and activists in the black community. They charged the AWVS with discrimination when segregated units were established in Harlem. They claimed that the AWVS did not encourage "full participation of the Negro in the defense program." Grace had been asked to serve on the national sponsoring committee when the AWVS was created, but she felt that her name was used as "window dressing" and that she was asked to participate only to mask the group's discrimination policies. Grace also criticized the AWVS for failing to include black women on their policy-making board. To show their displeasure with the AWVS, the three women resigned in February 1942. Their resignations were a way of protesting discrimination within the AWVS. But the AWVS called their actions "subversive"—a term that implied the black women were security threats during a time of war. An AWVS official remarked, "This is a subversive way of behaving. There has been an erroneous impression created by these ladies that they were more significant than they were."

The AWVS denied that they had discriminated against black women in Harlem. They said the two Harlem units included both black and white women. In addition, they pointed out that two black members of the Harlem unit were teachers for mixed black and white classes of volunteers.

Although black women charged that the AWVS didn't live up to its motto, "Unite and serve," they overcame the barriers of segregation in order to serve in a variety of ways in AWVS chapters throughout the country. Once again, they didn't let discrimination stand in the way of doing their part for the war effort.

WAND

Black newspapers called women to action in the fall of 1942. A new volunteer women's group had been established, and black women were encouraged to step up: "Give service to our country through the WANDs, whose wands point to VICTORY. No matter how little we give, remember, it looms large when all are giving."

The Women's Army for National Defense (WAND) was started in November 1942 by Chicago's Lovonia Brown. She had worked in other wartime organizations—including the OCD and American Red Cross. Through her work with those groups, Lovonia had seen women using executive skills that usually only men were given the chance to practice, such as leading and managing people. But typically these leadership positions were held by white women. Black women in those organizations were seldom given opportunities to lead or manage other members within the hierarchy. They did much of the work but received little of the glory, Lovonia said. Wanting to give black women the opportunity to sharpen their skills as leaders, she contacted nine other women and together they created the WAND.

The motto of the group was "Working for victory, planning for peace." It was a paramilitary group—part military, part civilian—with a structure similar to the US Army. Mary McLeod Bethune was the general. Lovonia Brown was lieutenant general. Marjorie Wickliffe, a social worker from Indiana, and Arenia Mallory, an educator from Mississippi, were colonels. They were assigned regions of the United States to recruit other women for the WAND. The organization was open to both black and white women. Each chapter was named for a well-respected black person. There was the Charlotta Bass Chapter named for the California newspaper publisher, the Margaret Simms Chapter named for a popular entertainer, and the Maudelle Bousfield Chapter to honor Chicago's first black public school principal.

Dedication of Women's Army for National Defense (WANDs) dormitory for war workers in Chicago. Left to right: Announcer Jonathan Cole of WBBM; Lt. Irma Cayton, for whom the dormitory was named; Austin Scott, regional minorities consultant for the Manpower Commission; and Lt. Gen. Lovonia H. Brown, organizer of the WANDs. *National Park Service; Mary McLeod Bethune Council House National Historic Site; National Archives for Black Women's History*

The WANDs took on a variety of causes. In Illinois a chapter made slippers for wounded soldiers. In Alabama a chapter offered nurse aide classes and gave parties for servicemen. In Tennessee a chapter sponsored USO shows. In Mississippi, WANDs went house to house collecting money for the Red Cross. Several WAND chapters in the Chicago area worked together to provide a residence where women who had come to the city to work in government offices during the war could live. Rooms were also available to Women's Army Corps members who were traveling through the city. They also maintained a childcare center for women who worked in war industries. The WANDs earned money to support their activities by holding teas. There were junior chapters in schools and colleges.

The WANDs took their motto seriously. They not only worked for victory during the war; they also made plans for the postwar world. Toward the end of the war in 1945 every chapter of the WAND prepared to help returning servicemen and their families—providing information about housing, recreation, education, nursery schools, and business opportunities. Returning servicemen and -women would need assistance finding civilian jobs after the war, and they would need help understanding their rights under the GI Bill. The WANDs were there to help during wartime, and they'd be there after the war.

In California, where state officials constantly feared enemy invasions along the coastline, the governor organized the Seventh Women's Ambulance and Nursing Corps as part of the California State Militia. Faustina Johnson was commissioned as lieutenant—the first black woman ever to be given a commission by a California governor—and headed up the corps. She led 75 black women who served as volunteers. They had to provide their own uniforms, but they were proud to serve their state and country. They would be called into service only in the event of an actual invasion, but they were prepared. Four platoons of volunteers included clerical workers, nurses, nurse aides, doctors, ambulance drivers, and stretcher bearers.

The United Service Organizations

Across the country in Boston, Massachusetts, another group of black women was prepared to volunteer service to the country. But in 1943 there were barriers that they had to overcome first. In Boston there stands a statue honoring the legacy of Crispus Attucks. He was one of the first casualties of the American Revolution in 1770. Crispus was a black man who died in the Boston Massacre. He became a symbol of freedom and equality. Because of Boston's commitment to the memory of such a famous black figure, many black people in the city found it especially disturbing when the United Service Organizations (USO) club located only about 50 feet from the Crispus Attucks statue on Boston Common was the site of racial discrimination in 1943.

The USO was formed in 1941 when six existing organizations combined their resources and their efforts to serve military personnel and their families. The YWCA, YMCA, National Catholic Community Service, the National Jewish Welfare Board, the Traveler's Aid Association, and the Salvation Army pooled their efforts under the newly created United Service Organizations (USO). It was authorized by the federal government to "serve the spiritual, social, and general welfare needs of soldiers and sailors." USO clubs were set up wherever men and women of the armed forces were located—in the United States as well as overseas. The USO also provided services for defense workers in some communities. The clubs were run by paid workers and thousands of volunteers. There were over 3,000 USO clubs in the United States during the war.

USO volunteers helped military wives who visited or wanted to live near their husbands at military camps around the country. It was difficult for these women to find places to stay, but it was even harder for black women because many boarding houses wouldn't allow black people. Sometimes the women had babies with them. In addition to finding lodging for the women, USO volunteers provided childcare and other services. They also conducted classes in first aid and budgeting and provided advice about marriage and family relationships during wartime.

In a New York City USO club a military wife could cook a meal for her husband and share it with him in a pleasant atmosphere. She could do her laundry or sew clothes. In Portsmouth, Virginia, the USO offered the Tiny Tots Checking Room where mothers could "park" their babies with volunteers while they ran errands or enjoyed a short rest. In Fayetteville, North Carolina, the USO offered military wives leisure-time activities such as music, arts and crafts, and discussion forums.

In addition to helping the families of soldiers and sailors, the USO clubs provided recreation for servicemen and -women who were far from their homes. At the clubs they could play games, read a book, or attend a social event. The USO looked for volunteers who they considered outstanding "socially, morally, educationally, and from a spiritual standpoint." Women volunteers trained to become hostesses. In their special training courses they learned how to greet visitors to the clubs. They wrote letters for the service personnel, organized games, and mended uniforms. Sometimes the volunteers were there just to talk to lonely servicemen and -women. Another duty of the volunteers was to dance with the servicemen at the USO dances.

The USO was required to open its buildings for the use of *all* men and women in uniform—but the clubs were usually segregated. So-called Negro USO Clubs were created for the black military personnel. And sometimes problems arose about the locations of the black clubs. In Salt Lake City, Utah, a USO center for black soldiers was scheduled to open in June 1943. But 17 white citizens presented a petition of protest to the city. The signers insisted they weren't opposed to the idea of a USO for black soldiers. But they thought a "more suitable" location could be found.

While the USO clubs were often segregated, that wasn't always the case. Many black women volunteered at USO clubs. Some worked at segregated clubs and others worked at integrated clubs. But wherever the women volunteered, they did it because they wanted to serve their country during a time of crisis.

There were integrated USO clubs at Sacramento, California; Pittsburgh, Pennsylvania; Ayer, Massachusetts; and in other communities. The New York Stage Door Canteen served both black and white guests. The volunteers who operated it were also of both races. There were 200 black hostesses who worked there. A black hostess named Osceola Archer said that sometimes there were problems related to race. Although men and women of both races danced with each other, some visitors to the club resented this. The hostesses were trained to reply, "I am dancing with the uniform of my country."

At the USO Soldiers and Sailors Recreation Center, not far from the Crispus Attucks memorial on Boston Common, black USO workers faced discrimination in 1943 when the board of directors of the Boston USO refused to allow black hostesses to volunteer at the center on Boston Common. The group said there weren't enough black soldiers using the club to justify the use of black hostesses. It explained that most black soldiers and sailors used another USO club on Ruggles Street, and there were black hostesses there. In May, after a month of negotiation with black leaders in Boston, the directors decided to allow black hostesses to volunteer at the Boston Common USO center. But in July, 25 white hostesses at the center threatened to resign if the black hostesses were allowed at the club. Finally, in August, 18 black women were certified by the USO to be hostesses in Boston. When five of them were requested to work at the Hotel Touraine USO center, they were told that they could dance only with black soldiers. The head of the board of directors who had approved the training of the black hostesses said he would never have approved the policy if he had known "mixed dancing was involved." Even the Boston police commissioner said he would not approve mixed dancing on the Boston Common.

Because the black hostesses were not allowed to serve without limitations, they decided to leave the club. In December 1943 a decision was reached by the Boston USO Committee and the black USO workers. A new "international" USO club was to be established in the exclusive Back Bay section of the city. The new club was open to all races, and volunteers of any race could work there. College co-eds of various races from nine colleges in the Greater Boston area pledged their support to the club. The women promised at least 200 volunteers would be ready by the time the new club opened in January 1944.

The establishment of the international USO was *not* a solution to the discrimination problem that existed at the Boston Common USO. While the black USO workers and members of the armed forces were promised a club where discrimination would be absent and which would be located in an exclusive Boston neighborhood, it didn't solve the problem of racism that existed in the Boston Common USO.

Saving Fat

The enemy knew what they were up against when it came to the force of the American military, but they couldn't have been prepared for the might of the American housewife. The military draft ensured a ready supply of soldiers. American factories furnished a steady stream of weapons and aircraft. And American housewives put their clout behind volunteer home front conservation efforts.

The American housewife was called upon to scrimp and save every scrap of fabric, paper, cardboard, metal, and even kitchen fat. These materials were taken to government collection centers and recycled into products for war use. Recycled magazines, games, and athletic equipment were used in military camps for leisure activities for the troops. Fabric was used to make military uniforms and parachutes. Recycled metal was used for weapons and aircraft. Paper and cardboard cartons were needed to ship food, medical supplies, and ammunition to the armed forces. And fat and oils were needed for the glycerin they contained. Glycerin was used for making explosives and in ointments for surgical dressings. During the first nine weeks of the nationwide campaign 4.5 million pounds of fat was collected at grocery stores. The Fat Salvage Committee estimated that was enough glycerin for 11,300,000 anti-aircraft shells. The goal was to collect 500 million pounds of fat.

A government agency, the Office of Price Administration (OPA), organized a plan for rationing food in American homes. There was a need for large quantities of food for the fighting armies in war zones and for citizens of warring countries where the production of food had been interrupted by the war. American farmers, workers, and housewives were called upon to help grow, harvest, and conserve food so those who couldn't produce their own had food. And American housewives stepped up to help. It meant eating and cooking differently—sometimes the usual ingredients were in short supply or not available at all. The OPA set up a system for rationing. They used a points system under which points were assigned to some products. Housewives got ration books from the county ration board. The books contained a limited number of stamps that could be used for the scarce items. Sugar, coffee, and red meat were rationed. Butter, milk, and eggs were also in short supply.

The rationing system could be a little tricky to understand. So in December 1942 black women's groups volunteered to help housewives understand the process. Representatives from several national black women's organizations attended a conference in Washington, DC, where they learned about rationing. Thomasina Johnson, Flaxie Pinkett, Elsie Austin, and Ethel Popel Shaw attended the conference and then went back to their communities and taught other women in their women's clubs about the system.

The Original Illinois Housewives Association existed before World War II but took on new duties after America joined the fight in late 1941. The group's motto was: "To give a greater knowledge to the housewife which will serve as power for an increased economic independence, that makes for better living." The organization offered monthly lectures and demonstrations on consumer problems and home economics, as well as a "circulating library" of literature about home economic issues. Consumer clinics were held with lectures, exhibits, and demonstrations on food and nutrition, fabrics and clothing, house furnishings, drugs and cosmetics, health and hospital insurance, savings, and gardens and flowers.

In October 1942, Lillian Le Vine, president of the Original Illinois Housewives Association, called a three-day conference. The theme was "Be prepared for vital war service." The group was taking on a new phase of war service work that fall and winter. Mothers, wives, sisters, and other female relatives of servicemen and -women were invited to join the organization. And all the group's board members signed the Consumers' Pledge for Total Defense, promising to buy carefully, take care of things they had, and waste nothing.

"Good, wholesome food puts the fight in our fighters." The federal government used catchy sayings such as this on posters and brochures to remind American farmers that they needed to help supply food to the military and to hungry people living in war-torn countries where food was in short supply. Through the US Department of Agriculture's Food for Freedom program, farmers were encouraged to grow more while using less. The government asked farmers to conserve fuel, machinery, and tires while producing more food with fewer workers. The government told farmers that in just one month the 7.5 million soldiers fighting the war ate a stack of food the size of the 102-story Empire State Building.

Since the increased demand for food directly affected farm families, black farming women played a key role in the war effort. Food production and food conservation were critical areas of focus. And black women on the farms came through for the war effort just as their counterparts in the cities did. Georgia's black farmers increased their poultry and egg production, enlarged their gardens, preserved fruits and vegetables, planted fruit trees, cured hams, and made lye soap from leftover cooking grease.

Even black women who didn't normally work on farms volunteered their efforts to help farmers meet the demands for increased food production. Because so many farm laborers had joined the military or gone to work at defense plants, farmers experienced a severe shortage of workers to help plant and harvest the crops. In the South, black wives of doctors, undertakers, teachers, preachers, and storekeepers in one county volunteered to help harvest the peanut crop in 1944. In Fitzgerald, Georgia, a group of women from the Baptist church volunteered to help a recently widowed woman harvest her Victory Garden in 1943. They picked, shelled, and prepared the produce from Ashley Johnson's farm. Then the volunteers took the produce to the local high school, where it was preserved by canning and dehydrating. The dehydrated food was taken to the community food bank for use in the winter months by families who were in need.

Sherman Coffee's family was in need of help in the fall of 1944. They operated an 840-acre farm near Frankfort, Kansas. Normally they had plenty of help during the harvest season—there were five sons in the family. But in 1944 those sons were all in the armed forces. When the local community turned out to help the family with the harvest, the appearance of one woman turned heads. Lucile Bluford, managing editor of the *Kansas City Call* newspaper, had driven 150 miles from Kansas City. She had taken her vacation time to help on the Coffee farm. Although Lucile had no experience in farm work, she drove a wagon as she helped with the threshing and loading of wheat. And she served as the assistant cook.

The Women's Land Army (WLA) was formed by the federal government in 1943. The goal was to recruit 60,000 women to help farmers throughout the country as they met the demands for food production. The government ran articles in black newspapers, encouraging women to join the WLA. But some states were reluctant to include black women in the WLA. An official in South Carolina explained that they planned to use white women initially—because if they started the program with black women, white women would refuse to join. However, in Arkansas by mid-1944 about 25,000 black women were WLA members.

The Red Cross

For many Americans in the 1940s the Red Cross was a symbol of generosity and goodwill. It was an organization known for its spirit of caring and compassion for people in need. But for many black people in the 1940s the admirable work of the Red Cross was overshadowed by its policies of racial discrimination.

The American Red Cross played a vital role during the war, providing aid to members of the armed forces and their families. The agency trained nurse aides to help alleviate the shortage of nurses in hospitals, provided care packages to civilians in war-torn countries and to American prisoners of war in enemy camps, and even followed Allied armies to the war zones. Some individuals in the Red Cross volunteered their time, while others were paid for their work. Many of those who were in paid positions had left successful professions to serve with the Red Cross for the duration of the war. The combined work of the 40,000 paid employees and 7.5 million unpaid volunteers had extraordinary results.

One service provided by the Red Cross was the collection and distribution of blood, which was available to people receiving transfusions in hospitals. The need for blood was great during wartime—especially by military hospitals for soldiers who had been wounded in battle. Americans were encouraged to donate at Red Cross blood banks, and many did. Many black people wanted to give blood to the Red Cross to help wounded soldiers, but the Red Cross would not accept it. The Red Cross defended its policy saying they were acting on orders from the military.

In January 1942 the agency changed its policy and accepted blood from black donors for the first time. Even so, it segregated the blood supplies. "Negro blood" was kept separate from "white blood." Blood from black donors was carefully labeled to ensure it was used only for black people.

In St. Louis, Missouri, Gabriel Jones and Ellise Davis went through a humiliating experience when they tried to donate blood to a Red Cross blood drive. The two women were workers at an ordnance plant and answered the call for blood when the Red Cross set up a blood bank at the plant. They were especially eager to donate because they had been told that few blacks had contributed to the bank. They were told by the Red Cross representative that their blood would not be labeled "Negro blood."

On the day of the blood drive the two women were standing in line with their white coworkers as they waited to donate their blood. To their surprise they were pulled from the line and escorted to an isolated room where Red Cross workers were preparing to withdraw their blood. The two women were surprised because Gabriel had talked to a woman at the Red Cross headquarters the day before the drive. At first she was told the Red Cross did not accept blood from blacks. Later she received a call from a woman at the Red Cross headquarters saying they *would* accept Gabriel's blood, but she didn't mention that Gabriel and Ellise would have to go through the experience in a separate area from their white coworkers. After being pulled into the separate room by officials, Gabriel and Ellise refused to give their blood to the Red Cross. They wanted to show their disapproval of the Red Cross segregation policy.

The policy of segregating blood continued because many Americans believed there was a difference between white people's blood and black people's blood. Many white people continued their racist beliefs that black people's blood must be kept separate so that it would not contaminate blood from white people. But even when scientists proved that blood characteristics were not related to race, the Red Cross continued to label blood by race. Finally, in 1950—five years after the end of World War II—the Red Cross stopped the practice.

The Red Cross trained women as volunteer nurse aides all across the country. Black and white women volunteered to "pledge myself before God, to practice my duties as nurses aide faithfully." And they agreed to fulfill their duties for no pay: "My only recompense will be satisfaction in a deed well done and in knowing that I am making a contribution to civilian defense and to suffering humanity." Each volunteer completed 80 hours of training and promised to complete at least 150 hours of service per year after her training.

The first "Negro Red Cross Nurse's Aide Corps" in the state of Texas graduated in April 1943, and its members went to work at Holy Cross Hospital, an "institution for the care of Negro patients" in Austin. In Harlem, New York, Grace Crump Jones was responsible for training the Red Cross volunteers at the hospital. Clerks, housewives, stenographers, factory workers, teachers, and newspaperwomen volunteered to become "the nurse's extra hand." Grace taught her first class of 25 volunteers to make beds, give baths, feed the sick, and admit and discharge patients. In Washington, DC, 54 prominent black housewives, civic workers, and community leaders made up the first class of Red Cross volunteer nurse aides at Howard University. After four weeks of lecture and classroom practice the volunteers completed three weeks of hospital probation. After they completed their training they served as assistants to the regular staff nurses in hospitals.

But not all Red Cross offices were open to black volunteers. Marie K. Clarke tried more than once to volunteer for nurse aide training with the Red Cross in Bridgeport, Connecticut. When she turned in an application in February 1942 the local Red Cross office accepted her. But before she began the training, local leaders contacted her and told her she couldn't enter the current training class because she was black. It was the second time she had offered her services to the Red Cross only to be refused.

Marie appealed the decision to the national office of the Red Cross in Washington, DC. In her letter she wrote, "Is that a democratic stand for a large organization to take? The organization's work is carried on with Negro's money. We certainly donate to your campaigns. Why can't we help to train so that in times of emergency we can do our part?"

An official from the Red Cross gave an explanation for Marie's rejection: After completing the Red Cross nurse aide training, the nurse aides would serve as volunteers in the hospitals in the city. But none of the Bridgeport hospitals had black nurses. Therefore, there was no need for black nurse aides. The official explained that the Red Cross was acting as an agent of the hospitals in training the volunteers and that the hospitals simply had no need for black aides.

One hospital in Washington, DC, was happy to accept black women who had completed a seven-week Red Cross course for nurse aides in May 1943. The women were government workers and housewives who entered the course expecting to volunteer in local hospitals after they received their certificates. They finished the course and were certified to assist nurses and doctors in the obstetrics and pediatrics departments of local hospitals. A white superintendent of nurses at one hospital gladly accepted the 37 black volunteers. She put them to work immediately— scrubbing floors, cleaning restrooms, and emptying bedpans!

The volunteers walked off the job and refused to return until the superintendent allowed them to assist in the areas in which they had been trained. The superintendent defended her actions, saying that the black volunteer nurse aides' presence had interfered with the training of "regular" student nurses. A representative for the black volunteers and the hospital officials met to settle the dispute. As a result, the superintendent allowed the black women to perform the duties for which they had been trained.

The Red Cross Overseas

The impressive work of the American Red Cross reached far beyond the cities, towns, and rural areas of America. When the Red Cross followed the American armies into battle at the fronts, black women were there to give their support. And while they may have been ignored by many Americans back home, they were revered by American soldiers across several continents.

In the fall of 1942 the Red Cross sent out a call for black men and women to volunteer for overseas duty. Articles appeared in black newspapers stating: "Help Wanted! Red Cross Seeks Qualified Colored Specialists for Overseas Assignments." There were black soldiers fighting across the globe, and because white Red Cross workers typically didn't serve black soldiers—either because they refused to, or because they didn't have the opportunity to because of segregated facilities—there was a need for black Red Cross workers. There was a need for directors, associate directors, and recreation officers for the Red Cross service clubs located around the world. Some of the positions were paid positions. Black men and women answered the call. Typically, only men could fill the club directors' jobs, but women were placed as associate directors and staff assistants.

The first black female Red Cross workers who volunteered for overseas duty arrived in London in October 1942. Henrine Ward, C. Gladys Martin, Magnolia Latimer, Carol Jarrett, and Sydney Taylor Brown won the hearts of the British according to newspaper reports. Their job was to supervise the recreation activities of the black soldiers and to promote good relations between black troops and British citizens. The newly opened Red Cross club they were to work at was a place where soldiers on leave from the front could enjoy wholesome cultural activities.

The staff at the London club was thrilled when in December they had a visit from First Lady Eleanor Roosevelt. Henrine Ward and Carol Jarrett were chosen to escort her to the reception room, where an official committee was waiting to greet her. The First Lady walked through the club chatting with soldiers. Henrine described how she felt that day. "I was thrilled and proud when the First Lady of our land heartily shook my hand 3,000 miles from home. I couldn't help but realize what a big thing she was doing to come so far to visit our troops and give spirit to those of us who had left home to make our colored warriors comfortable."

There were three major branches of the Red Cross overseas—service clubs, field services, and clubmobiles. The service clubs were located in urban centers and served men on leave from the battlefield. The clubs had libraries, gyms, and auditoriums for dances. There were pool tables, darts, ping-pong, and pinball machines for use by the soldiers. The clubs had dining halls, and staff served three meals a day. There were beds and showers for the soldiers. The field services branch provided facilities wherever there was a large concentration of troops in remote places. The field services set up facilities near the troops using any buildings they could find—even if they were just huts. But the Red Cross workers rolled up their sleeves and made the facilities comfortable for troops who needed a break from the fighting. The clubmobiles were huge, specially designed "luxury" trucks. They traveled to remote places where soldiers were stationed and where there was no train service. The clubmobiles were outfitted with playing cards, chewing gum, cigarettes, and candy—and doughnuts freshly made by the female Red Cross workers who were assigned to the trucks.

By May 1943 the Red Cross had sent black female Red Cross workers to Europe. Some were stationed at service clubs in England—in Liverpool, Bristol, and London. Others were assigned to clubmobiles or to field service.

Many soldiers thought the American women they met at the Red Cross clubs were special. But some seemed to have a distinctive appeal for the soldiers who were far from home. Camille King Jones of Chicago was always cheerful and endeared herself to the soldiers by participating in any club activities with a smile and a friendly word. Her attractive personality earned her recognition as the "unofficial sweetheart of all the colored soldiers" who came to London.

But the fact that a woman wore a Red Cross uniform didn't automatically mean she would be treated with respect. A black journalist named Vincent Lushington "Roi" Ottley reported an incident that illustrated how ugly some American servicemen could be when it came to living and working with black women—even those wearing Red Cross uniforms.

J. Clarice Brooks was a social worker in New York when she decided to join the Red Cross and volunteer for overseas duty. One of her assignments was at a club for black servicemen in Belfast, Ireland. One night five white American soldiers saw Clarice at a Red Cross club for white soldiers as she was waiting for a ride to her living quarters.

"There's the b— that's runnin' the club for n—," one of the soldiers shouted.

Clarice replied, "This is a Red Cross club for American soldiers if they behave themselves."

The soldiers wouldn't leave her alone. "What do you mean? N— are better behaved than we are?" one of them sneered.

Another soldier said to his friend, "Are you going to let her talk to you like that?"

"Let's beat her up," another chimed in.

"Yeah, we know how to treat n—!" agreed another.

As the white soldiers began to move in on Clarice, a white officer approached the group and prevented the soldiers from harming her. Afterward, Clarice reported the incident to authorities and wanted to press charges against the soldiers. But, she said, nothing was ever done about the ugly incident.

Roi Ottley wrote about Clarice's experience in an article titled "Dixie Invades Britain." He believed that British behavior toward black Americans was negatively influenced by white American soldiers. Some of those Americans were racist—like the ones who threatened Clarice—and Roi reported that those Americans encouraged the British to follow racist policies. The title of his article reflected his belief that the Jim Crow practices of Dixie—the American South—had traveled across the Atlantic. But the reality was that racism could be found in Britain as well as in Dixie. Racism was not exclusively American.

In 1943 when Carol Jarrett, Henrine Ward, Lucille McAllister, and Gertrude Furlowe arrived at the Red Cross club building in Bristol that was designated for black servicemen and -women, they found the building in rubble. It had been hit by enemy bombs, and the rooms were open to the skies. The floors were wet from rain, and only two rooms were livable. Within a year the Red Cross women—with help from the citizens of Bristol—had transformed the building. The newly refurbished Red Cross club had a cafeteria, sleeping rooms, and recreation facilities. Soldiers who needed a respite from the war could get a tasty meal and a peaceful night's sleep in a clean room. They could dance with a pretty girl, and play basketball, tennis, badminton, horseshoes, ping-pong, and billiards.

The arrival of the first black Red Cross women in England caught the attention of British civilians and caused a sensation among the black American servicemen. But it was nothing compared to the commotion created when a single black woman reported for duty along the Alcan Highway in March 1943. About 1,300 men turned out to witness the arrival of Hazel Dixon Payne in *minus*-70-degree temperatures at Dawson Creek, British Columbia.

The men were part of the all-black 95th Engineers regiment of the US Army, and they were building a highway through Canada and Alaska. The road was known as the Alcan Highway. The soldiers had been in Alaska for a year and a half and hadn't seen a black woman in all that time. Hazel reported that, "The expression on their faces exhibited tension, anxiety, and a grand appreciation for a Negro woman."

Hazel was the assistant field director of the Red Cross club located at the 95th Engineer army post. She was taken by car over a dirt road to her new home—a room in a wooden hut. When she arrived in her room she saw a dressing table, washstand, and chest of drawers made from odd pieces of wood. Hazel found a note on the dressing table that read,

To the first lady of the Alcan, we are pleased to have you and hope that you will enjoy the use of this furniture as much as we have enjoyed making it for you. You are brave and have done a fine thing to leave all the comforts of civilian life to come to us and may God guide you and keep you always. We feel as if this war is really worth fighting for now that you have come to us, and we know we will win this war.

Hazel was determined to open the Red Cross Club as soon as possible. She spent her first day sewing curtains, cleaning windows, and arranging furniture. She also spent some time interviewing the soldiers about their welfare. Over the next few months Hazel made the club into a "home away from home" for the soldiers. She managed to get a couple of pool tables and ping-pong tables. A stage was built where the men produced a play called *Dozing Along*, which was about their lives on the Alcan Highway, where bulldozers were the common form of transportation. Hazel said her experience on the Alcan Highway was something she'd never forget. She was grateful that she was able to serve her country and the Red Cross. "It also makes me believe that this democracy is worth fighting for and I know we will win this war. I intend to do my part."

In July 1943 Hazel was sent to London, England, where she supervised the Home Hospitality Committee at a Red Cross club for black service members. It was her duty to help create positive relations between black American soldiers and the British citizens. Hazel did do her part for the war effort, but she didn't live to see the end of the war. In October 1944 she died after a surgery and was buried in England.

Some Red Cross assignments were definitely more enviable than others. Three black Red Cross workers arrived at their destination in February 1944. Sara R. Johnson, Helen Chequita Lonewolf, and Ruby Kelly had been sent to operate a "negro-staffed club" for the Red Cross "somewhere in North Africa." Ruby, a former teacher, had requisitioned a beautiful farmhouse with a view of the Mediterranean Sea for use as the Red Cross clubhouse. Thousands of black troops in the area visited the Country Club, as it was known. Ruby was astonished one day when a soldier threw his arms around her, picked her up, and carried her into the clubhouse. The soldier was her brother-in-law; he had heard she was in North Africa, where he was stationed. He had been looking for her whenever he had a spare moment. He finally spotted her at the Country Club and was so happy he couldn't resist sweeping Ruby off her feet. She was embarrassed by the whole thing, but the soldiers who watched the spectacle were delighted.

Cheers and applause greeted four black Red Cross volunteers when they arrived at the Doctor Carver Club in Australia in August 1943. They were the first black volunteers to arrive in Australia, and the black soldiers were thrilled at the sight of Grace Outlaw, Clara Wells, Rosemary Spears, and Geraldine Randall. Grace had been a social worker in New York City before volunteering to go overseas with the Red Cross. Clara had a master's degree in physical therapy and was excited about her first trip abroad although her seasickness made the trip a little less enjoyable. Rosa had worked in Oregon for the YWCA before joining the Red Cross. And it was expected that Geraldine would be especially popular with the soldiers because she "could make the piano talk."

In October 1944 another family reunion took place "somewhere in the Southwest Pacific." Thelma Holman Raynor was serving with the Red Cross when she met James Newman, a sailor from Virginia. She remembered meeting a sailor named Frank Newman just a few days before this. She asked James if he had a brother. James said he did have a brother named Frank, and he thought his brother was in "this part of the world." Thelma told James she *knew* with certainty that he was, because she had just met him. It didn't take long for Thelma to get the brothers together. She immediately planned a special dinner at the Red Cross club where she worked. The Newman brothers, along with Thelma, enjoyed a happy reunion.

"Somewhere in New Guinea," in January 1944, the *Pittsburgh Courier* newspaper reported, six black "goddesses" stepped off a ship to the awe of hundreds of black soldiers. The women were Red Cross workers who had volunteered for overseas duty. But to the soldiers—some who hadn't seen a woman in months—they were goddesses. Rosa Spears, Clara Wells, Norma Manley, Nola "Kitty" Cox, Laura Anderson, and Mary Parker had come to operate the Club Papua. The soldiers had walked miles to get a glimpse of the women. Some of the soldiers brought gifts. Some talked and talked. Some were silent. Some just stared. Others had tears in their eyes.

Clara Wells must have been a very levelheaded woman, or she could have been swept off her feet. She arrived at Club Papua from her former assignment at the Doctor Carver Club. Clara said she received hundreds of marriage proposals while she was in Australia. And while that might sound like a glamorous life, Clara described her typical day at a Red Cross club as far from glamorous: no time for breakfast, no coffee, no juice, no ice, no bath, no mouthwash, plenty of ants and mosquitoes, and—thankfully—plenty of deodorant brought from home. After a game of cards and a ride in an amphibious jeep—a vehicle that traveled on land and water, she ate her lunch of beef and corn. Then she read some of her 188 letters—mostly from soldiers—and one from her boyfriend. She wrapped packages for a soldier, wrote a letter to an anxious mother, and sent a sympathy letter to a bereaved family. Late in the afternoon a group of soldiers leaving for a "destination unknown" asked her to sing their favorite song for them—"Baby, Don't You Cry."

> *"No matter what you say*
> *I'm gonna leave you right away*
> *So now, baby, baby, don't you cry."*

Kitty Cox was one of the black women who worked at the Club Papua, and it prepared her well for her next assignment at Oro Bay, a city of tents, crude wooden structures, and thatched huts carved out of the jungle. It was home to 10,000 soldiers. And those 10,000 soldiers idolized the only woman at Oro Bay—Kitty Cox.

When Kitty arrived in April 1944 she was one of two black women sent to operate the Red Cross recreation hall called Club Paradise. The other woman—Laura Anderson—stayed for a couple of months before she left for her home in the United States. Kitty was left to manage the club alone. Kitty decided to take advantage of the 10,000 soldiers and put them to work. The men organized committees to operate the club. They elected officers and had a constitution.

Although the soldiers took on much of the work of running the club, Kitty had plenty to do. She had a knack for locating scare supplies—ice cream, jam, cheese, chess sets, ping-pong balls, paper cups, lumber, bolts of cloth, books, and even circus tents. She even managed to hustle up aluminum from wrecked airplanes when the soldiers needed materials for their hobby workshop. She had to get the clubmobile—a big van stocked with snacks and soft drinks—out to isolated locations for the men who couldn't get in to Club Paradise. And the fact that the club's committees were operated by soldiers presented a unique problem. Sometimes an entire committee was wiped out overnight by the enemy. When that happened, Kitty had to assume the responsibilities of that committee until replacements could be found. Most days Kitty spent 12 to 14 hours a day at the club before returning to her sleeping quarters at the Banana Manor.

By the end of 1944, France had been liberated from German occupation. Black American soldiers were stationed in France, and Red Cross officials moved black workers from England to set up and manage clubs for the soldiers. Geneva Holmes had already spent 10 months in Plymouth, England, where she provided services for the thousands of black soldiers who participated in the D-day invasion at Normandy, France, in June 1944. Now she was off to Paris. Olive Blackwell, Estelle Trent, Geraldine Ross, and Thelma Pratt left England for Paris as well. Sydney Taylor Brown was sent to operate a club at Le Mann, France; and Lucille McAllister went to Rennes. La Verne Birch and C. Gladys Martin were sent to operate the Liberty Club at Cherbourg.

Some of the newly arrived women would be attached to clubmobiles on the famous Red Ball Express. After the liberation of France the Allied armies had the Germans on the run. As the Allies chased the retreating Germans across France and Germany, they needed huge amounts of supplies—especially gasoline. The Sherman tanks were gas guzzlers—moving only one to two miles on a gallon of gasoline. But it wasn't easy getting supplies from the port cities to the fighting men. So the military came up with a plan to take over two roads just for their use. Six hundred miles of roadway—the

Clubmobile in France, March 1945.
Courtesy of the American Red Cross/All rights reserved in all countries

Red Ball Express—was designated for military use only. One road was used solely by the trucks loaded with supplies; the other road was used solely by the returning trucks. The trucks ran 24 hours a day. Most of the truck drivers were black servicemen. They were whom the black Red Cross women were sent to France to serve. With the exhausting schedule, the soldiers were in need of rest and relaxation when they could get it. The Red Cross workers were there to offer it.

Mines, mud, mountainous terrain, and bitterly cold floodwaters made the fighting especially miserable for the all-black 92nd Division of the army in western Italy in late 1944 and early 1945.

Sara B. Johnson (left), Geraldine Dyson (middle), and Evelyn G. Vaughan (right) with the Red Cross serve hot coffee and doughnuts to troops manning anti-aircraft defenses with the Fifth Army in Italy in 1943. *Courtesy of the American Red Cross by Ollie Atkins/All rights reserved in all countries*

Red Cross club girls Wilhelmina Barrow and Juanita Morrow, both from New York City, serve troops of the 27th Chemical Company after traveling 100 miles by truck to deliver cookies and doughnuts, October 1945. *American Red Cross photo by Gerald Waller, courtesy of the American Red Cross/All rights reserved in all countries*

Add to that constant, heavy shellfire from the enemy. It was almost unbearable for the soldiers. But not far behind the front lines, Red Cross workers Geneva Howard, Marie Leach, Sybil Gowby, and Elizabeth Coppin offered a break from the misery. They operated a portable club unit that provided facilities for reading, writing, and recreation, along with a snack bar. And for those soldiers who were fighting in isolated areas and not able to get to the portable units, Ruth Pius, Viola Miller, and Gladys Powell drove a clubmobile to the soldiers. They got as close to the front lines as possible to deliver coffee and fresh doughnuts.

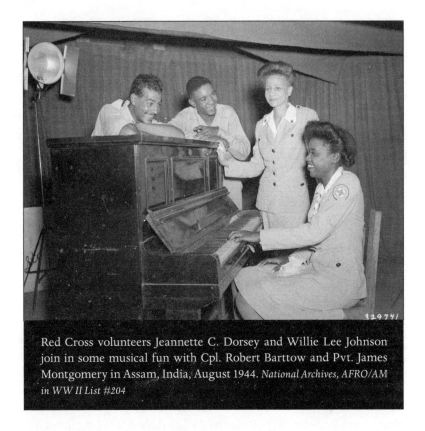

Red Cross volunteers Jeannette C. Dorsey and Willie Lee Johnson join in some musical fun with Cpl. Robert Barttow and Pvt. James Montgomery in Assam, India, August 1944. *National Archives, AFRO/AM in WW II List #204*

The Red Cross club located at Margherita, India, was a unique club that served both black and white servicemen. It was staffed by black Red Cross personnel. The facility looked like a country club situated at the top of a hill at the end of a winding road. Servicemen and Red Cross staff could sit on the balcony that overlooked fields of green tea plants. The club had a library, card rooms, and a canteen that offered sandwiches, doughnuts, apple pie, and ice cream. The club was a popular place. Between 400 and 1,200 servicemen visited every day. Willie Lee Johnson, Faye Sandifer, M. Virginia Bailey, and Jeannette C. Dorsey were Red Cross workers who served as staff assistants at the club.

As spring approached in 1945, the war was beginning to wind down in the European theater. And by summer, the war would be over in the Pacific region too. Red Cross workers who had been in war zones for years were beginning to think of home and postwar America.

Thoughts of Home

In May 1945, J. Pericles McDuffie was passing through London on her way home to the States. She carried her luggage through the train station and made her way through the city on VE Day (Victory in Europe Day) while all of London's train porters and taxi drivers were out celebrating. Pericles didn't mind the inconvenience though. She had reached London from her assignment in Paris in only 14 hours—amazing considering it had taken her 14 *days* traveling from London to Paris at the height of the fighting a few months earlier. It was wonderful to get back to a city that was now free of bombs.

"At least 10,000 people were milling around Buckingham Palace, and everyone in the city was wearing red, white and blue," said Pericles of her return to London. She was surprised to see the usually conservative Londoners in "a peace-happy mob that kissed the bobbies [policemen] 'til their faces were red from lipstick as well as embarrassment."

While Pericles was on her way back to the United States, two other American women were still in Europe and only dreaming of home. Mary Stamper had enjoyed being stationed in France, but in her opinion San Francisco was the most beautiful city in the world. Henrine Ward Banks was operating the Canebiere Club in Marseille, France, and got word that she was going home after three years away. When she arrived at her mother's house she planned to first kiss her mom and then head straight to the kitchen, where she would drink a big bottle of ice-cold milk from the refrigerator.

Lolita Espadron looked forward to going back home to New Orleans after the war. Even though it is known as a city with terrific food, fabulous music, and plenty of lively night-clubs, all Lolita wanted was to spend some quiet evenings at home listening to her radio. It wasn't that she didn't like socializing with her friends at clubs. But Lolita had filled an unusual role with the Red Cross in Sydney, Australia. After working her usual eight-hour day at the Booker T. Washington Red Cross Club, she organized outings for groups of service-men and -women to nightclubs in the city. Most of the clubs that served black servicemen reserved a table for Lolita and her group of war-weary soldiers who were looking for a break from the fighting. Lolita was just the "organizer"—the soldiers brought their girlfriends. Everybody looked forward to an eve-ning of good music, great dancing, and a meal that wasn't in the mess hall.

Lolita commented at the end of the war that she never knew going to nightclubs could be work. Many nights after working her long shift at the Red Cross club all she wanted to do was go to her room and relax, but she didn't want to let the fun-seeking soldiers and their girls down. By the end of her duty in Austra-lia, Lolita had had her fill of the nightlife. She looked forward to returning to New Orleans to take up her old job as a social worker. But she did spend a little time wondering if she would be satisfied with her social work after the "glitter and glare" of the night life in Sydney. "I wonder how I'll fit in," she said about her return to the postwar world.

Backing the Attack for Democracy

Segregation and discrimination were part of American life in the 1940s. It was a time when black people were intentionally excluded from civic organizations and government programs. It was a time when black people were forced to sit in separate sections of buses, trains, and public buildings. It was a time when black people were told their blood was inferior to white people's blood. Segregation and discrimination were two evils of American society in the 1940s. Most white Americans accepted and didn't question the racism that existed.

It was also an unusual time. The country was at war with forces that threatened the ideals of democracy. Many Americans feared their way of life was in danger. And when the country went to war, many Americans volunteered to help win the war and preserve their way of life.

Thousands of black women who had been victims of segregation and discrimination volunteered to serve their country in a variety of ways. Many of them were treated cruelly in return. Five black entertainers who volunteered to entertain American servicemen at a camp in Arizona were forced to sit up all night on a train because the rail company refused to give them sleeping berths. Marie K. Clarke volunteered to join a nurse aide class and was told she wasn't needed because she was black. Gabriel Jones and Ellise Davis volunteered to donate blood and learned it would be labeled "Negro blood." And Mildred McAdory volunteered to organize a scrap drive only to end her day bruised and in a roach-infested jail cell.

Why did these women, and so many others like them, volunteer to serve a country that tolerated segregation and discrimination? The black Red Cross volunteers who took the pledge of nurse aides hoped to make a "contribution to civilian defense and to suffering humanity." Eva White, the mother of six who volunteered as a nurse aide when her children were in school, said she got great satisfaction knowing that she was doing something for her country. Henrine Ward, who served with the Red Cross in England and France, said she wanted to "make our colored warriors comfortable" when they were 3,000 miles from home. Hazel Payne, nicknamed the First Lady of the Alcan, said she volunteered because "this democracy is worth fighting for."

5

ENTERTAINERS

"We Don't Take Your Kind"

We don't take Negroes here. —Hotel clerk in Ohio

I'm sorry, we don't take your kind.
                                    —Hotel manager in Washington, DC

You'll have to eat in the kitchen. —Waitress in Missouri

All across the United States in the 1940s black citizens met with discrimination when they tried to stay in hotels and eat in restaurants. It meant that black people planned ahead when they took trips. Travelers prepared sack lunches at home so they wouldn't have to face the possibility of being turned down for service in a restaurant. Friends and relatives were contacted along the route to provide overnight lodging for travelers. And it didn't make a difference if the traveler happened to be one of the most well-known and talented entertainers of the time or that she had raised thousands of dollars for the war effort.

By the fall of 1945, when Hazel Scott entered a café in central Missouri and was told she'd have to eat in the kitchen, she had won acclaim as a Broadway performer and Hollywood film star. Trained as a classical pianist by a Juilliard teacher, she had made a name for herself by "swinging the classics"—uniquely blending classical music with jazz in her performances: Beethoven with Basie, Tchaikovsky with jive, Chopin with boogie-woogie. She said she just couldn't resist the temptation to jazz up her classics. And she did it with such success that audiences couldn't resist her. She reportedly made $5,000 a week and dined at New York hot spots such as Sardi's and El Morocco.

Hazel's star status granted her access to some of the best restaurants in the country. But for those out-of-the-way roadside diners where the workers didn't recognize her, Hazel was just another "colored" trying to eat with whites.

It was while she was on her way to a performance in St. Louis, Missouri, in October 1945 that Hazel and her companions entered a small café along the way. When she approached the counter and asked for service, the waitress said, "You'll have to eat in the kitchen."

"I'm sorry, but I don't eat in kitchens," Hazel replied.

When Hazel asked if she could get some sandwiches to take out, she was told she could but that she couldn't stand at the counter to wait for them. Hazel Scott, a star of stage and screen, remained at the counter as she waited for her food.

Later someone asked Hazel why she didn't identify herself to the café workers—surely she would have been served if they had known who she was. Hazel explained, "I don't want any special privileges. There are 13 million Hazel Scotts in America. They just don't play the piano."

Star Power

Throughout the war years, Hazel Scott made valuable contributions to the war effort. It wasn't unusual for her to make as many as five benefit performances for wounded servicemen in a week. And she visited hospitals that others chose to forget. "I have played in many tropical disease wards where the fellows are so badly mangled that screens are kept in front of them," Hazel said. "I know I'm using what talent I have to do something for America and my people too."

In January 1942, Hazel performed in a show titled "Salute to Colored Troops" where she helped raise funds for a recreation center for servicemen and -women in New York. Although she could command a lucrative sum for her appearances, Hazel refused to take any money for her work. Later in the same year Hazel performed at a "monster bond rally"—called "Win the War"—in Carnegie Hall in New York. Early in 1943, Hazel volunteered again in a Carnegie Hall concert—this time to raise funds to help an ally of the United States. Five hundred seats were reserved for anyone who brought a watch in good working condition. The donated watches were sent to the Soviet Union for army officers, soldiers, doctors, and nurses at the front. In February 1944, Hazel performed in the "Million Dollar War Bond Show" at the Roxy Theater in New York. And on July 4, 1944, at Lewisohn Stadium in New York, Hazel took part in a four-hour-long bond rally that required anyone who wanted to attend to purchase a war bond.

Hazel Scott was one of thousands of entertainers who used their star power to help win the war. Musicians, singers, dancers, actors, and comedians were eager to do their part to support the war. Many famous Hollywood stars helped raise money for the war by participating in war bond rallies. Providing soldiers with wholesome entertainment was a major part of the war effort. The nation's leaders knew it was important to provide US soldiers with uniforms, food, weapons, and ammunition, but they also recognized it was important to keep morale high. One way to do that was to give soldiers opportunities to rest, relax, and forget the war for a short time. President Franklin Roosevelt understood the importance of entertainers to the war effort when he said, "Entertainment is always a national asset; invaluable in time of peace, it is indispensable in wartime."

Chairwoman of the Hollywood Victory Committee's Negro Division Hattie McDaniel (center) takes time off from rehearsals to lead a caravan of entertainers and USO hostesses for a performance and dance for soldiers stationed at Minter Field in Southern California. *National Archives, AFRO/AM in WW II List #216*

In April 1942 some Hollywood stars formed the Hollywood Victory Committee. Members of the committee pledged to provide support for the war through appearances at bond rallies and through performances at military training camps and hospitals. Big-name stars joined the group—Clark Gable, Bette Davis, Carole Lombard, Dale Evans. Some entertainers volunteered their time—others were paid. But the Hollywood Victory Committee segregated the black entertainers in the organization.

A black actress named Hattie McDaniel was selected to head up the "Negro talent" for the black Hollywood Victory Committee. Hattie encouraged other black entertainers to join the committee, and together they coordinated the work of black performers who did their part for the war effort through radio broadcasts and live appearances. Hattie not only organized, she also performed at camps at least once a week. Hattie's work helped contribute hundreds of thousands of dollars to the war bond drives, and her personal appearances helped boost the morale of thousands of American servicemen and -women.

But Hattie's contributions to the war effort meant nothing to a group of homeowners who lived near her in a Los Angeles neighborhood. They didn't see Hattie as a person who had worked to help America win the war; they saw a black woman living in a white neighborhood. And that was not acceptable to them.

A Maid, but Not a Servant

Black Americans who wanted to work in Hollywood in the 1940s had few choices when it came to movie roles. Black actors seldom appeared in movies. And when they did, men were cast as buffoons and women as maids. On the occasions when black actors and actresses were portrayed in roles outside the stereotypes, Hollywood sent special versions of the films to movie theaters in the southern states—versions with the scenes racist white moviegoers would deem "offending" cut out. When it wasn't possible to cut scenes, the movie producers assured the southern theater managers that black theaters and white theaters would get the movies at the same time so white moviegoers wouldn't have to worry about black moviegoers trying to see the movie in the white theaters.

Hattie McDaniel was a talented actress, singer, songwriter, and comedian and could have performed well in many different roles. But she ended up as a maid more times than not. Hattie looked at it this way: "It's better to get $7,000 a week for playing a servant than $7 a week for being one."

While Hollywood was only interested in seeing Hattie as a maid, black soldiers appreciated her rousing song and dance performances. They forgot—just for a while—that they were soldiers about to ship out when they heard her comedy routines. Hattie took her job as the head of the black Hollywood Victory Committee very seriously.

In April 1942, Hattie wowed newly arrived soldiers at an army camp near San Bernardino, California, with her singing and dancing. The soldiers brought down the house with applause and crowded around her begging for autographs so they could prove to their families back home that they'd seen the famous star. In June Hattie coordinated a star-studded show for soldiers at Camp Hahn in San Bernardino County in California. In July Hattie organized an event in Hollywood for servicemen on leave. It included a parade and bowling party. Hattie and the other stars she had lined up bowled along with the soldiers. At the end of the day, the soldiers enjoyed Hattie's hilarious comedy act. In August 1942, Hattie organized a caravan of stars to the southwestern mountains where the soldiers of the segregated black 10th Cavalry Unit of the US army were training. By October Hattie was on the road to Indiana, where the US Treasury Department had asked her to drum up interest in the "Interracial War Bond Rally." She had special leave from the Hollywood studio where she was in the midst of filming a movie. In April 1943, Hattie organized a group of black entertainers for an event at Camp Young near Indio, California. The 85-mile-per-hour winds from a desert dust storm didn't stop the singers and dancers from entertaining the 25,000 soldiers who had come to see them. After the stage performance the stars headed to the hospital to visit with the patients. In June 1943, Hattie performed at an event to launch a campaign to raise $175,000 in war bonds to buy a bomber.

Hattie McDaniel was admired for the work she did with the Hollywood Victory Committee, and she was respected by many Americans for being the first black actor to win an Oscar. Some people criticized her because she accepted movie roles in which she played a stereotype—a black "mammy" with a kerchief on her head in Gone with the Wind. It gave the impression that Hattie McDaniel was a meek, submissive type. But in 1945, Hattie did something that made everyone look at her with renewed respect.

Sometimes when Hattie and the Hollywood Victory Committee were planning their events they met at Hattie's house in an area of Los Angeles known as the Sugar Hill neighborhood. A number of black stars and businesspeople had purchased homes there after they had made it in Hollywood.

In the 1940s some cities or neighborhoods had racially restrictive covenants, which were contracts that prohibited the purchase, lease, or even occupation of property by specific groups of people—often black people. It meant that black people were frequently denied housing based on the color of their skin. And at that time it was legal.

A typical covenant read like this: "No person or persons of African or Negro blood, lineage, or extraction shall be permitted to occupy a portion of said property."

After Hattie paid for her house and moved in, a group of white residents in the neighborhood filed a legal complaint against the black homeowners. The complaint said the original owners of the homes did not have the right to sell to blacks. Therefore, Hattie and the other black homeowners were living in their Sugar Hill houses illegally and had to leave. If they refused, they would be evicted!

Hattie and some of her black neighbors decided to fight back. They found an attorney who agreed to take their case. In December 1945 the case was heard in a Los Angeles courtroom. Judge Thurmond Clarke presided. For two hours the judge listened to the opposing lawyers. Spectators in the courtroom noticed a portrait of Abraham Lincoln—the president who had freed the slaves—behind Judge Clarke. "I hope that judge has eyes in the back of his head," one black man commented.

The next morning the judge had reached his decision: "It is time that members of the Negro race are accorded, without reservations or evasions, the full rights guaranteed them under the 14th Amendment to the federal Constitution. Judges have been avoiding the real issue too long." And with that, Judge Clarke threw the case out of court!

Hattie McDaniel had played the part of an obedient servant in movies because Hollywood wouldn't let her show her true strengths as a singer and performer. When she was confronted with an unjust law in the real world, Hattie showed that she had plenty of strength. She refused to play the part of an obedient servant. She had gone above and beyond to serve her country in its time of need, and she refused to let a few of her neighbors force her out of her home.

"Whatever I can contribute I am only too anxious to. When I look around me and see how the men and women of Hollywood all are joined in magnificent support of the war effort, I realize how completely this is a struggle which demands the most of all of us," Hattie explained.

Lena Quits

Lena Horne was one of the rare black performers who had starred in Hollywood movies—not with speaking parts, but as a singer. That made it easier to cut her scenes from the movies when they played in the South. Still, Lena was gaining acclaim as a performer—from white as well as black audiences. Her tour of the South was part of a USO tour arranged by the Hollywood Victory Committee.

Lena Horne kisses Montrose Carrol, a worker at the Kaiser Company Shipyard in Richmond, California, May 1943.

Photographs and Prints Division, Schomburg Center for Research in Black Culture; The New York Public Library; Astor, Lenox and Tilden Foundations; US Office of War Information, E. F. Joseph, Photographer

One night in 1944 when she was scheduled to perform, Lena peeked out at the audience from backstage. She saw only white soldiers. Lena had performed many times at military camps, and she was used to seeing white soldiers in the front seats of the auditoriums while the black soldiers sat in the back or in a balcony. That was typical, and it always made Lena angry. But she wanted to perform for the soldiers, and she knew that the military was segregated so there wasn't much she could do about it. But on this occasion Lena didn't see *any* black soldiers in the auditorium. When she asked where the black soldiers were, she was told that she would be performing for them the next morning—in their mess hall. It meant Lena and her band would have to stay overnight—something she hadn't planned. But she agreed so that the black soldiers at the camp could see her perform.

The next morning Lena arrived at the black mess hall. This time when she looked out at the audience she saw more white men in the front rows. The black soldiers were in the back.

"Now who the hell are *they?*" Lena asked.

"They're the German prisoners of war," someone explained.

Lena was furious. She stepped down from the stage, moved to where the black soldiers sat, turned her back on the German prisoners, and sang a few songs to the black soldiers. But she wasn't able to complete the performance because she was so upset about the disrespect shown the black soldiers.

Lena Horne quit her USO tours after the incident. She didn't quit performing for the soldiers, however. She continued to visit bases all over the country throughout the war. But she paid her own way—so she could show the black soldiers the respect they deserved.

Morale Builders

Lena Horne's tour to the South in 1944 had been sponsored by the USO. The organization had begun to play a major role in providing entertainment for the troops in October 1941. The USO tours were called camp shows. These live shows toured the United States military training camps, and eventually shows went overseas. Actors, musicians, singers, dancers, and comedians were eager to show their patriotism by performing.

The camp shows were segregated—white entertainers in white shows for white soldiers, black entertainers in black shows for black soldiers. By 1942 black camp show units were touring military camps across the country. Many black women—singers, dancers, musicians, actresses, and comedians—performed, and they were a hit. Each show comprised a variety of acts combined under one title. *Swing Is the Thing, Harlem on Parade, Sunset Orchestra Revue, Swingin' On Down, Sepia Swing Revue,* and *Rhythm and the Blues* featured unknown performers and big-name stars. The Three Cabin Girls, Caterina Jarboro, the Three Spencer Sisters, Julie Gardner, Rosetta Williams, Gwen Tynes, the Smith Sisters, Sandra Lee, Rosalie Young, Laura Pierre, and Martha Please were black entertainers who worked for the "Negro talent" division of the camp shows.

Ella Fitzgerald sang in a camp show at Fort Jay, New York, in early 1942. She sang some of her favorites—"You Showed Me the Way," "Good Night My Love" and "I'm the Lonesomest Gal in Town—for the servicemen. Blues singer Bette St. Clair and tap dancer Evelyn Keyes traveled with the *Sepia Swing Revue* in 1942. The camp show *Keep Shufflin'* traveled throughout the Midwest in 1943 and starred the Three Shades of Rhythm, a "girl group" from California. Late in 1943, soldiers about to ship out were entertained by Una Mae Carlisle and Ann Cornell at Camp Shanks, near New York City. Camp Shanks, nicknamed Last Stop, USA, by the soldiers, was a camp used exclusively for deployment of troops overseas. Una sang two songs she had written—"Walkin' by the River" and "I See a Million People." Ann sang "You'll Come Back."

In April 1943 the *Afro American* newspaper reported that the USO had 266 entertainers in 45 units in overseas shows, but not one black entertainer was among them. But by fall 1943 the first black camp shows had begun to perform in a series of shows known as the Foxhole Circuit.

The first overseas show starring black entertainers performed for British and American servicemen in Cuba, the Bahamas, Haiti, Jamaica, the Virgin Islands, Antigua, Puerto Rico, Trinidad, and British and Dutch Guiana. Comedian Willie Bryant acted as the master of ceremonies, introducing acts that included blues singer Betty Logan and Julie Gardner, an accordionist and singer.

While playing one of their first stops on the tour, the entertainers received a call from a supply ship stocked with a crew eager to see a live performance at sea. The entertainers were bundled onto a plane and within a few hours they were aboard a troop ship with all its identification marks carefully covered. They went aboard, put on their show, and flew back to the base. None of the performers ever knew where they had been, but they all knew how much the sailors appreciated their efforts. While they were aboard the ship, they said they were treated like royalty. Julie Gardner had performed her rendition of "Pistol Packin' Mamma." Betty Logan, known as the Brown Bombshell, sang the new hit "Chicken Ain't Nothin' But a Bird."

When Julie Gardner, blues singer Ann Lewis, and comedian Flo Robinson arrived with a camp show in New Caledonia in the Southwest Pacific in June 1944, the military police were called out to clear the roads for the 8,000 soldiers who had heard that the women were in the area. The black soldiers had been in the jungles of New Caledonia for two years and hadn't seen any women in a very long time. The men weren't disappointed by the show. Flo and her husband performed their comedy act, ending with a jitterbug swing. Julie was the star of the show with her accordion, playing and singing "Hit That Jive, Jack," "Kow Kow Boogie," and "Don't Cry, Baby." Ann Lewis, with her flame-red upswept pompadour, followed Julie's act. She finished with her performance of "St. Louis Blues" and danced the boogie and the shorty George.

Julie Gardner headed off to Alaska in October 1945 along with three other black entertainers—pianist Gladys Cooper, singer Rosetta Williams, and acrobatic dancer Dollie Pembrook. The four were part of a camp show sent to entertain black troops on the Aleutian Islands. Their first stop was Attu, at the end of the island chain. Bad weather kept the show on Attu for more than a week, but the soldiers didn't mind. They hadn't seen a black woman in three years, and some of them cried at the sight of the three entertainers. They honored the women by naming their jeeps after them.

Five black USO entertainers were in Italy in late 1944 with USO Unit 249—the first black troupe in the European theater of operations. Along with master of ceremonies Doc Wheeler, pianist-accordionist Jack McGuire headed up the male segment of the show. But the real hits were the three women: "the exotic darling of the unit" singer Ethyl Wise, "the bluest of blues" singer Sandra Lee, and "five foot package of dancing dynamite" Iva Bowen.

Caterina Jarboro was trained as a classical singer and had made a name for herself as a soprano in the opera world in the United States and Europe. In 1944 she headed up a USO tour in Italy. USO Show Number 384—*Concert Time*—featured Caterina in New Year performances in Naples and Rome. From there the show toured the entire front, entertaining the soldiers of the 92nd Division. Caterina was accustomed to performing for audiences in fine concert halls, but she adjusted to entertaining in wartime Europe too. When war first broke out, Caterina was living and working in Europe; sometimes she could be found singing in air raid shelters as bombs dropped from the skies.

USO Troupe Number 339 arrived in the Persian Gulf in early 1945. The all-black troupe had come to entertain the soldiers of the 380th Port Battalion, the 675th Port Company, and the 153rd Bakery Unit. Lillian Thomas and Cora Green were performers with the troupe and the first American black women the soldiers had seen in two years. Lil Thomas played the "St. Louis Blues" with "a solid bass that brought raves from the packed house." And she finished her set of several encores with "My Ideal" in a "sultry sweet and low voice." Cora Green was a hit with her renditions of "The Laziest Gal in Town" and "Stormy Weather."

In September 1945 the black USO show *Plenty Potent* arrived in the Dutch East Indies to entertain soldiers and sailors who had been in the Pacific theater of operations for 30 months. It was the first black troupe to appear there. The 75-minute shows that were offered for seven nights featured pianist Bernice Harris and Iva Bowen, who tap-danced to boogie-woogie. Rosalie Young sang for the troops—"Save All Your Honey for Me," "When They Ask About You," "I'll Get By," and "I'll Walk Alone." The soldiers and sailors sent this message back home: "Please send more colored performers!"

The Gal Who Set Two Continents on Fire

When Alberta Hunter set out on her USO tours across the globe in 1944 she already had made a name for herself as the "gal who set two continents afire" in the 1920s and '30s. A captivating performer, Alberta was a regular at the Chez Florence, Paris's "smartest café." It was at the Chez Florence that England's Prince of Wales—the future King Edward—came to hear Alberta sing "Time on My Hands." She played at the famous Dorchester Hotel in London and had a six-week engagement at the Palladium. It was reported that Alberta Hunter had "seared the hearts of men" across Europe.

Alberta's dazzling career was interrupted by Hitler's advancing armies. She fled Europe with unfulfilled contracts in Denmark, Greece, and Germany. Alberta's star power was as bright in the United States as it had been in Europe. And for a few years Alberta was happy to work her magic on American audiences. But when the USO offered her the opportunity to travel the world again, she couldn't resist.

"We are in the jungles of Burma," wrote Alberta Hunter in her column for the *Afro American* newspaper in late 1944. "Before arriving in this area, we witnessed our first actual air raid and have become quite accustomed to stepping over dead bodies. We have to keep our doors and windows closed for fear that some kind of wild animal will pay us an unwelcomed visit. One recently plunged through the screen window of a hut and mangled its occupant."

Alberta took her USO show *Rhythm and Blues* to the black servicemen who were carving a road through the jungles on the legendary Ledo Road. Alberta planned to be in the China-Burma-India theater of war for six months. In addition to managing the show, she sang; during her spare time, she wrote for the *Afro American* newspaper back home in Baltimore, Maryland.

In February 1945, Alberta wrote from Assam, India, where she and her troupe—consisting of Taps Miller, a male trumpet player; the Three Rhythm Rascals, three male musicians who specialized in boogie-woogie; and Mae Gaddy, a female singer from New York City—were a treat for the weary soldiers.

In her newspaper column Alberta reminded readers that she and her fellow performers were doing their part for the war by entertaining the troops: "We are in one of the most picturesque countries of the world making history. We are the first colored unit to play this country; in fact, we are blazing a trail, where no artists have played." She begged readers to do their part for the war effort by sending more mail to the troops.

While Alberta entertained the troops in Burma and India in the winter of 1945, the war in Europe entered its final stages. In May 1945 victory was declared by the Allied troops in Europe. General Dwight D. Eisenhower of the US Army—nicknamed Ike—had established his Allied headquarters in Frankfurt, Germany. Ike and military leaders from two of America's allies— Field Marshall Sir Bernard Montgomery from Britain and General Gregori Zhukov of the Soviet Union—met to discuss what to do with defeated Germany.

The challenges facing the leaders were enormous. The world was watching them as they made decisions that would affect millions of people across the globe. With so much responsibility on their shoulders, the generals needed an occasional break from their work. Alberta Hunter's energetic USO show was just what the generals needed to take their minds off their obligations for a few hours. The black press reported that Ike had passed up a list of popular white stars who were in Europe—including Sonja Henie, Mickey Rooney, and Marlene Dietrich—and requested

Alberta Hunter's USO Troupe *Rhythm Carnival* to provide the respite for the generals. Ike's personal aide ordered a special plane to transport Alberta, the Three Rhythm Rascals, singer Mae Gaddy, and trumpeter Jean Starr to Frankfurt. The three generals reportedly hummed along to the popular American songs—"Straighten Up and Fly Right," "G.I. Jive," and "Deep in the Heart of Texas." And Ike—the supreme commander of the Allied Expeditionary Force—sang along with Alberta Hunter as she performed one request after another. When the general refused to let the entertainers depart, word had to be sent to the next camp where the stars were scheduled to perform to cancel their show. It had to be disappointing to the soldiers at the next stop, but who could say no to the three war heroes who were deciding the future of the postwar world?

Alberta wrote her newspaper column in July from France. She and her troupe had just left Paris, where they had performed. She reported running into some black Americans who had been freed from Nazi concentration camps where they had spent the war years—famous trumpeter Arthur Briggs and Edgar Wiggins, a reporter for the *Chicago Defender* newspaper.

In September 1945, Alberta wrote about performing in Zell am See, Austria, where they toured the palatial home of Nazi Hermann Goering. She reported that the walls of the house were covered in thick satin and lined with priceless paintings of religious scenes. The dining room held a silver table that she wrote would require "10 to 15 men to move." She commented on the beautiful horse stables at the estate, which was hidden among the trees. She wrote about performing at Bad Gastein in Austria and observed, "Words cannot describe the beauty of Austria."

From Austria, Alberta and her troupe returned to France, where they entertained the soldiers of the 482nd Medical

Battalion at the city of Metz. Then on to Reims, where the treaty ending the war in Europe had been signed. She said the soldiers were so excited about her show they stood in line in the streets and alleys waiting to get in. Alberta wrote from Dijon, France, in November 1945.

Although the war was over in Europe by May 1945, the USO and government officials knew it was still important to keep soldiers' morale high as they occupied the war-torn lands in Europe. That's why the USO sent a rash of shows to Europe in mid-1945. Alberta Hunter was called upon to set out on her world tour for the USO, and the International Sweethearts of Rhythm were called to Europe.

The Sweethearts

Black entertainer Anna Mae Winburn was in France about the same time as Alberta Hunter. For Anna Mae the journey to Europe was in some ways exciting, but it was also very sad. She was the leader of an all-girl band that was making history: it was the first integrated girl band to tour the war front. And Anna Mae hoped this trip would give her the chance to run into her brother, who was serving somewhere in Germany. But Anna Mae knew she wouldn't run into her other brother—he had died in Normandy, France, during the D-day invasion in 1944.

Some Americans didn't seem to care about the sacrifices Anna Mae's family had made for the war effort. When they looked at Anna Mae they didn't see a young woman whose family had made the supreme sacrifice for their country. They didn't see a young woman who had two brothers who fought to defend democracy in a dangerous war zone. They didn't see a talented musician and singer. When they watched petite Anna Mae Winburn as she led an 18-piece swing band, they saw a black girl mixing with white girls—and for many Americans that was unacceptable. In fact, they had made it against the law in some states, and they believed that law should be enforced.

Anna Mae was the beautiful and talented leader of the International Sweethearts of Rhythm. The band had been a hit in the United States since 1941 when they had gone professional. Originally the International Sweethearts of Rhythm had comprised girls from the Piney Woods Country Life School, a school for black children in Mississippi. The group had been formed to help raise money to support the school. But by 1941 when the band went pro, the members were no longer students; they were talented female musicians who loved to perform—and made money doing what they loved. What made the International Sweethearts of Rhythm unusual was not that they were women—there were other "all-girl" bands performing across the United States in the 1940s.

What made the International Sweethearts of Rhythm stand out was that the band members were from a variety of racial backgrounds. That's how the word "international" became part of the band's name. The African American, Mexican, Asian, American Indian, and Puerto Rican part of the band didn't cause a problem for most people—because none of these musicians was white. Nonwhites working, traveling, and eating together were of little interest to most white Americans—as long as they didn't use white restaurants and restrooms. But it was the *white* part of the band that caused problems.

The International Sweethearts of Rhythm traveled from coast to coast in their own sleeper bus—Big Bertha. Traveling in Big Bertha made life easier for the women in the band because it was difficult to find hotels that would allow the black women— including Anna Mae Winburn, Helen Jones, Evelyn McGee, Pauline Braddy, Clora Bryant, Vi Burnside, Tiny Davis, and

Johnnie Mae Rice—to stay. It also made it easier to conceal the white women in the band—including alto sax player Roz Cron.

The fact that Roz Cron and other white women played with the band caused problems in the southern United States, where Jim Crow laws made it illegal for white people to work, socialize, or eat with black people. It was illegal for black and white people to share a park bench. It was illegal for a black person to stay on a sidewalk when he or she met a white person. The black person had to step off into the gutter to let the white person pass. And it was illegal for black Anna Mae Winburn to head a band that included white women. Yet the International Sweethearts of Rhythm defied the law and played throughout the South. But when they performed it was not unusual to see white police officers pacing back and forth in front of the bandstand—trying to figure out if any of the band members were white. Roz Cron wore dark makeup to cover up her white skin and permed her hair to make it curlier.

In Birmingham, Alabama, the International Sweethearts of Rhythm ran into a potential problem with police one night after a performance. The women were on Big Bertha preparing to travel to their next show in St. Louis, Missouri, when they heard from some friends that the police were suspicious about a few of the Sweethearts. The band manager got the white girls—and the ones who *looked* white—off the bus as quickly as she could. They hailed a cabbie, who demanded the girls ride out of sight on the floor of his cab, and made their way to the train station, where they boarded the whites-only train compartment to meet up with the rest of the band in St. Louis.

Finding restaurants that would serve the band members in the South posed a huge dilemma for the Sweethearts. Sometimes they had to go for hours between meals. Sometimes the white band members went into a restaurant and ordered takeout for the black members. Usually the white café owners required black customers to come to the back door to get the food—and to leave the parking lot immediately afterward. And some café owners refused to serve even takeout orders when they saw black women in the bus. When the Sweethearts played at military camps around the country, the black soldiers knew about the difficulties of traveling and made sure the band members had plenty of food from the camp mess before they set out for their next show.

The Sweethearts did their part for the soldiers too. In May 1943 the US Office of War Information's Radio Section started producing special programs over the Armed Forces Radio Service (AFRS). The programs were beamed by shortwave radio to fighting men in all corners of the globe. A special weekly variety show called *Jubilee* was produced for black men and women serving overseas. Many black entertainers performed on the *Jubilee* programs—Hattie McDaniel, Billie Holiday, Ethel Waters, Lena Horne, Butterfly McQueen, and the International Sweethearts of Rhythm.

When black servicemen heard the Sweethearts on the *Jubilee* programs, they began a letter-writing campaign to the USO begging for the Sweethearts to travel overseas to entertain the black troops. Letters came from all over the world where black soldiers were serving—Alaska, North Africa, Australia, Burma, the South Pacific, and Europe. The USO contacted the Sweethearts' manager and arranged for their overseas tour. They promised the band members a weekly salary of $84—a definite improvement over the $20 weekly salary most Sweethearts earned touring in the States. When the Sweethearts heard that they were going overseas for a six-month tour they were delighted, but they weren't told *where* they were going. It wasn't until they boarded the ship that they learned they were headed to Europe—France, Germany, and Italy—where the war was over but where there were thousands of black soldiers waiting to see them.

Anna Mae Winburn directed the Sweethearts as they performed in the Olympia Theater in Paris in August 1945. Their show was recorded and played on the radio for those soldiers who couldn't attend the performance in person. Next they played at the University of Paris, where the Sweethearts reported that the soldiers whistled and stomped their feet "until the roof appeared to be descending upon us." In Italy the Sweethearts, featuring trumpeter Tiny Davis and tenor sax player Vi Burnside, entertained the soldiers of the 36th Division. It was reported that by the end of each show the soldiers were "eating out of their palms." In Germany the Sweethearts were attached to the Third Army and performed two shows every night everywhere the soldiers were stationed—small towns and large cities. The Sweethearts wore Women's Army Corps (WAC) uniforms while they performed and while they traveled. But they weren't prepared for the harsh weather as winter approached. The soldiers in charge of supplies at the military camps made sure the Sweethearts had warm coats, scarves, boots, and long underwear. The Sweethearts had three army trucks—and three GIs—assigned to them as they traveled across the continent.

Traveling and eating weren't a problem for the Sweethearts while they were in Europe. They were treated like queens at the military camps—getting comfortable beds and the best food available. Sometimes they stayed in fine hotels where servers in formal attire attended to their needs. They reported stopping in Nuremberg at the Grand Hotel for a meal and seeing the lavish rooms where Hitler had stayed when he was in the city. In Munich some of the Sweethearts actually slept in a room that Hitler had occupied. While in Germany, the Sweethearts lived for a time in a sumptuous house with 25 rooms, sunken gardens, expansive porches, and stately windows with views of the flower gardens.

Anna Mae Winburn and her Sweethearts said they would never forget how they had been treated during their time in Europe. No cramped bunks on Big Bertha. Just clean, comfortable accommodations at the end of each long day. No stale takeout meals eaten on the run. Just fine food provided by servers dressed in formal attire. No police officers peering into their faces, searching for signs of whiteness. Just adoring soldiers gazing with admiration and gratitude.

The Sweethearts had done their part for the war effort—in the United States and in Europe. But they had to travel to war-torn Europe to experience the respect they deserved.

The Nightingale of the European Theater

Margaret Simms was a black woman living in Jacksonville, Florida, who wanted to do her part for the war effort. In December 1942 she decided to join the Red Cross. She was accepted and got her assignment. Her education in business administration made the Red Cross think she would be an excellent assistant club director in England, so they arranged her passage on a troop ship filled with soldiers headed to the battlefields of Europe. Many of the soldiers must have been frightened as they made their way across the Atlantic. But someone had heard that the black Red Cross volunteer could sing. The commanding officer thought a little music could be just the thing to take the soldiers' minds off their destination. Margaret was asked to give a shipboard concert, and she was a hit.

By the time the ship reached England, the Red Cross had heard about Margaret's singing abilities and reassigned her to a position that allowed her to use her musical talents—rather than her business administration skills. Margaret was assigned to entertain the troops stationed across Great Britain. Sometimes she went to the military camps, where she persuaded the soldiers to sing along with her as she performed their favorites: "My Buddy," "When Day Is Done," and "You'd Be So Nice to Come Home To." Margaret's repertoire was a blend of Negro spirituals and the classics. Posters advertising Margaret's shows proclaimed: SHE SINGS, YOU SING, EVERYBODY SINGS. At Red Cross clubs Margaret sang solo, performing "Still as the Night," "The Lord's Prayer," "None but the Lonely Heart," and Brahms's "Cradle Song." By August 1943, Margaret had traveled back and forth across Great Britain, covering 40,000 miles and performing for 300 audiences. She'd been all over England and to Glasgow and Edinburgh in Scotland. Margaret's rich, beautiful voice was described as "magic-like." Her reputation had earned her the titles Nightingale of the European Theater and Songbird of the South.

In Cherbourg, France, Margaret was near exhaustion after giving 10 concerts in seven days at hospitals for wounded soldiers. But she didn't stop. Back in England she borrowed a pair of boots from a soldier as she journeyed into the outlying regions through knee-deep mud to sing spirituals at an open-air concert in which she performed without accompaniment. The soldiers joined in when she sang their favorites—"Swing Low, Sweet Chariot," "Why Adam Sinned," and "On My Journey Now."

"Mud? I like it! And I'm perfectly happy here, singing in the mud!" laughed Margaret.

In 1944, Margaret took a break from the mud for a visit back to the United States. By September 1945 Margaret was back in France, heading up a trio of performers. Constance Randall of Washington, DC, and Minto Cato of New York City joined

Margaret in entertaining troops who were waiting for deployment to their next assignments. The Nightingale of the European Theater was once again doing her part for the war effort—making homesick soldiers feel a little less lonely.

"Arriving in camp, all the weariness you may have felt immediately drops away at the sight of hundreds of soldiers in fatigues with mess kits in the chow line—smiling, grinning, kidding, welcoming you—glad for the sight of someone in a dress from home," Margaret explained.

The Toast of Europe

Intriguing stories seemed to follow Josephine "Jo" Baker wherever she went. She had grown up in poverty in America but in the 1920s had made her way to Paris, where she became a celebrated singer and dancer. Her singing abilities were questionable, but there was no doubt that her dancing skills were exceptional. Josephine Baker became the rage of Paris—and all of Europe. She was a glamorous star and became a very wealthy woman. A black woman with Josephine's power and influence was a fascinating spectacle to many Europeans in the years leading up to World War II, and Josephine took advantage of her star status. She attended lavish social events and struck up friendships with prominent people across Europe.

But Josephine was much more than a pretty face and a glitzy entertainer. She was a woman who loved her adopted country and hated the Nazis who were invading France's neighbors in 1939. When Josephine was asked to become an undercover spy for the French, she was eager to undertake this risky assignment.

She continued to travel—entertaining and partying with high-level officials. But now Josephine did much more than sing and dance. She came into contact with people who had valuable information about the enemy. Before Italy entered the war on the side of Germany, she spent time with Italian officials and learned about their activities. She listened as she mingled with military and political leaders. As she traveled, she watched the movements of the enemy's military. And when she was alone, she took notes and hid them in her underwear or wrote messages with invisible ink on her sheet music. As Josephine traveled to southwestern France, Portugal, Spain, and North Africa to perform she acted as a courier, passing her secret messages and documents to other spies along the way.

Very few people knew about Josephine's spy work at the time. But every serviceman in Europe and North Africa knew about Jo Baker, the entertainer. Every serviceman wanted to see her, and Josephine wanted to meet as many of these soldiers as possible. She knew they needed some relief from the horrors

Josephine Baker in Paris, 1949. *Library of Congress, Carl Van Vechten Collection, LC-DIG-ppmsca-07816*

of the war. So Josephine went out on tour to sing and dance to entertain the troops—for free—wherever they were stationed.

She performed at Red Cross clubs, hospitals, airports, and military camps in Oran, Casablanca, and Fez. In Algiers Josephine performed a benefit concert for the children's department of the Red Cross. High-ranking French, British, and American military officers attended and contributed money to the children's fund. Wherever she went she sang the soldiers' favorite songs: "Thanks for Everything," "Two Loves Have I," "Mama, I Want to Make Rhythm," "Tipperary," "Over There," "The Only Girl in the World," and "Gertie from Bizerte."

In August 1943, Josephine was performing in Algiers to a crowd of 2,000 when her voice became weaker and weaker. Weeks of constant touring and entertaining without rest had caused her to lose her singing voice. But she refused to leave the stage and finished her concert by softly reciting the words of her songs rather than singing them. The soldiers were just as happy with her speaking voice as they had been with her singing voice.

At another camp in 1943, Josephine was performing during an evening show on an improvised wooden stage in a dusty field. Thousands of soldiers sat on the ground around the stage. As Josephine strode onto the stage in her flamboyant gown of purple and red stripes and swept up to the mike, the crowd erupted in a roar of approval. She sang in both French and English. After two encores she reappeared on the stage in a tight-fitting, low-cut evening dress of green and gold—just as the air raid sirens wailed and the camp bugles sounded. A voice came over the loudspeaker: "Air raid! Air raid! Disperse into the fields at once." The soldiers and Josephine scattered, running for cover. They watched as the sky lit up with flashes of light from exploding bombs. They heard the crack of gunfire and the sound of exploding shells. The "air show" went on for some time. Then suddenly, it stopped. The all-clear siren sounded. Josephine stepped back up on the stage and picked up where she had left off. She closed her show with the singing of the "Star-Spangled Banner."

Josephine Baker's reputation as an entertainer was well known and controversial. Her risqué costumes and evocative dancing were offensive to some. During the war Josephine's performances were appreciated by soldiers who needed a break from the horrors of war. It wasn't until after the war that everyone learned of her life as a spy. The French government honored Josephine with their Croix de Guerre for feats of bravery. Josephine Baker's contributions to the performing arts may be questionable, but her role in helping to win World War II was undeniable.

A Long Way from Harlem

When Coretta Alfred was a young girl singing in her Baptist church in Harlem, New York, she couldn't have imagined the adventurous life she would lead as an adult. But those years as a choir singer prepared her for what was to come.

The situation in the Soviet Union was bleak in June 1941. Hitler's army had invaded from the west. The Soviet citizens had heard many stories about the atrocities committed by the German soldiers. By October the Germans were close to the capital city. German planes were dropping bombs on Moscow daily.

For most Americans the happenings in the Soviet Union were too distant to cause immediate concern. War was not yet part of American life. But for Coretta Alfred, the German army was not in some foreign land 4,000 miles away. It was fast approaching her apartment in Moscow.

In 1901 Coretta Alfred had been invited to join a group of black female singers who called themselves the Louisiana Amazon Guards. They packed their bags and set sail for a singing tour of Europe. Three years later the women performed in Russia (the future Soviet Union) in theaters in Moscow and St. Petersburg. Coretta began to study opera at the Russian conservatories of music, and by 1920 she had become a well-known opera star. After marrying a Russian professor, she became known as Madame Coretti Arle-Titz.

As the German army approached the city of Moscow and bombs dropped from the skies, Madame Coretti Arle-Titz shared an air raid shelter with her neighbors. It was probably the only shelter in the city where the occupants were entertained by a renowned opera star. Coretta's lovely soprano voice competed with the sounds of exploding bombs and distant gunfire. But her performance helped to distract the frightened men, women, and children huddled below ground in the shelter.

Coretta also did her share for the war effort by giving concerts to farmers, coal miners, and war plant workers in the Siberian region of the country. She visited hospitals, where she sang to wounded soldiers of the Soviet army. She read to the soldiers and wrote letters for them. She even taught English to the soldiers and answered their questions about life in America. The Soviet soldiers were curious about life in America for black citizens. Some people called Coretta the brown-skinned sister of mercy.

Coretta was eager to do her part for the war effort in her adopted country. But her contributions didn't stop with her work with the Soviet people. Far from her homeland, Coretta found an opportunity to help Americans too.

As the German army made its way by land across the western part of the Soviet Union, Soviet soldiers desperately needed military supplies and equipment. Without help the Soviet army would soon be defeated by the advancing Germans. They turned to the British, Canadians, and Americans for help, but there were limited options for getting supplies to the Soviets from the outside world.

The most likely route was also the most dangerous. It was known as the Murmansk Run, and parts of the route were known as Suicide Alley because the possibility of death was very real. Murmansk and Archangel were two Soviet port cities in the northern part of the country—near the Arctic Circle. Beginning in the fall of 1941, British, Canadian, and American ships traveled in convoys through the Barents Sea and the Arctic Ocean to bring badly needed supplies to the Soviets.

The sailors on the Murmansk Run knew their chances of survival were slim. If they managed to escape the German submarines, torpedoes, or aircraft they couldn't be certain the icy hurricane-strength winds wouldn't bring disaster to their ships. With the frigid winds forcing sea spray onto the surfaces of the ships, the decks were covered with ice. They faced constant danger of capsizing and from equipment freezing. Their cargoes of jeeps, trucks, tanks, rifles, machine guns, and millions of pairs of boots could land at the bottom of the sea. And the same could be said for the sailors themselves. The ships couldn't stop to help anyone who fell overboard—a stopped ship was an easy target for the Germans.

For those sailors who managed to survive the Murmansk Run, there was a bit of rest and relaxation on land. American sailors and civilian ship workers took advantage of time off in the port cities. That's why Coretta and her pianist husband headed for Murmansk and Archangel late in 1943, where Coretta gave a series of concerts at the international seamen's clubs. Coretta was a hit with all the sailors who needed to calm their jangled

nerves after the deadly seas of the Murmansk Run. Her sooth-
ing voice gave them a sense of peace before they set out on their
return trip through the treacherous waters. But it was the black
sailors who were especially pleased—and surprised—to find
Coretta in a land so far from home. It was for these sailors that
Coretta sang the old Negro spirituals that she had sung in her
church in Harlem.

The black American sailors in Murmansk and Archangel
made Coretta think about her old home in America. While
happy memories of her life in Harlem stayed with her in her
new home, other experiences haunted Coretta.

"I returned to America to see my mother, but my heart
remained in Russia, where among the Russian masses I could
forget that I am colored. I found America with its oppression,
frustration, Jim Crow and hypocrisy unbearable and soon
returned to my beloved Russia."

Although Coretta Alfred decided to make her home in Russia, she never forgot her roots. And when her countrymen
needed her, Coretta was eager to help. Music, to Coretta, was a
universal language that could offer a sense of calm to frightened
people—regardless of nationality.

A Texan in Paris

Growing up in Bonham, Texas, Roberta Dodd was in high
demand as a singer in church choirs and at school parties.
Roberta wasn't the only black girl in America with a voice that
made the citizens of her hometown sit up and take notice. However, not many black girls from small towns in Texas ended up
in Nazi-occupied France, entertaining European royalty.

Roberta left Bonham after graduating from high school.
She studied piano and voice at Fisk University in Nashville,

Tennessee, and then went on to Chicago, where she studied with a voice teacher who honed her skills in the French language. Roberta made her musical debut at Kimball Hall in Chicago and prepared to embark on a tour of the United States. She concluded her national tour with a concert at the Bonham Courthouse, where she performed to a packed house.

Roberta traveled to France to study under a renowned voice teacher named Blanche Marchesi. In Paris she married an African lawyer and political activist named Kojo Marc Tovalou-Houenou, who claimed to be a prince (although some people questioned his alleged royal status). They shared a passion for music, and when they married, the home of Prince and Princess Tovalou-Houenou, as they were called, became a gathering place for the international music society of Europe. Roberta's career flourished. She was presented in concert at the French Colonial Exposition, where King Albert and Queen Elizabeth of Belgium requested an introduction. Roberta and her husband lived in Porto Novo in French West Africa for a time—where Kojo Marc owned an estate. When he died of typhoid fever, Roberta moved back to Paris. In 1940 when the German army invaded France, Roberta was living there with friends. Although she had little money and relied on friends for financial support, Roberta was still referred to as Princess Tovalou-Houenou.

When the Allied armies liberated France in 1944, Roberta was eager to do her part to make the American soldiers feel at home. She sang for wounded soldiers in hospitals, and she worked every day at the information desk of the Left Bank Red Cross club that was operated by black Americans. Roberta's royal status wasn't of concern to the soldiers who saw her at the Red Cross club thousands of miles from home. They saw a woman with a welcoming smile and a lovely voice. They didn't care if she was a princess or a commoner.

The 404th Army Service Forces Band

WAC Band #2 found it difficult to keep up with all the invitations to perform for war bond drives. The band was made up of black Women Army Corps (WAC) musicians stationed at Fort Des Moines, Iowa, late in 1943. The band had made its debut at a service club in Des Moines in September. The musicians were under the command of Second Lieutenant Alice McAlpine from Springfield, Massachusetts, and they had played all across the state of Iowa in small towns and large cities by the summer of 1944. The predominantly white communities throughout the state came out to see and hear the black musicians. And, most important, they bought war bonds to help support the fighting men and women in the armed forces.

Members of the all-black 404th Army Service Forces Band. *Fort Des Moines Museum and Education Center; Vera Campbell Collection*

There was a WAC Band #2 because WAC Band #1—the 400th Army Service Forces (ASF) Band—was all white. Many talented black WACs had auditioned for the ASF band. Some of the women who tried out had been college music majors, music teachers, or even professional musicians in civilian life. But *not one* black WAC ever made the cut. They decided to start their own band—WAC Band #2.

When the band first formed they didn't have instruments—nor did they have "official" status in the army. They eventually got both.

Although the US Army didn't recognize the black WAC band as an official army band, army officers at Fort Des Moines did allow the formation of the group in September 1943. It took about a month to find enough instruments to complete a band. So while the search went on, the black musicians trained as a chorus to improve their music-reading abilities. The result was that by the time instruments had been rounded up, the women sounded very good as a singing group. But it was their reputation as a band that brought the invitations to perform.

Finally, in June 1944—after the black band had become so popular and had been so successful at war bond drives—the army staff at Fort Des Moines recognized the black musicians by making WAC Band #2 official—still segregated, but official. However, the official designation was short lived. Within a month, the women received notice that their group had been disbanded. The reasons given by the army were that the band had not been authorized by the US Army headquarters in Washington and that only one band was allowed on each base—and Fort Des Moines had the 400th. The commander at Fort Des Moines said the budget no longer allowed for a second band. It was not possible for WAC Band #2 to continue.

The all-black WAC band had become a source of pride for many black Americans. The women had just returned from a grand parade in Chicago where crowds had cheered them and celebrated their new official status. They had performed at the University of Chicago to a packed house. How could the army deactivate them?

Black leaders, community members, and members of black organizations across the country learned of the injustice and felt it was intolerable. They instigated a massive protest directed at policymakers in the army and the War Department. Officials were bombarded with letters and telegrams. Black newspapers encouraged the movement. By August the army had reversed its decision to deactivate WAC Band #2 and reinstated the band with an official name—404th AFS Band.

The black WACs were elated. But by November 1944 they were more puzzled than elated. When the original band was disbanded in the summer, the members had been reclassified into non-band positions and the band's instruments was taken away. Two months had passed since the reinstatement of the new band, and very few members had instruments. In fact, the instruments were coming in from the army supply depot at a rate of only about one every week. At that rate, it would be *years* before they had enough instruments to begin performing again. Despite the barriers that seemed continually to crop up, the women of the 404th AFS Band refused to give up. The instruments did eventually come and by December they were once again performing. In May 1945 the 404th AFS Band performed in the Mighty Seventh War Bond Drive in Chicago at the Savoy Ballroom. The drive began on May 14 and ended on June 30 and brought in over $26 billion for the war. The army hadn't made it easy for them, but the women of the black WAC band insisted on doing their part for the war effort.

Home Sweet Home

As the war ended and soldiers began returning home in large numbers, entertainers welcomed them home with special performances. One of those entertainers was concert and stage star Muriel Rahn, who had been told by a hotel clerk in 1942 that she was not welcome because they did not "take your kind."

In August 1945, 10,000 weary soldiers arrived in New York from Europe on the *Queen Elizabeth*. The soldiers were so happy to see home that some cried as they disembarked; others kissed the ground. From the ship the soldiers were taken to nearby Camp Kilmer, New Jersey, where Muriel headed up a homecoming show for the returning heroes. Although Muriel was a superstar and could have earned thousands of dollars for her performance, she sang for free.

If Muriel Rahn and other black female entertainers who had helped boost the morale of American ser-

Soprano Muriel Rahn volunteered to sing for returning troops.
Library of Congress, Carl Van Vechten Collection, LC-USZ62-114454 DLC

vicemen and -women fighting to rid the world of fascism and Nazism hoped that life would be better for black Americans after the war, they were seriously disappointed.

The Jim Crow laws that prohibited black and white people from associating with one another were still very much in place in the southern United States. Shortly after the war ended the Darlings of Rhythm performed in Georgia. The band's trumpet player, Toby Butler, was arrested by authorities. It was alleged that she was a white girl associating with the black members of the band—something that was prohibited in the state of Georgia. Jessie Turner, the leader of the Darlings, explained, "My sole interest is in building the best musical unit possible and as long as my girls conduct themselves properly and display ability, I do not see that it would matter even if there were a few women from Mars mixed in."

The International Sweethearts of Rhythm performed in St. Louis, Missouri, a few months after the war ended. After finishing a three-week engagement they planned to travel to their next appearance—a music festival in North Carolina. Before they left, bandleader Rae Lee Jones received a call from a man who identified himself as a Ku Klux Klan member. He warned that there would be Klan "activity" in North Carolina if white women performed with the Sweethearts. The Sweethearts ignored the warning and played to a crowd of 10,000—with no disturbances. It was thought the swarm of police milling around the grounds deterred the Klan from taking any action.

In 1939 a famous black singer named Marian Anderson had been denied access to a building called Constitution Hall in Washington, DC. The hall belonged to the Daughters of the American Revolution (DAR), and they didn't allow black performers to use their building. It caused a stir at the time. Eleanor

Roosevelt severed her membership with the group to protest the discrimination against Marian Anderson.

By 1945 thousands of black men and women had fought and died in a war against fascism and Nazism. Black Americans had contributed generously to war bond drives. They had worked in war plants ensuring that American soldiers had the planes and equipment they needed on the battlefields of Europe, Africa, Asia, and the Pacific. And black performers had traveled to battlefields to entertain the weary troops.

Hazel Scott had performed in concerts to help raise money in war drives. She had entertained servicemen and -women at military camps around the country. She had visited military hospitals to cheer the wounded. Although she was a famous star and could have demanded a hefty sum, she refused payment for her war work.

So why would the DAR refuse to allow Hazel Scott to use Constitution Hall—their national headquarters in Washington, DC—for a concert? Why would the president of the United States allow such a thing to happen? And, why would the First Lady seem to approve of the actions of the DAR?

In October 1945, Hazel asked to rent Constitution Hall for a piano concert. The DAR said no. They weren't interested in changing their rule that restricted the use of the hall to "white artists only." When President Harry Truman was asked to intercede on Hazel's behalf, he seemed to voice his disapproval of the DAR's actions. He reminded Americans that America had fought a world war for democratic principles. He said, "We have just brought to a successful conclusion a war against totalitarian countries which made racial discrimination their state policy. One of the first steps taken by the Nazis when they came to power was to forbid the public appearance of artists and musicians whose religion or origin was unsatisfactory to the 'master race.'"

Still, the president didn't think he could force the DAR to change their policy of racial discrimination. He said he couldn't get involved because the DAR was not a public agency. "I am sure that you will realize, however, the impossibility of any interference by me in the management or policy of a private enterprise such as the one in question," the president explained. The DAR blamed their actions on the laws of the District of Columbia. They said the existing laws in the city required separate schools, churches, and other public buildings for blacks and whites. They were just following the laws by refusing Hazel's request. But they followed up by saying their policy of "white artists only" was "not intended to and should not be considered to imply the inferiority of either race to the other." If the ladies of the DAR thought this would make Hazel Scott feel better about their racism, they were wrong. Hazel said, "If I weren't allowed to use the hall because my music was unsuitable, it would be a different matter. But to refuse to let me play because of race is both stupidly reactionary and vicious."

First Lady Bess Truman had accepted an invitation for tea at the Washington DAR headquarters about the same time as the Hazel Scott incident. Some black people hoped she would decline. Hazel said she hoped the First Lady would show her disapproval of the DAR's racial discrimination by avoiding the tea, much like Eleanor Roosevelt had done years earlier. But the First Lady went to the DAR event and stayed for almost an hour. The *Afro American* newspaper reported that when a reporter asked her if she would accept future invitations from the DAR, the First Lady replied, "Why not?"

Hazel was disappointed that the First Lady decided to attend the tea. She said, "I wish she had refused to go because in the midst of this unfortunate discrimination her presence there gives sanction to their action against me."

Many black female entertainers had made sacrifices in order to do their part for the war effort. Some had traveled in the southern United States to perform for servicemen despite the dangerous Jim Crow laws that made racial discrimination the law. Some had volunteered to perform for the troops without pay. Some had followed the troops to the fronts in Europe, North Africa, and the Pacific—facing many of the same dangers as the soldiers, sailors, and marines. Some had lived in tents and braved jungles, deserts, and stormy seas to give the servicemen and -women a few moments of relief from the war. After the war, most returned to the United States to confront the racism that they hoped would have subsided just a little. A few, like Josephine Baker and Coretta Alfred, chose to remain in their adopted countries, where they knew they would not have to face the cruel racism that ruled American society.

When she was asked about life after the war, Josephine Baker replied, "After the war? Who knows? Paris again? I suppose so. America? I think not."

EPILOGUE

In 2009 a black woman, Michelle Obama, moved into the White House with her family. She was not there to work as a White House servant, a position that had typically been held by black men and women in previous generations. She was the First Lady. Her husband, Barack Obama, had just become the first black person to be elected president of the United States. His election in November 2008 was a milestone in American history. It was an event that would have been inconceivable in the 1940s.

What monumental events transpired between 1940 and 2009 that made it possible for a black family to occupy the White House? And who were the individuals that helped transform the society that allowed such change?

There were many factors that led to change for black Americans. And there were many courageous people who fought for changes to the unjust system that created segregation and racism. Landmark court decisions—including *Brown v. Board of Education* in 1954, which ended legal segregation in public schools—changed the portrait of American education. Federal legislation—including the Civil Rights Act of 1964, which outlawed discrimination on the basis of race and gender—had an impact on the American workplace. Rosa Parks, who in 1955 refused to give up her bus seat to a white person, sparked a city-wide boycott in Montgomery, Alabama, altering transportation in America. And Dr. Martin Luther King Jr., who led the fight for equality through peaceful resistance, helped bring about a new America.

The actions of many ordinary citizens, who resisted discrimination in many everyday ways, helped change America. Many of the black women who overcame race and gender barriers to help win World War II continued their fight for equality after the war ended in 1945. Some did it in quiet, discreet ways; others were more outspoken in their resistance to injustice.

In 1942 when Juanita Jackson Mitchell led a group of black citizens to the state capitol in Maryland to demand civil rights from Governor O'Conor, she and her fellow marchers were laying the foundation for the civil rights marches of the 1960s. Juanita's activism in the 1940s continued throughout her lifetime.

Juanita became known as "the first lady of Maryland's leading civil rights family" for her fight to end segregation and discrimination in the state. In 1950 she was the first black woman to become a lawyer in Maryland, and she served as counsel to the Maryland NAACP. She used her legal expertise to fight segregation in public places and in the state's schools. She brought lawsuits to end discrimination in hiring and to end a jury system that segregated black and white jurors. In the 1960s she fought to integrate restaurants, and President John F. Kennedy named her to the White House Conference on Women and Civil Rights. She organized a group named Stop the Killing Campaign in 1985 in response to a rash of killings of black teens. When Juanita Jackson Mitchell died in 1992 the governor of Maryland said the state had lost a "great lady."

When Inda DeVerne Lee led the Fourth of July protest at the Red Cross club in India in 1945, she wanted to call attention to the injustice of segregation in the armed forces. Her fight against injustice became a lifelong mission. Settling in St. Louis, Missouri, after the war, DeVerne organized a chapter of the Congress on Racial Equality (CORE), a leading civil rights activist group. She protested the segregation policies of the bus and train companies. And she took on the banks that refused loans to residents of black neighborhoods. She worked to help ensure fair housing and employment for blacks. She fought for laws to protect the rights of women. She became the first black woman in the Missouri state legislature in 1962 and served until 1982. As a state legislator DeVerne was an advocate for children, disabled, and elderly people. She also worked for reform in the state's prisons. When she died in 1993 she was called "a giant" for her commitment to civil rights for all people.

When E. Pauline Myers told A. Philip Randolph in 1941 that she wasn't a party girl and that she wanted to build a movement, she meant it. After the war Pauline worked in the labor movement demanding equal rights for workers. She had been a key organizer in the 1941 March on Washington, and when another March on Washington took place in 1963, Pauline took part in it—alongside A. Philip Randolph. In 1983, Pauline was still doing the work she loved—demanding equality for American citizens. When she was asked to speak to a journalism class at Howard University and a friend warned her that there might be student protests to contend with because of an unpopular decision made by an administrator, she said, "If there wasn't any trouble, I wouldn't want to go."

In 1998 the *Washington Post* ran an obituary for 89-year-old E. Pauline Myers. She was described as a "social activist" who contributed to "historic events that laid the groundwork for what came to be known as the civil rights movement."

Layle Lane, the woman who met with President Franklin Roosevelt in 1941 to demand equality for blacks in employment and the military, continued to "hammer away at the walls of segregation" as she put it, until her death in 1976. Layle's work with the American Federation of Teachers (AFT) union continued to shape her life after the war. When the AFT was asked to provide an amicus (from the term *amicus curiae*, "friend of the court") brief to the Supreme Court for *Brown v. Board of Education*, Layle led the writing team. Throughout the 1950s she worked to end Jim Crow practices in teachers' unions across the country. She wrote a monthly column—"Debits and Credits"— about the gains and losses for social justice in education. And she put her words into actions by offering her farm in Pennsylvania as a camp for poor inner-city kids. Layle, who believed education was a road to equality, devoted her life to education and equality.

Army nurse Daryle Foister spent the war years serving in hospitals across the globe. When she returned to the United States after her war duty she wanted to further her education and applied to the nursing school at Louisiana State University. But Daryle was denied admittance to the nursing program, and she believed it was because of the color of her skin. She brought a lawsuit against the university in 1951 and won. Because of Daryle's suit the university's law school and medical schools were opened to black students.

The black women who broke race and gender barriers to help win World War II could only dream of a day when a black woman and her family would live in the White House of the United States. And because of their determination and courage in the 1940s, their dreams became a reality.

NOTES

||||||||||||||||||||||||||||||||||||||||||||||||||||||||||||||||||||||||||||||||||||||||||||||||||||||||||||||||||||||||||||||||||||||||||||||||||||||||||||||||||||||||||||||

Chapter 1: War Workers

"I stood in line with the others": Afro American 8-12-1944

Ethel was one of the many women who were eager: Telephone interview with Florence Hawthorne, 9-29-2011

A government official from the War Manpower Commission: Time 9-21-1942

A spokesman for the agency said he had 500 openings: Afro American 9-29-1942

"While agencies struggle toward a nationwide": St. Petersburg Times 12-21-1941

But not all businesses were ready: Telephone interview with Florence Hawthorne, 9-29-2011

"when the imperative need of utilizing": Chicago Daily Tribune 6-4-1942

"all had sweaty hands": Chicago Defender 11-6-1943

"Colored women just do not have": Afro American 12-22-1942

"Negroes could not be used": Chicago Defender 11-23-1940

Two black women in Ohio: Journal of Negro Education, Summer 1943

"has experienced no difficulty": Chicago Defender 3-10-1945

"It is as toothless as a month-old baby": Afro American 12-22-1942

When an arsenal in New Jersey: Chicago Defender 2-17-1945

Toilets became a major issue: Chicago Defender 10-16-1943

President Roosevelt became involved: Chicago Defender 12-25-1943

"They say they need food": Chicago Defender 3-18-1944

In some cases, auxiliaries were formed: Chicago Defender 11-27-43

The wives who followed their soldier husbands: Crisis 1-1943

"It was a discouraging process": Chicago Daily Tribune 10-11-1942

"Every cadet in all the CAP squadrons": Chicago Daily Tribune 8-18-1944

"*The most delicate job*": *Afro American* 3-31-1945
"*For though I have witnessed two lynchings*": *Afro American* 3-18-1944
"*Indeed, visibility in the community*": *Notable Black American Women*, 62
"*There is a world revolution*": *Chicago Defender* 11-14-1942
"*One thing seems certain*": *Chicago Defender* 1-29-1944
"*It's a man's war no longer*": *Chicago Defender* 9-26-1942
She was hospitalized for a couple of months: E-mail exchange with Benjamin
    Phillips 9-11-2011

Chapter 2: Political Activists

but everybody said they were ace: *Chicago Defender* 3-6-1943
What happened next is: *Time* 10-26-1942; *Chicago Defender* 3-6-1943; *Chicago
    Defender* 10-17-1942
"*the most dangerous Negro*": *Chicago Defender* 6-28-1941
"*I want all America to understand*": *Pittsburgh Courier* 6-27-1942
"*After this world conflict is over*": *Pittsburgh Courier* 6-27-1942
In Chicago, Ethel Payne: *Chicago Defender* 7-4-1942
In St. Louis, Thelma McNeal: *Chicago Defender* 8-15-1942
How Can We Die Freely: *Marching Together: Women of the Brotherhood of Sleeping
    Car Porters*, 170
For five days in June 1943: *Chicago Defender* 5-1-1943, 6-5-1943, 6-19-1943
And E. Pauline Myers reminded the delegates: *Afro American* 7-10-1943; *Pittsburgh
    Courier* 7-10-1943; *Chicago Defender* 6-19-1943 (David Lucander, in "It Is a
    New Kind of Militancy: March on Washington Movement, 1941–1946,"
    indicated that Myers was not able to attend the We Are Americans, Too,
    conference because she was hospitalized. But two newspaper accounts
    report she was in attendance and delivered speeches. An earlier news-
    paper account reported her hospitalization, but also stated that she was
    expected to recover in time to attend the conference.)
Pauli and a friend were on their way: Documenting the American South: Oral
    Histories of the American South
A year before Hattie protested: *Chicago Defender* 4-24-1943
"*time to begin training Americans*": *Marching Together: Women of the Brotherhood
    of Sleeping Car Porters*, 17
The Double Victory Girls Club: *Chicago Defender* 12-11-1943
In December 1942, Ethel had taken: Women in Journalism Oral History Project
Anna Arnold Hedgeman was a black woman: *Chicago Defender* 9-16-1944
The well-organized event was supported: *Pittsburgh Courier* 5-2-1942
"*friends of Mrs. Roosevelt*": *Free Lance-Star* 10-5-1944

"drive a hard bargain": *Chicago Defender* 6-16-1945

Norma Green was a black army nurse: *Chicago Defender* 10-3-1942

In fact, there were fewer than 200: *The Army Nurse Corps: A Commemoration of World War II Service*, 9

Compared to about 20,000: *A History of the U.S. Army Nurse Corps*, 270

This question came after it was learned: *Chicago Defender* 1-20-1945

The city hospital in Baltimore: *Afro American* 6-8-1943

After a while, her superintendent suggested: Western Historical Manuscript Collection University of Missouri–St. Louis, www.umsl.edu /~whmc/guides/t016.htm

It released a statement: *Pittsburgh Courier* 10-3-1942

Chapter 3: The Military

"I went to the coffee shop": *Pittsburgh Courier* 8-11-1945

"Will all the colored girls move over on this side.": *One Woman's Army: A Black Officer Remembers the WAC*, 19

At the mess hall the black WAACs: Telephone interview with Violet Hill Askins Gordon, 4-25-2008

"with heads high": *Chicago Defender* 8-15-1942

"firm of step": *Chicago Defender* 8-15-1942

"breathing defiance to Hitler, Hirohito, and Mussolini": *Chicago Defender* 8-15-1942

Tessie O'Bryant sent three daughters: *Pittsburgh Courier* 6-12-1943

Tessie Theresa, Ida Susie, and Essie Dell O'Bryant had decided to join: Veterans' History Project of the Library of Congress, Essie Dell O'Bryant Woods

"laundries, mess units, or salvage": *When the Nation Was in Need: Blacks in the Women's Army Corps During World War II*, 74

When the day of departure arrived, Charity: *One Woman's Army: A Black Officer Remembers the WAC*, 131

The entire city seemed to have been leveled: Veterans' History Project of the Library of Congress, Essie Dell O'Bryant Woods

"We wanted the Negro WACs out": *Chicago Defender* 7-7-1945

"colored boyfriends coming to call on them": *Chicago Defender* 7-7-1945

"lead to general social intermingling": *Chicago Defender* 7-7-1945

"Negroes got the idea that": *Chicago Defender* 7-7-1945

"Welcome these Negro": *We Served America Too!: Personal Recollections of African Americans in the Women's Army Corps During World War II*, 190

"no place for them": *Afro American* 8-21-1943

Other branches of the military: *Our Mothers' War: American Women at Home and at the Front During World War II*, 216

"We will be the first group": Sammie M. Rice Collection
One of the nurses, Alma Favors: Chicago Defender, 3-13-1943
Sammie continued to send: Sammie M. Rice Collection
"bedlam broke loose": Pittsburgh Courier, 12-11-1943
"the nurses received an ovation": Pittsburgh Courier, 12-11-1943
"We are extremely anxious to get to work": Afro American 4-11-1944
silk from a military parachute: Veterans' History Project of the Library of Congress, Interview Transcript: Prudence Burns Burrell
A picture of a black soldier lying in a hospital bed: Flagstaff Oral History Project
From the newspaper account: Pittsburgh Courier 6-30-1945
Before patients could be treated: Roundup 5-31-1945
"I haven't minded": Roundup 5-31-1945
"They just accept us": Chicago Defender 9-22-1945

Chapter 4: Volunteers

At the end of one day, Mildred boarded a bus: California Eagle 12-18-1942 (In *Carry Me Home: Birmingham, Alabama—The Climactic Battle of the Civil Rights Revolution*, Diane McWhorter describes Mildred boarding a street car. And she writes that the two men were fellow members of the Southern Negro Youth Conference [SNYC].)
Dora Lewis was less successful: Chicago Defender 7-11-1942
"Every one of us, no matter where he lives": Chicago Defender 12-6-1941
One night in September 1942 a black couple: Chicago Defender 10-10-1942
When the US Army Air Forces requested: Chicago Defender 10-18-1941
"blackout of Negroes": Pittsburgh Courier 3-14-1942
These troubling events in New Orleans: Chicago Defender 3-20-1943
"My children are all at school": Pittsburgh Courier 12-19-1942
"widely diversified": Afro American 6-20-1942
"destined to be a great hit": Chicago Defender 2-28-1942
Twelve black AWVS members: Pittsburgh Courier 10-10-1942
"This is a subversive": Pittsburgh Courier 3-7-1942
In Salt Lake City, Utah: Chicago Defender 6-26-1943
"mixed dancing was involved": Chicago Defender 11-20-1943
On the day of the blood drive: Chicago Defender 9-30-1944
"Is that a democratic stand": Pittsburgh Courier 2-28-1942
"I was thrilled and proud": Chicago Defender 12-19-1942
"There's the b— that's runnin'": Negro Digest September 1944
"The expression on their faces": Chicago Defender 7-3-1943

"*At least 10,000 people were milling*": *Chicago Defender* 6-16-1945
"*I wonder how I'll fit in*": *Chicago Defender* 10-21-1944

Chapter 5: Entertainers

"*You'll have to eat in the kitchen*": *Chicago Defender* 10-27-1945
Throughout the war years, Hazel Scott made valuable: E-mail exchange with
    Adam Clayton Powell 9-3-2011
"*Entertainment is always*": Hope for America http://myloc.gov/Exhibitions
    /hopeforamerica/causesandcontroversies/entertainingthetroops
    /ExhibitObjects/BolsteringMorale.aspx
"*It's better to get $7,000*": *Our Mothers' War*, 222
"*I hope that judge*": *Time* 12-17-1945
"*It is time that members*": *Time* 12-17-1945
"*Now who the hell*": *Chicago Defender* 1-6-1945
"*the exotic darling of the unit*": *Chicago Defender* 10-28-1944
"*the bluest of blues*": *Chicago Defender* 10-28-1944
"*five foot package of dancing dynamite*": *Chicago Defender* 10-28-1944
"*a solid bass*": *Pittsburgh Courier* 1-13-1945
"*sultry sweet and low voice*": *Pittsburgh Courier* 1-13-1945
"*gal who set two continents afire*": *Afro American* 5-2-1942
"*seared the hearts of men*": *Afro American* 5-2-1942
"*We are in the jungles of Burma*": *Afro American* 12-23-1944
"*We are in one of the most picturesque*": *Afro American* 11-18-1944
The black press reported that Ike: *Afro American* 6-30-1945
"*Words cannot describe*": *Afro American* 9-15-1945
The International Sweethearts of Rhythm traveled: www.riverwalkjazz.org
    /jazznotes/intl_sweethearts
Traveling in Big Bertha made life easier: http://americanhistory.si.edu/webcast
    /jam2011_women.html
In Birmingham, Alabama: http://americanhistory.si.edu/webcast/jam2011
    _women.html
Anna Mae Winburn directed the Sweethearts: *Chicago Defender* 8-25-1945
"*eating out of their palms*": *Chicago Defender* 12-15-1945
Nightingale of the European Theater: *Pittsburgh Courier* 5-15-1943
Songbird of the South: *Pittsburgh Courier* 5-20-1944
"*Arriving in camp, all the weariness*": *Pittsburgh Courier* 5-20-1944
At another camp in 1943: *Negro Digest* December 1943
In 1901 Coretta Alfred: *The Music of Black Americans: A History*, 306

As the German army approached: Chicago Defender 12-18-1943

That's why Coretta and her pianist husband: Chicago Defender 12-18-1943

"I returned to America to see my mother": Crisis 7-37

Roberta left Bonham: "Bonham Musicians Back Future Opera Star"

They shared a passion: Chicago Defender 9-1-1945

WAC Band #2 found it difficult: Iowa Bystander 7-24-1944, Interview with Novella Cromer 10-6-2011

But by November 1944: Iowa Bystander 11-16-1944

"We don't take Negroes here": Chicago Defender 10-3-1942

Shortly after the war ended: Chicago Defender 7-13-1946

"My sole interest is in building": Chicago Defender 7-13-1946

The International Sweethearts of Rhythm performed in St. Louis: Pittsburgh Courier 6-29-1946

"We have just brought to a successful conclusion": Chicago Defender 10-20-1945

"I am sure that you will realize": Chicago Defender 10-20-1945

The DAR blamed their actions: Chicago Defender 12-22-1945

"Why not?": Afro American 1-5-1946

"After the war? Who knows?": Pittsburgh Courier 5-19-1945

Epilogue

"the first lady of Maryland's": Baltimore Sun 7-8-1992

Settling in St. Louis, Missouri: St. Louis Post-Dispatch 1-25-1993

When she was asked to speak: Washington Post 9-3-1998

Layle's work with the American Federation of Teachers: American Educator Winter 2000–2001

BIBLIOGRAPHY

Books

Adams Earley, Charity. *One Woman's Army: A Black Officer Remembers the WAC*. College Station: Texas A & M University Press, 1989.

Atwood, Kathryn J. *Women Heroes of World War II*. Chicago: Chicago Review Press, 2011.

Bellafaire, Judith L. *The Army Nurse Corps: A Commemoration of World War II Service*. U.S. Army Center of Military History, 1993.

Carew, Joy Gleason. *Blacks, Reds and Russians: Sojourners in Search of the Soviet Promise*. Piscataway: Rutgers University Press, 2008.

Carney Smith, Jessie, ed. *Notable Black American Women*. Detroit: Gale Research, 1992.

Chateauvert, Melinda. *Marching Together: Women of the Brotherhood of Sleeping Car Porters*. Urbana: University of Illinois Press, 1998.

Guzman, Jessie Parkhurst, ed. *Negro Yearbook: A Review of Events Affecting Negro Life, 1941–46*. Tuskegee, AL: Tuskegee Institute, 1947. www.archive.org /stream/negroyearbookrev00guzmrich/negroyearbookrev00guzmrich _djvu.txt.

Honey, Maureen, ed. *Bitter Fruit*. Columbia: University of Missouri Press, 1999.

Kersten, Andrew E. *Race, Jobs, and the War: The FEPC in the Midwest, 1941–46*. Champaign: University of Illinois Press, 2007.

Litoff, Judy Barrett, and David C. Smith, eds. *American Women in a World at War: Contemporary Accounts from World War II*. Wilmington, DE: Scholarly Resources, 1997.

McCabe, Katie, and Dovey Johnson Roundtree. *Justice Older than the Law: The Life of Dovey Johnson Roundtree*. Jackson: University Press of Mississippi, 2009.

Moore, Brenda L. *To Serve My Country, To Serve My Race: The Story of the Only African American WACs Stationed Overseas During World War II*. New York: New York University Press, 1996.

Morehouse, Maggie. *Fighting in the Jim Crow Army: Black Men and Women Remember World War II*. New York: Rowman & Littlefield, 2000.

Olson, Lynne. *Freedom's Daughters: The Unsung Heroines of the Civil Rights Movement from 1830 to 1970*. New York: Touchstone, 2001.

Putney, Martha S. *When the Nation Was in Need: Blacks in the Women's Army Corps During World War II*. Metuchen, NJ: Scarecrow Press, 1992.

Rollins, Judith. *All Is Never Said: The Narrative of Odette Harper Hines*. Philadelphia: Temple University Press, 1995.

Sarnecky, Mary T. *A History of the U.S. Army Nurse Corps*. Philadelphia: University of Pennsylvania Press, 1999.

Shaw, Stephanie J. *What a Woman Ought to Be and to Do: Black Professional Women Workers During the Jim Crow Era*. Chicago: University of Chicago Press, 1996.

Southern, Eileen. *The Music of Black Americans: A History*. New York: W. W. Norton and Company, 1997.

Sugrue, Thomas J. *Sweet Land of Liberty: The Forgotten Struggle for Civil Rights in the North*. New York: Random House, 2008.

Tucker, Sherrie. *Swing Shift: "All-Girl" Bands of the 1940s*. Durham, NC: Duke University Press, 2000.

Yellin, Emily. *Our Mothers' War: American Women at Home and at the Front During World War II*. New York: Free Press, 2004.

Dissertations

Lucander, David. "It Is a New Kind of Militancy": March on Washington Movement, 1941–1946" (2010). *Open Access Dissertations*. Paper 247. http://scholarworks.umass.edu/open_access_dissertations/247.

Sims-Wood, Janet. "We Served America Too!: Personal Recollections of African Americans in the Women's Army Corps During World War II." Graduate School of the Union Institute, 1994.

Interviews

Telephone interview with Violet Gordon, April 25, 2008.

Telephone interview with Rosemary Skipper, June 13, 2011, and August 20, 2011.

Telephone interview with Ora Pierce Hicks, June 17, 2011.
Telephone interview with Frances Hawthorne, September 29, 2011.
Telephone interview with Novella Cromer, October 6, 2011.

Journals

Ransom, Leon. "Combating Discrimination in the Employment of Negroes in War Industries and Government Agencies." *Journal of Negro Education* 12, no. 3 (Summer 1943): 405–416.
Schierenbeck, Jack. "Lost and Found: The Incredible Life and Times of (Miss) Layle Lane." *American Educator* (Winter 2000–2001).

Letters

Sammie M. Rice Collection, Betty H. Carter Women Veterans Historical Project, Martha Hodges Special Collections and University Archives, University Libraries, University of North Carolina at Greensboro, NC.

Magazines

"California: Victory on Sugar Hill." *Time*, December 17, 1945.
"Crime: Lynch Week." *Time*, October 26, 1942.
Eustis, Morton. "Double Bill in North Africa." *Negro Digest*, December 1943.
Gorham, Thelma Thurston. "Negro Army Wives." *Crisis*, January 1943.
Hall, Chatwood. "A Black Woman in Red Russia." *Crisis*, July 1937.
Murray, Pauli. "A Blueprint for First Class Citizenship." *Crisis*, November 1944.
"U.S. at War: The Vanishing Servant." *Time*, September 21, 1942.

Newspapers

"A Rebuke Opens Air Raid Posts for NY Women." *Chicago Defender*, October 18, 1941.
"Alberta Hunter Abroad." *Afro American*, September 15, 1945.
"Army Nurse Jim Crowed at Airfield and on Plane." *Pittsburgh Courier*, August 11, 1945.
"Army Nurse, Preparing to Go to War, Beaten." *Chicago Defender*, October 3, 1942.
"Avers New Deal Slights Negro Civil Air Cadets." *Chicago Daily Tribune*, August 18, 1944.

"Before the Dream: Pauline Myers, Foot Soldier in a Long-Ago March for Civil Rights." *Washington Post*, August 26, 1993.

"Blackout Test Shows Fallacy of Jim Crow in Civilian Defense." *Pittsburgh Courier*, March 14, 1942.

Bolden, Frank. "Burma Hospital Has All-Negro Personnel." *Pittsburgh Courier*, June 30, 1945.

Briggs, Diana. "Women Power in War." *Chicago Defender*, September 26, 1942.

Buchanan, Sgt. C. M. "Negro Hospital." *Roundup*, May 31, 1945. http://cbi -theater-1.home.comcast.net/~cbi-theater-1/roundup/roundup053145 .html0.

"City Hospitals Asked to Use Colored Nurses." *Afro American*, June 8, 1943.

"Claims Trained Negroes Can't Get War Jobs." *Chicago Daily Tribune*, June 4, 1942.

"Deactivate Negro WAC Band at Ft. Des Moines." *Iowa Bystander*, July 20, 1944.

"Defense Jim Crow Bared in Philly." *Afro American*, January 11, 1941.

"Domestic Service Is on the Way Out." *Afro America*, September 29, 1942.

"8 Chicagoans in N. Africa Hospital Unit." *Chicago Defender*, March 13, 1943.

Estrada, Louie. "Social Activist E. Pauline Myers Dies." *Washington Post*, September 3, 1998.

"Experiences in Europe Thrill Red Cross Aide." *Chicago Defender*, June 16, 1945.

"FBI Can't Find Any 'Eleanor Clubs.'" *Pittsburgh Courier*, October 3, 1942.

"FEP Told of Job Bans in West Coast Shipyards." *Chicago Defender*, November 27, 1943.

Fletcher, Michael. "Juanita Jackson Mitchell: Civil Rights Leader Battled Bias in Court." *Baltimore Sun*, July 8, 1992.

Fraser, Edna. "Courier Correspondent Finds La Baker Easy to Meet, Know." *Pittsburgh Courier*, May 19, 1945.

"GIs Like All-Girls' Band." *Chicago Defender*, December 15, 1945.

"Glory Gals Demonstrate Their Skill." *Afro American*, June 20, 1942.

Hall, Chatwood. "Harlem Choir Singer Tours Red Army Camps, Hospitals to Bolster Morale." *Chicago Defender*, December 18, 1943.

"Harlem Women Relieve Jersey Work Shortage." *Chicago Defender*, February 17, 1945.

Haynes, S. A. "Historic Year Marks Passing of an Era." *Afro American*, January 5, 1946.

"Highlights, Footnotes on New York's Protest Rally." *Pittsburgh Courier*, June 27, 1942.

Hill, Herman. "AWVS Members Have Bitter Experience on Crack Train." *Pittsburgh Courier*, October 10, 1942.

"Hit Red Cross Jim Crow of Nurses at Bond Rally." *Chicago Defender*, March 20, 1943.

"Hotel Bars Muriel Rahn Famous Concert Artists." *Chicago Defender*, October 3, 1942.

Hunter, Alberta. "Alberta Hunter Meets Tan Yanks Along Ledo Road." *Afro American*, December 23, 1944.

"Ike Selected Hunter Sextet Over America's Biggest Stars." *Afro American*, June 30, 1945.

"Jail Girl Musician in Georgia; All-Male Show Hits." *Chicago Defender*, July 13, 1946.

"Jo Baker, Entertainer, Dies Penniless in Europe." *Iowa Bystander*, November 19, 1942.

Jones Garrett, Lula. "Lipstick." *Afro American*, March 31, 1945.

Jones Garrett, Lula. "Strange Fruit Fine Foil for White Supremacy Lore." *Afro American*, March 18, 1944.

Jones, Scoop. "Soldiers Cheer as First Nurses Reach Australia." *Pittsburgh Courier*, December 11, 1943.

"Josephine Baker Dies Penniless." *Chicago Defender*, November 21, 1942.

"Josephine Baker Reported Dead in Morocco Following Long Illness." *Afro American*, November 21, 1942.

"Life on Alcan Highway Described by First Race Woman to Serve There." *Chicago Defender*, July 3, 1943.

Lopez, Jacqueline. "Nazis Talk of Wives, Children to Negro Nurses." *Chicago Defender*, September 22, 1945.

"Many Protest WAC Band Demobilization at Fort." *Iowa Bystander*, July 24, 1944.

"March Plans Big Parley in Chicago." *Chicago Defender*, May 1, 1943.

McAlpin, Harry. "Howard Students Picket Jim Crow Restaurant." *Chicago Defender*, April 24, 1943.

McCray, George. "12,000 in Chicago Voice Demands for Democracy." *Chicago Defender*, July 4, 1942.

"McQuay-Norris Says It Won't Hire Women." *Afro American*, August 12, 1944.

"Mercedes Welcker Writes Song for Women's Volunteer Service." *Chicago Defender*, February 28, 1942.

"Mississippi on Another Rampage; Two 14-Year-Old Boys Lynched!!" *Chicago Defender*, October 17, 1942.

"Mixed Dancing Barred by USO." *Chicago Defender*, November 20, 1943.

"'Most Dangerous Negro in America' to Blast Charges by Rep. Mitchell." *Chicago Defender*, June 28, 1941.

"MOWM Asks Roosevelt to Appoint Race Commission." *Pittsburgh Courier*, July 10, 1943.

"Nazi Prisoners Gloat as U.S. Nurses 'Get the Works.'" *Chicago Defender*, January 20, 1945.

"N.J. Law Bars Jim Crow in Raid Shelters." *Chicago Defender*, October 10, 1942.

"Not a Toot from WAC Band Since Reorganization." *Iowa Bystander*, November 16, 1944.

"Nurses' Aide Applicant Turned Down Flatly by Red Cross." *Pittsburgh Courier*, February 28, 1942.

"Nurses' Aides Play Vital Role in Our Country's War Effort." *Pittsburgh Courier*, December 19, 1942.

"Only Two Per Cent of N.Y. War Workers Colored." *Afro American*, December 22, 1942.

Ottley, Roi. "Dixie Invades Britain." *Negro Digest* 3, September 1944.

"Outlook for 'Americans' Meet Bright." *Chicago Defender*, June 19, 1943.

Pearson, Drew. "The Washington Merry-Go-Round." *Free Lance-Star*, October 5, 1944.

Phillips, B. M. "What They Said and Did at March-on-Washington Confab." *Afro American*, July 10, 1943.

"Plan Big, 'Americans Too,' Chicago Conclave." *Chicago Defender*, June 5, 1943.

Porter, Amy. "Servant Problem of Yesterday Now Domestic Crisis." *St. Petersburg Times*, December 21, 1941.

"Princess Makes a Paris Comeback." *Chicago Defender*, September 1, 1945.

Rea, E. B. "Alberta Hunter, Enchantress Who Set Two Continents Afire, to Settle Down." *Afro American*, May 2, 1942.

Rea, E. B. "Encores and Echoes." *Afro American*, November 18, 1944.

"Refuse to Give Blood After Red Cross Jim Crow." *Chicago Defender*, September 30, 1944.

"Refuse to Give War Bond Pledge to Negro Woman." *Chicago Defender*, July 11, 1942.

"Refused Service in Senate Café, Women Protest." *Chicago Defender*, September 16, 1944.

Reid, James M. "Maryland Citizens Stage March on Capital; Protest Killings." *Pittsburgh Courier*, May 2, 1942.

"Residents of Capital Told 'Be Prepared.'" *Chicago Defender*, December 6, 1941.

Rivera, A. M., Jr. "'Sweethearts' Defy Threats; Play Festival." *Pittsburgh Courier*, June 29, 1946.

"Roosevelt Seizes War Plan in Jim Crow Dispute." *Chicago Defender*, December 25, 1943.

"Salt Lake City Whites Object to Negro USO." *Chicago Defender*, June 26, 1943.

Sanders, James A. "Doc Wheeler's USO Unit Hit on European Fronts." *Chicago Defender*, October 28, 1944.

"St. Louis Set for City-wide Protest Meet." *Chicago Defender*, August 15, 1942.

"Secretary Claims Wrong Impression Has Been Created." *Pittsburgh Courier*, March 7, 1942.

Shephard, Joseph. "Bring on D.C. Heat Wave." *Afro American*, August 21, 1943.

Smith, Alfred E. "Lena Horne Quits USO Tour in Row over Army Jim Crow." *Chicago Defender*, January 6, 1945.

"'Southern Songbird' Does Grand Job for Red Cross." *Pittsburgh Courier*, May 20, 1944.

Spraggs, Venice. "'Lady Lobbyist' Blazes Path in Nation's Capital." *Chicago Defender*, June 16, 1945.

Spraggs, Venice Tipton. "President Truman Raps DAR Ban on Hazel Scott." *Chicago Defender*, October 20, 1945.

Spraggs, Venice Tipton. "Women in the National Picture." *Chicago Defender*, January 29, 1944.

Stiles Taylor, Rebecca. "Activities of Women's National Organizations." *Chicago Defender*, November 14, 1942.

"Sweaty Hands Prevent Hiring of Negro Girls." *Chicago Defender*, November 6, 1943.

"'Sweethearts' Get Groovy in Paris." *Chicago Defender*, August 25, 1945.

"3 Sisters Now in WAAC; 5 Cousins in Army." *Pittsburgh Courier*, June 12, 1943.

Tubbs, Vincent. "Nurses Overseas Anxious to Get to Hospital Posts." *Afro American*, April 11, 1944.

"'Unholy 3' Fight WACs in 'Black Ghetto' Plot." *Chicago Defender*, July 7, 1945.

"Urge WAAC to Steer Clear of Jim Crow." *Chicago Defender*, June 20, 1942.

"USO Troupe Thrills Doughboys in Persia." *Pittsburgh Courier*, January 13, 1945.

"WAACS Make First Public Bow in Style at Fort Des Moines, Iowa." *Chicago Defender*, August 15, 1942.

"WAC Disbanded at Ft. Des Moines." *Iowa Bystander*, July 24, 1944.

Ward, Henrine. "Local Girl in Britain Tells of First Lady's Welcome." *Chicago Defender*, December 19, 1942.

Waters, Enoch P. "Red Cross Girl Has Fill of 'Night Life.'" *Chicago Defender*, October 21, 1944.

Waters, Enoch P. "Two Lynched Boys Were Ace Scrap Iron Collectors in Mississippi Town." *Chicago Defender*, March 6, 1943.

"Western Electric Strike Asks Jim-Crow Toilets." *Chicago Defender*, October 16, 1943.

Wheatley, Tom. "DeVerne Calloway Dead at 76." *St. Louis Post-Dispatch*, January 25, 1993.

Wilhelm, John. "A Chicagoan Wins Air Unit for Her Race." *Chicago Daily Tribune*, October 11, 1942.

"Woman, 64, Supervises 80 Truck Farm Workers." *Chicago Defender*, March 18, 1944.

"Women Barred from Defense Project Jobs." *Chicago Defender*, November 23, 1940.

"Women Protest USES Job Bias in Cincinnati." *Chicago Defender*, December 11 1943.

Wong, Willie Lee. "Nazis Gone, Germans Rave over Sweethearts of Rhythm Band." *Chicago Defender*, September 8, 1945.

Woods, Howard B. "Hazel Scott Jim Crowed Again; St. Louis Café Bars Pianist." *Chicago Defender*, October 27, 1945.

Woods, Howard B. "Negro Women in St. Louis Plant After FEP Probe." *Chicago Defender*, March 10, 1945.

"Youth Leader Jailed, Beaten by Ala. Cops as Jim Crow Sign Moved." *California Eagle*, December 18, 1942.

Zack, Eugene C. "DAR Blames U.S. Laws for Hazel Scott Ban." *Chicago Defender*, December 22, 1945.

Video

Army Pictorial Service, Signal Corps, "The Stilwell Road." www.youtube.com/watch?v=6aQdcAd-ERA.

Websites

Documenting the American South: Oral Histories of the American South. Oral history interview with Pauli Murray, February 13, 1976. Interview G-0044. Southern Oral History Program Collection. http://docsouth.unc.edu/sohp/G-0044/menu.html.

Flagstaff Oral History Project. Oral history interview with Grady and Hazel Neal, January 16, 1976. http://archive.library.nau.edu/cdm4/item _viewer.php?CISOROOT=/cpa&CISOPTR=64416&CISOBOX=1& REC=12.

Goldthwaite, Carmen. "Bonham Musicians Back Future Opera Star." www .carmengoldthwaite.com/images/003sample%20robertadodd.doc.

Interview with DeVerne Calloway. Western Historical Manuscript Collection. University of Missouri–St. Louis. http://www.umsl.edu/~whmc /guides/t016.htm.

Library of Congress. Hope for America. http://myloc.gov/Exhibitions/hope foramerica/causesandcontroversies/entertainingthetroops/Exhibit Objects/BolsteringMorale.aspx.

The Missouri Women's Council Presents "Outstanding Women of Missouri" Travelling History Exhibit. http://www.womenscouncil.org /cd_web/Calloway.html.

Riverwalk Jazz. "International Sweethearts of Rhythm: America's #1 All-Girl Band." JazzNotes, March 10, 2011. www.riverwalkjazz.org /jazznotes/intl_sweethearts.

"Roberta Dodd Crawford." Texas State Historical Association. http://tsha online.org/handbook/online/articles/fcr69.

Veterans' History Project of the Library of Congress. Interview Transcript: Prudence Burns Burrell. http://lcweb2.loc.gov/diglib/vhp/story/loc .natlib.afc2001001.04747/transcript?ID=sr0001.

Veterans' History Project of the Library of Congress. Interview Transcript: Essie Dell O'Bryant Woods. http://lcweb2.loc.gov/diglib/vhp-stories /loc.natlib.afc2001001.04741/transcript?ID=sr0001.

Willie Mae Cotright, Mary Newson, Aller Hunter interviews. Regional Oral History Office, The Bancroft Library, UC Berkeley Library. http: //bancroft.berkeley.edu/ROHO/projects/rosie.

"Women and Jazz: International Sweethearts of Rhythm." National Museum of American History. Live Webcast from Carmichael Auditorium, March 30, 2011. http://americanhistory.si.edu/webcast/jam2011_women.html.

"Women in Journalism Oral History Project." Washington Press Club Foundation. http://beta.wpcf.org/oralhistory/payn3.html.

INDEX

Page numbers in *italics* indicate photographs.

acting roles, 199–200, 201
"Activities of Women's National Organizations" (Taylor), 34
Adams, Charity, 91, 109–10, 111
Adams, Osceola Macarthy, 161
Adelmond, Charlotte, 147
African Campaign Ribbons, 123–24
Afro American (newspaper), 15, 24, 32, 206, 209, 210
AFRS (Armed Forces Radio Service), 215
AFT (American Federation of Teachers), 45, 238
Aikens, Mattie L., *122*
air raid drills, 149–51
Albin, Thelma, 113
Alcan Highway, 181, 182
Alexander, Frances, 105, 108
Alexander, Hattie, 22, 23
Alfred, Coretta, 222–25
Alpha Kappa Alpha (AKA), 72
Amalgamated Clothing Workers Union, 24
American Association of Nurses (ANA), 74

American Federation of Teachers (AFT), 45, 238
"American Women for Defense" (Welcker-Jordan), 157–58
American Women's Volunteer Service (AWVS), 156–62
ammunition workers, 15–16
Amos, Helen, 105
Anderson, Birdie Beal, 60–61
Anderson, Laura, 184, 185
Anderson, Marian, 3, 231–32
Anderson, Mildred, 35
Annapolis, Maryland, 65–67
Argonaut (train), 160
Arle-Titz, Coretti, 223
Armed Forces Radio Service (AFRS), 215
Armstrong, Henry "Hurricane Hank," 159
Army Air Corps, 44
Army Nurse Corps, 73–74, 77. *See also* nurses
army posts, 26–27
Army Service Forces (ASF) Band, *227–29*
Ashmore, Mayvee, 107
Askins, Violet, 105
Askins, Ward, 91

Atlanta University School of Social
Work, 147
Attucks, Crispus, 165
Austin, Elsie, 170
Austria, 211
aviation industry, 10, 27–31

Baham, Rita, 59
Bailey, M. Virginia, 189
Baker, Josephine "Jo," 219–22, 220,
234
Baldwin, Beulah, 125
Baltimore, Maryland, 146
Banks, Henrine Ward, 190–91
Barger, Sylvia, 59
Barnes, Margaret, 106
Barrow, Wilhelmina, 188
Barttow, Robert, 189
Bass, Charlotta, 33
Bates, Alva, 147
Bearden, Bessye, 52
Beauticians Volunteer Corps, 148
Bell, Ethel, 7
Bell, Roberta, 23
Bennett, Blanche, 147
Bethune, Mary McLeod, 52, 69–72,
71, 88, 91, 95–96, 162–63
Bethune-Cookman College, 70
Big Bertha bus, 213
Birch, La Verne, 186
Black Cabinet, 71–72
blackout tests, 150–51
black-owned newspapers, 31–37
Blackwell, Olive, 186
Bland, Consuela, 105–6
Bland, Marjorie, 106
block plan system, 144
blood drives, 173–75, 192
Bluefield Daily Telegraph, 101
Bluford, Lucile, 172
Boggess, Eva, 123
bond drives, 147, 148–49, 197–98,
229
bond rally incident, 151–52

Booker T. Washington Red Cross
Club, 191
Boston Common USO center,
167–68
Bowen, Iva, 207, 208
Boyd, Norma E., 72
Bracey, Eleanor, 108
Braddy, Pauline, 213–14
Branker, Dorothy, 125
Briggs, Arthur, 211
Briggs, Diana, 34–35
Bristol, England, 180–81
Brooks, J. Clarice, 179–80
Brotherhood of Sleeping Car Porters
(BSCP), 24, 42
Brown, Birdie, 125, 126, 128
Brown, Jeanetta Welch, 26
Brown, Lovonia, 162–63
Brown, Sydney Taylor, 177–78, 186
Brown, Willa, 27–31, 28
Brown v. Board of Education, 235, 238
Bryant, Clora, 213–14
Bryant, Willie, 206
Burma, 209
Burma Road, 134–35
Burnham Park, 115
Burns, Prudence, 125, 126, 127–28,
129
Burnside, Vi, 213–14, 216
Burrell, Lowell, 129
Burrell, Rose, 24–25
Burton, Katherine, 148
Burtos, Flossie, 18
buses/busing, 3, 55, 75, 142–43
Butler, Toby, 231

CAA (Civil Aeronautics Authority),
27, 29
California Eagle (newspaper), 33
Calloway, Thelma, 119–20, 123, 130
Campbell, Vera, 90, 91, 99
Camp Shanks, 206
camp shows, 205–12, 215–17
CAP (Civil Air Patrol), 30

Carlisle, Una Mae, 206
Carpenter, Hattie, *18*
Carrol, Montrose, *203*
Carter, Mildred, 91
Caserne Tallandier, 113
Cato, Minto, 218–19
Cayton, Irma, 105, *163*
Chez Florence, 209
Chicago Coliseum protest, 52–53
Chicago Daily Tribune, 29
Chicago Defender (newspaper), 34
Chumley, Ruth, 63
Civil Aeronautics Authority (CAA),
    27, 29
Civil Air Patrol (CAP), 30
civilian defense groups, 144–52
civilian industries, 22
Civilian Pilot Training Program
    (CPTP), 28
Civil Rights Act, 3, 235–36
Clarke, Marie K., 175–76, 192
Clarke, Thurmond, 202
clubmobiles, 178–79, *186*, 188
Club Papua, 184
Club Paradise, 185
Coast Guard, 118
Coffee, Sherman, 172
Coffey, Cornelius, 28
Coffey School of Aeronautics, 28,
    29–30
Cole, Jonathan, *163*
Coleman, Burneda, 12–13
Combre, Hattie, 12–13
Committee on Civilian Defense,
    146
Concert Time USO tour, 208
Congress of Industrial
    Organizations (CIO), 24
Congress on Racial Equality
    (CORE), 237
conservation efforts, 168–70
Constitution Hall, 231–32
Consumer Information Service,
    147–48

Consumers' Pledge for Total
    Defense, 171
Cooper, Gladys, 207
Coppin, Elizabeth, 188
Cornell, Ann, 206
Cosmos (Red Cross club), 82
Cotright, Willie Mae, 20–21
covenants, 115, 201–2
Cox, Elestia, 135, 136
Cox, Nola "Kitty," 184, 185
CPTP (Civilian Pilot Training
    Program), 28
Cron, Roz, 214
Culpepper, Geneva, 125, 128
Currie, Fannie, 22–23

Dailey, Phyllis Mae, 77–78
Daniels, Cleopatra, 91, 92
Daniels, Eula, 105
Darlings of Rhythm, 231
Daughters of the American
    Revolution (DAR), 3, 231–33
Davis, Bette, 199
Davis, Ellise, 192
Davis, Lois Mae "Peaches," 35
Davis, Madine H., 135
Davis, Tiny, 213–14, 216
Dawson Creek, British Columbia, 181
"Debits and Credits" column (Lane),
    238
defense contracts, 5, 9, 43–44, 48
Defense Councils, 144
defense plants, 5–6, 10–11, 18–19,
    48–49
Defreese, Hulda, 107–8
Des Moines, Iowa, 97
Dewey, Thomas E., 68
direct action, 50–51, 53, 54
distribution centers, 137–39
"Dixie Invades Britain" (Ottley), 180
Doctor Carver Club, 183
Dodd, Roberta, 225–26
domestic workers, 6–7, 10–11, 24–25,
    83–86

Domestic Workers Alliance, 25
Donaldson, Natalie, 105
Dorsey, Jeannette C., 189, 189
Double V campaign, 62–63
Double Victory Girls Club, 63
draft, of nurses, 76
draft, military, 44
Duvall, Hattie, 56, 60
Dyson, Geraldine, 187

Eaton, Rebecca, 25
Eisenhower, Dwight D., 210–11
Eldridge, S. T., 52
Eleanor Clubs, 83–86
Elliott, Rose, 135
entertainers, war efforts, 197–98, 234
Espadron, Lolita, 191
Europe, respect for blacks in, 217
Evans, Bessie, 125
Evans, Dale, 199
Executive Order 8802, 9, 13–14,
    48–49

factories, 5–6, 10–11, 18–19, 48–49
factory workers
    civilian industries, 22–23
    job security, 25–26, 70
    labor shortages, 5, 7
    labor unions, 24–25
    racial discrimination, 5–6, 8, 9,
        11–18
    recruitment of women, 7, 8–9
    training programs, 9–10, 11, 16
    wages, 7, 10–11
    work conditions, 18–20, 21–23
Fair Employment Practices
    Committee (FEPC), 9, 14, 48, 64
farmers/farming, 122–23, 171–72
Fat Salvage Committee, 169
Fauset, Crystal Bird, 67–69
Federal Bureau of Investigation
    (FBI), 85
Federal Council on Negro Affairs,
    71–72

Ferguson, Lessie, 101–2
Fisher, Bernice, 59
Fisher, Thelma, 125
Fitzgerald, Ella, 205
Fleming, Maggie, 160
Florence, Arizona, 137–39
Foister, Daryle, 125, 135, 137, 238
Food for Freedom program, 171
food production, 171–72
Fort Des Moines, 93, 228
Fort Huachuca, Arizona, 27, 104–5,
    106, 107, 160
four freedoms, 43, 45, 62
Foxhole Circuit, 206
Freeman, Susan E., 121, 124
Fuller, Jacquelyn, 111
Fuller, Winona, 111
Furlowe, Gertrude, 180

Gable, Clark, 199
Gadsden, Maude, 148
Gant, Florie E., 133
gardening, 122–23
Gardiner General Hospital, 115
Gardner, Julie, 206–7
garment industry, 24
Garrett, Lula Jones, 32
gender discrimination, 8, 103
gender roles, 1–2, 6–7, 8, 34–35, 72
German prisoners, 137–39
Gill, Roby, 122, 123, 130
Glass, Agnes B., 135
Glover, Rosemae, 135, 136
Goering, Hermann, 211
Gowby, Sybil, 188
Gowdy, Myrtle, 106
Grand Hotel, 216
Grant, Thelma, 60
Grayson, Wilnet, 107
greatest generation, 2
Green, Cora, 208
Green, Ernest, 40–41
Green, Leola M., 122
Green, Norma, 75

Greer, Hazel, 102
Greer, Mazel, 102
Grimes, Chinkie, 160
Gunter, Patricia, 101

Hamilton, Joan, 125, 128
Hammond, Velma, 116–17
Harlem American Women's
    Volunteer Service (AWVS), 158
Harris, Bernice, 208
Harris, Georgia, 106
Harris, Sarah, 35
Harrison, Vera, 105
Hart, Fannie, 125, 135, 137
Hedgeman, Anna Arnold, 64
Hobby, Oveta Culp, 88, 92
Hold Your Job clinics, 70
Holiday, Billie, 39
Hollywood, California, 199–200
Hollywood Victory Committee,
    198–99, 200
Holmes, Geneva, 186
Holmes, Inez, 125, 126
Home Hospitality Committee, 182
Hoover, Gladys, 59
Hope, Lugenia Burns, 161
Horne, Lena, 203–4
hotels, racial discrimination at, 195,
    213
Hotel Touraine USO center, 168
housewives, 168–70
housing, 19, 81, 114–16, 201–2
Howard, Geneva, 188
Howard University, 56–57
Huggar, Bernice, 113–14
Hughes, Ernestine, 106
Hunter, Alberta, 209–12
Hunter, Aller, 21
Hunter, Irene, 63
Hunter, Jane Edna, 76
Hunter, Patsy, 160

Illinois Central Railroad, 22–23
"In a Man's World" (Briggs), 34–35

International Ladies' Garment
    Workers' Union, 24
International Sweethearts of
    Rhythm, 212–17, 231
"Interracial War Bond Rally," 201
Ivory, Gertrude, 124

Jackson, Alfonso, 149–50
Jackson, Dorothy, 149–50
Jackson, Juanita, 35
Jackson, Lillie M., 66
Jackson, Priscilla, 59
Jacobs, Bernice, 116–17
James, Ruth L., 112
"James Parker Blues" (Calloway),
    119–20
Japanese American detainees,
    80
Jarboro, Caterina, 207–8
Jarrett, Bessie Mae, 93
Jarrett, Carol, 177–78, 180
Jefferson, Althea, 116–17
Jim Crow laws, 213, 214, 231
job security, 25–26, 70
Joe Louis Service Guild, 155
Johnson, Alice, 82
Johnson, Ashley, 172
Johnson, Claretta, 13
Johnson, Cordelia Green, 54
Johnson, Dovey, 71, 91–92
Johnson, Faustina, 164–65
Johnson, Grace Nail, 161
Johnson, Sara B., 187
Johnson, Sara R., 182
Johnson, Thelma, 106
Johnson, Thomasina "Tommie"
    Walker, 72–73, 170
Johnson, Willie Lee, 82, 189, 189
Jones, Camille King, 179
Jones, Elnora, 125
Jones, Gabriel, 192
Jones, Grace Crump, 175
Jones, Helen, 213–14
Jones, Rae Lee, 231

journalists, 31–37
Jubilee radio show, 215

Kansas City Call (newspaper), 172
Kearney, Mary Frances, 92
Keep Shufflin' USO tour, 205
Kelly, Ruby, 182–83
Kendrick, Margaret, 135
Kennedy, John F., 236
Keye, Alice, 160
Keyes, Evelyn, 205
King, Lula, 22
King, Martin Luther, Jr., 3, 236
Ku Klux Klan, 231

labor camps, 137
Labor Division of the War
    Production Board, 8–9
labor shortages, 7, 10–11, 76, 153
labor unions, 24–25, 42, 45
LaGuardia, F. H., 148, 150
Landrum, Anna, 125, 135, 137
Lane, Layle, 45–46, 47, 48, 51, 54, 238
Lang, Charlie, 40–41
Lang, Zola Mae, *122*
Lathion, Polly, 135
Latimer, Magnolia, 177–78
Lawson, Senora B., 54
lawsuits
    against AWVS, 161–62
    against black homeowners, 202
    against LSU nursing program,
        238
    against racial discrimination,
        13–14, 236
    against school segregation, 235
Leach, Marie, 188
Ledo Road, *134–35*, 209
Lee, Hazel, 116–17
Lee, Inda DeVerne, 81–83, 237
Lee, Sandra, 207
Le Havre, France, 112
Lend-Lease Act, 43
Lesesne, Lillie L., 135

Le Vine, Lillian, 170–71
Lewis, Ann, 206–7
Lewis, Cleomine, 116–17
Lewis, Dora, 148
Lewis, Mary, 105
Liberia, 121–25
"Liberia Blues, The" (Calloway), 123
Liberian Humane Order of African
    Redemption, 124
Ligon, Eloise, 82
"Lipstick" (Garrett), 32
lobbyists, black, 72
Logan, Betty, 206
Lombard, Carole, 199
London, England, 190
Lonewolf, Helen Chequita, 182
Los Angeles riots, 4
Louis, Marva, *154–55*
Louisiana Amazon Guards, 223
Louisiana State University, 238
Lowther, Dolly, 147
Lucas, Olive, 135
lynchings, 39–41

Maddox, Pearl, 60–61
Madison Square Garden protest,
    51–52
malaria, 121, 123–24
Mallory, Arenia, 162–63
Manley, Norma, 184
Marchesi, Blanche, 226
March on Annapolis, 65–67
March on Washington, 42, 45–48,
    49, 237
March on Washington Movement
    (MOWM), 50, 52–54
Marine Corps, 44, 118
Martin, C. Gladys, 177–78, 186
Mary Mahoney Award, 124
Mathews, Claudia, 125
Maxwell, Chrystalee, 123
Maxwell, Doris, 113
Mayers, Marjorie, 125, 128
Mayo, Lucille, 106

McAdory, Mildred, 141, 192
McAllister, Lucille, 180, 186
McAlpine, Alice, 227
McDaniel, Hattie, 198, 199–203
McDuffie, J. Pericles, 190
McGee, Evelyn, 213–14
McGuire, Jack, 207
McKreever, Lawrence, 128
McNeal, Thelma, 53
McNeely, Eloise, 113–14
Metropolitan Council of Negro
  Women, 147
Mighty Seventh War Bond Drive,
  229
military police, 113
Miller, Louise, 125, 129–30, 140
Miller, Taps, 210
Miller, Viola, 188
"Million Dollar War Bond Show,"
  197
Mitchell, Juanita Jackson, 65, 66–67,
  236
Monroe, Clara, 105
Monroe, Millie, 160
Montgomery, Bernard, 210–11
Montgomery, James, 189
Morrow, Juanita, 188
MOWM (March on Washington
  Movement), 50, 52–54
Murmansk Run, 224
Murray, Pauli, 54–56, 57
Myers, E. Pauline, 50–51, 53, 54,
  237–38

NAACP (National Association for
  the Advancement of Colored
  People), 2
National Association of Colored
  Graduate Nurses (NACGN), 74,
  78, 124
National Association of Colored
  Women (NACW), 70
National Council of Negro Women
  (NCNW), 70

National Negro Airmen's
  Association of America, 27, 30
National Negro Congress, 25
National Non-Partisan Council on
  Public Affairs, 72
National Nurse Training Act, 73
National Youth Administration
  (NYA), 69
Navy Nurse Corps, 77–78
Navy Yards, 14
Neal, Grady, 133–34
Neal, Hazel, 133–34, 136, 137
Negro Committee for United Action
  to Defeat Hitler and Hitlerism, 149
Negro Employment and Training
  Branch, 8–9
Negro Nurses in the War
  conference, 76
Negro Red Cross Nurse's Aide
  Corps, 175
Negro USO Clubs, 166–67
"Negro Women War Workers"
  bulletin, 37–38
neighborhood associations, 114–16,
  201–2
Newman, Frank, 183
Newman, James, 183
New Orleans, Louisiana, 151
Newson, Mary, 20
newspapers, 31–37
New York Amsterdam News, 1
19th Amendment, 2
nonviolence, 50–51, 53, 54
Non-Violent, Good Will, Direct
  Action campaign, 53–54
Non-Violent, Good Will, Direct Action
  (Myers), 50
Norford, Thomasina Walker
  Johnson, 1–2
nurse aides, 152–53, 175–77
nurses
  in Australia, 125–28, 127
  in CBI theater, 133–37
  civilian, 79–81

in Europe, 130–32
in Florence, Arizona, 137–39, *138*
in Liberia, 118–25, *120*
in military, 73–78, *118*, *131*, 139–40
in Philippines, 129
shortages, 76, 153
training programs, 73, 75, 80, 238
NYA (National Youth
Administration), 69

Obama, Barack, 235
Obama, Michelle, 235
O'Bryant, Essie Dell, 102, 111–12
O'Bryant, Ida Susie, 102
O'Bryant, Tessie Theresa, 102,
111–12
O'Connor, Sandra Day, 3–4
O'Conor, Herbert R., *, 65, 66–67
Office of Civilian Defense (OCD),
67–68, 144–49, 150–51, 152
Office of Price Administration
(OPA), 169
Office of War Information, 7
Oliver, Glennye, 106
"On the Sidewalk" (Bass), 33
Original Illinois Housewives
Association, 170–71
Osby, Mildred, 91
Ottley, Vincent Lushington "Roi,"
179, 180
Outlaw, Grace, 183

Pace, Marie Harding, 60
pamphlets, 8, 50
Parker, Mary, 184
Parks, Rosa, 3, 236
Paterson, Jewell, 122
Payne, Ethel, 52, 53, 63–64
Payne, Hazel Dixon, 181–82, 193
Pembrook, Dollie, 207
Pennsylvania House of
Representatives, 67
Pettiford, Ruth, 148
Petty, Mary L., 130

Philippines, 129
Phillips, Bettye Murphy, 35–37, *36*
Pickens, Harriet Ida, *117*
Pierce, Ora, 137–38, *139*
Pinkett, Flaxie, 170
Pitts, Lucia, 113–14
Pittsburgh Courier (newspaper), 62,
126, 133, 184
Pius, Ruth, 188
Plenty Potent USO tour, 208
point-rationing system, 147, 169–70
police brutality, 65, 66, 142–43
pools, 82
Postal Directory Service, 110, 111–14,
112
Powell, Gladys, 188
Pratt, Thelma, 186
prisoner of war hospitals, 131–32,
137–39
protests
against discrimination, 51–54
of Lend-Lease Act, 43
March on Annapolis, 65–67
March on Washington, 42,
45–48, 49, 237
restaurant sit-ins, 56–62

racial discrimination. *See also* racism;
segregation
in AWVS, 161–62
at Boston USO center, 167–68
in CAP, 30–31
in civilian defense groups, 146,
149–52
covenants, 114–16, 201–2
damage to war effort, 41, 86
by DAR, 3, 231–33
in government agencies, 64
government programs, 14, 48–49
in hospitals, 75, 80–81, 115,
176–77
in hotels, 195, 213
in job market, 3, 5–8, 9, 11–16, 44
laws against, 3, 44, 150, 235–36

in military, 28, 44–45, 50, 140
against nurses, 73–75, 76–77,
    79–81
prevalence of, 140, 192, 195, 234
in Red Cross, 82–83, 151–52,
    173–76
in restaurants, 56–62, 64–65,
    129–30, 140, 195–96, 214–15
in US Navy, 73, 116–17
in WAAC, 89, 100
in workplaces, 16–18
racism. *See also* racial discrimination;
    segregation
    American attitude, 140, 180, 192,
        225, 234
    beliefs about blacks, 12, 98
    British attitude, 180
    education about, 68
    European attitude, 217
Rahn, Muriel, *230*
railroad workers, 22–23
Randall, Constance, 218–19
Randall, Geraldine, 183
Randolph, A. Philip, 42–43, 45,
    47–48, 49, 51
rationing, 169–70
Raynor, Thelma Holman, 183
Red Ball Express, 186–87
Red Cross
    blood drives, 173–75, 192
    clubmobiles, 178–79, *186*, 188
    Motor Corps, 148
    overseas service, 177–79
    racial discrimination, 82–83,
        151–52, 173–75
    recruitment of blacks, 177
    segregation, 173–75, 177
Red Cross Clubs
    in Australia, 183, 191
    in British Columbia, 181–82
    in Europe, 185–86, 187–88
    in Great Britain, 178, 180–81,
        182, 217–18
    in India, 189

in New Guinea, 184, 185
in North Africa, 182–83
Register and Vote campaigns, 67
restaurants, 64–65, 129–30, 140,
    195–96, 214–15
restaurant sit-ins, 56–62
Rhythm and Blues USO tour, 209–10
Rhythm Carnival USO troupe, 211
Rice, Johnnie Mae, 213–14
Rice, Sammie M., *118*–19, 121, 125,
    130
Ricketts, Adele, 113–14
riots, 4
Robinson, Ellen L., 120, *122*
Robinson, Flo, 206–7
Robinson, Mary, 82
Robinson, Rose, 135, 136
Rogers, Edith Nourse, 88
Roosevelt, Eleanor, 55, 69, 85, 178,
    231–32
Roosevelt, Franklin D.
    anti-discrimination stance, 9,
        17, 48
    on entertainment, 198
    Faucet and, 67, 68
    on four freedoms, 42–43
    on March on Washington, 47–48
    WAVES, 117
Ross, Geraldine, 186
rubber plantations, 121
Russell, Anna, 108
Russia, 222, 225

"Salute to Colored Troops," 197
Sandifer, Faye, 189
Schenck, Caroline, 125, 135, 137
school segregation, 3, 54–55, 235
Scott, Alivia, *18*
Scott, Austin, *163*
Scott, Hazel, 196–97, 232–33
scrap drives, 141–43
segregation. *See also* racial
    discrimination; racism
    acceptance of, 140, 192

in airplanes, 130
in AWVS, 156, 161–62
on buses, 55, 75, 142–43
in civilian defense classes, 146
in court system, 236
in housing, 115, 201–2
Jim Crow laws, 55, 213, 214, 231
in journalism, 31
in labor unions, 24
laws against, 235–36
in military, 27, 44–45, 73–74,
   76–77, 79, 87, 140, 204
in military bands, 228–29
in OCD, 150–51, 152
in Red Cross, 173–75, 177
in restaurants, 56–62, 129–30,
   140, 196
in schools, 3, 54–55, 235
of toilets, 17–18
on trains, 20, 160
in US Army, 73–74, 89, 109
in USO, 166–67, 204, 205
in WAC/WAAC, 87–88, 89,
   93–94, 97–98, 109, 228
Selective Training and Service Act,
   44
Semper Paratus, Always Ready
   (SPAR), 118
Sepia Swing Revue USO tour, 205
service clubs, 97
Seventh Women's Ambulance and
   Nursing Corps, 164–65
sexism, 8, 103. See also gender roles
Shaw, Bertha, 82
Shaw, Ethel Popel, 170
Sherard, Corrie, 105
Shubuta, Mississippi, 39–41
Simms, Margaret, 217–19
6888th Central Postal Directory, 110,
   111–14, 112
Smith, Alberta, 125
Smith, Betty Jane, 111
Smith, Geraldine, 82
Smith, Shermine, 60–61

social welfare agencies, 147
Southern Pacific Railways, 160
Soviet Union, 222, 225
SPAR (Semper Paratus, Always
   Ready), 118
Spears, Rosa, 184
Spears, Rosemary, 183
Spragg, Venice, 34
spy activities, 219
Stallworth, Bertha, 20
Stamper, Mary, 190
Staupers, Mabel, 73–76, 77
St. Clair, Bette, 205
Stewart, Esther, 120
Stewart, Mattie W., 148
Stilwell Road, 134–35, 136
Stimley, Eula Loucille, 78
St. Louis protests, 53, 60–62
Stop the Killing Campaign, 236
Strange Fruit (Garrett), 32
"Strange Fruit" (Meeropol), 39
Sublett, Marie, 102–3
Sublett, Robert, 102–3
Sugar Hill neighborhood, 201–2

Taylor, Dorcas, 131
Taylor, Rebecca Stiles, 34
Ten Percenters, 88
Terry, Jessie L., 145
"These Versatile Women" (Garrett),
   32
Thomas, Lillian, 208
Thomas, Sarah, 120
Thompson, Vora, 60–61
Thornton, Modestine Crute, 60
335th Station Hospital, 135–36
Three Rhythm Rascals, 210
Three Shades of Rhythm, 205–6
Tiny Tots Checking Room, 166
Tovalou-Houenou, Kojo Marc, 226
Townscent, Elcena, 125, 128
training programs, government,
   9–10, 11
Trent, Estelle, 186

Truman, Bess, 233
Truman, Harry, 232–33
tuberculosis wards, 79
Turner, Effie Mae, 13
Turner, Helen, 78
Turner, Jessie, 231
Tuskegee Institute, 29, 75

United Domestic Workers' Union,
    24–25
United States Employment Service
    (USES), 14–15
University of Maryland, 2–3
US Army, 74, 82. *See also* Army
    Nurse Corps
US Army Air Corps, 28
US Army Air Forces, 29
US Navy, 14, 44, 73, 77–78, 116–17
USO (United Service Organizations),
    165–68
USO clubs, 165–68
USO tours, 205–12, 215–17
USS *James Parker,* 119

Vaughan, Evelyn G., 187
Vinson, Rosemary, 125, 135, 136–37
volunteering, reasons for, 143, 145,
    192–93
voting rights, 2

WAAC (Women's Army Auxiliary
    Corps), *104, 106, 107*
    admittance of blacks, 70–71
    auxiliaries, 100–103
    basic training, 93–98
    field assignments, 103–8
    gender discrimination, 103
    graduation ceremonies, 99–100
    military benefits, 108–9
    officer candidate training, 88–89,
        92–93, *95*
    pressure to perform, *95–96,* 105
    racial discrimination, 89, 100
    recruitment efforts, 71, 89–93

    segregation in, 87–88, 89, 93–94,
        97–98
    specialist training, 101, 103
WAC (Women's Army Corps)
    military benefits, 108–9
    neighborhood associations,
        114–16
    news articles, 32
    overseas service, 109–14
    segregation, 109, 228–29
WAC Bands, 227–29
WADCA (Women's Ambulance
    Defense Corps of America), 155
Wade, Ruth, 106
wages, 7, 10–11, 25–26, 85
Walowitz, Shirley, 59
WAND (Women's Army for
    National Defense), 162–65
war bonds, 147, 148–49, 197–98, 201,
    229
Ward, Henrine, 177–78, 180, 193
War Emergency Volunteer Services
    (WEVS), 155–56
war industry, 5, 9, 43–44, 48. *See also*
    defense plants
War Manpower Commission, 7
War's Greatest Scandal, The (Myers),
    50
war workers. *See* aviation industry;
    factory workers; journalists
Washington Post, 237–38
Waters, Virgie, 66
Watkins, Doshia, 135
WAVES (Women Accepted for
    Volunteer Emergency Service),
    116–17
WDCA (Women's Defense Corps of
    America), 153–55
We Are Americans protest, 53–54
Webb, Idell, 122–23, 130
Weir, Vernice, 105
Welcker-Jordan, Mercedes, 106,
    157–58
Wells, Clara, 183, 184

"We're the WAACs" (Welcker-
    Jordan), 106
Western Electric Company, 17–18
WEVS (War Emergency Volunteer
    Services), 155–56
Wheeler, Doc, 207
Wheeler, Eva, 135
Wheeler, Ruth Mattie, 60–61
White, Eva, 153, 193
Wickliffe, Marjorie, 162–63
Wiggins, Edgar, 211
Wilkins, Roy, 41
Williams, Alexander (Jake), 37
Williams, Rosetta, 207
Wills, Frances, 117
Winburn, Anna Mae, 212–17
WINGS (Women in Ground
    Service), 10
"Win the War" bond rally, 197
Wise, Ethyl, 207
WLA (Women's Land Army), 172
Women Accepted for Volunteer
    Emergency Service (WAVES),
    116–17
Women in Ground Service
    (WINGS), 10
"Women in the National Picture"
    (Spragg), 34
Women Ordnance Workers
    (WOW), 10
"Women Power in War" (Briggs), 34

Women's Ambulance Defense Corps
    of America (WADCA), 155
Women's Army Auxiliary Corps
    (WAAC). See WAAC
Women's Army Corps (WAC). See
    WAC
Women's Army for National Defense
    (WAND), 162–65
Women's Bureau of the US
    Department of Labor bulletin,
    37–38
Women's Defense Corps of America
    (WDCA), 153–55
Women's Division for the Sale of
    War Bonds, 147
Women's Land Army (WLA), 172
Women's Motor Corps, 147
Woods, Esther, 35
Wool Conservation Program, 148
Works Progress Administration
    (WPA), 27, 67
WOW (Women Ordnance Workers),
    10
Wright, Cora, 116–17
Wrights, Eleanor, 59

Young, Rosalie, 208
YWCA, 23

Zhukov, Gregori, 210–11
Zurita, Juan, 159